French Historical Studies

VOLUME 38 ■ NUMBER 2 ■ APRIL 2015

SPECIAL ISSUE:
FOOD AND FRANCE: WHAT FOOD STUDIES
CAN TEACH US ABOUT HISTORY
EDITED BY BERTRAM M. GORDON AND ERICA J. PETERS

Introduction

Bertram M. Gordon and Erica J. Peters

The publication of a special issue of *French Historical Studies* on French food history highlights the increased attention paid to gastronomic studies in academic circles on both sides of the Atlantic. One observer at a recent American Historical Association meeting noted that "every major publisher seems to have at least one new book on some aspect of food history."[1]

Evidence indicates a growth of interest in food history during the last generation, notably in the Anglophone world. The Oxford Symposium on Food and Cookery, established in 1981 along with its published proceedings, was cochaired that year by Alan Davidson, author of *The Oxford Companion to Food*, and Theodore Zeldin, a historian of France. The Association for the Study of Food and Society (ASFS) was created in 1985. It holds annual meetings and publishes the quarterly journal *Food, Culture and Society*.

In 1989 Hans-Jürgen Teuteberg of the University of Münster led the initiative to create the International Commission for Research into European Food History, which continues to sponsor conferences and publish a newsletter in English. Under the leadership of Jacques Pepin and Julia Child, Boston University established a Masters in Gastronomy program in 1994, said at the time to be the first in the United States.[2]

Bertram M. Gordon is professor of history at Mills College in Oakland, California, where he regularly teaches a course in "cuisine history," and is author of chapters on eating "as God in France" in *Voyage, Reisen und Essen* (2002); the history of *Gourmet Magazine*'s perceptions of French food in *Gastronomie et identité culturelle française* (2007); and the history of chocolate in France in *Chocolate: History, Culture, and Heritage* (2009). Erica J. Peters is director of the Culinary Historians of Northern California and author of *Appetites and Aspirations in Vietnam: Food and Drink in the Long Nineteenth Century* (2012) and *San Francisco: A Food Biography* (2013).

The editors appreciate the invaluable assistance of Rachel Fuchs, Kent Wright, Amy Long, Richard Hopkins, and the anonymous readers who reviewed the many submissions, and they thank the new editors, Kathryn A. Edwards and Carol E. Harrison, for managing the transition so smoothly.

1 Donald A. Yerxa, "Beyond Logistics: Food as an Instrument of Modern Warfare," *Books and Culture*, Sept.–Oct. 2013, 30.

2 Bob Thomas, "Julia Child, Jacques Pepin Team Up on PBS," *Seattle Times*, Sept. 7, 1994, community.seattletimes.nwsource.com/archive/?date=19940907&slug=1929179. See also Dena

French Historical Studies, Vol. 38, No. 2 (April 2015)   DOI 10.1215/00161071-2842530

Since 2001 the University of California Press has published *Gastronomica*, a quarterly that focuses on the history and culture of food.

At the same time, non-Anglophone researchers have also developed a rich set of approaches to food history and food studies in general. The Institut Européen d'Histoire et des Cultures de l'Alimentation was founded in 2001, bringing together scholars such as Francis Chevrier, Julia Csergo, Jean-Louis Flandrin, Massimo Montanari, Jean-Robert Pitte, Jean-Pierre Poulain, Françoise Sabban, and Peter Scholliers. According to an overview published in 2012, half of the articles published in the institute's journal, *Food and History*, have been in English, 40 percent in French, and 6 percent in Italian.[3]

Students are also interested in food studies. In 2003 ASFS listed seventy-five university food studies courses, and in 2008 it named ten university food history programs in the United States, Europe, and Australia.[4] Further, the general public has also developed an interest in food history; as of 2014 the Food History News website listed fifteen culinary history organizations in the United States, Canada, and Australia.[5] In her online manual on how to do food history, Rachel Laudan lists twenty-two academic periodicals devoted to food studies.[6] Food was also the topic of at least eighteen presentations at the 2014 meeting of the American Historical Association.

The focus on food history in this issue of *French Historical Studies* mirrors this growing academic interest in food studies and raises the question of the particular case of French culinary history within the larger field. Anglophone writers have shifted over time in their appraisal of French cuisine, from scattered attacks on French food in the early modern era to the preeminence of champagne, French wines, and French haute cuisine in the nineteenth century. In *All Manners of Food* Stephen Mennell notes that medieval aristocratic cuisine styles were similar in France, Italy, and England.[7]

An early English-language reference to French cooking appeared

Kleiman, "A University Offers Food for Thought," *New York Times*, Nov. 20, 1991, www.nytimes.com/1991/11/20/garden/a-university-offers-food-for-thought.html.

[3] Peter Scholliers, "Ten Years of Food and History," *Food and History* 10, no. 2 (2012): 28–29.

[4] For the 2003 course syllabi, see Jonathan Deutsch, *Teaching Food: Agriculture, Food and Society Syllabi and Course Materials Collection: A Publication of the Association for the Study of Food and Society and the Agriculture, Food and Human Values Society*, 2003 ed., June 12, 2003, cafs.landfood.ubc.ca/en/wp-content/uploads/Teaching_Food_-_Agriculture_Food_and_Society_Syllabi_2003.pdf. The 2008 ASFS Food Studies Programs list was accessed at food-culture.org/FoodStudies.html on Nov. 17, 2008, but is no longer available on this site.

[5] "Resources and Links," *Food History News*, foodhistorynews.com/yellow.html (accessed Aug. 17, 2014).

[6] Rachel Laudan, "Getting Started in Food History," in *A Historian's Take on Food and Food Politics*, www.rachellaudan.com/getting-started-in-food-history (accessed Aug. 17, 2014).

[7] Stephen Mennell, *All Manners of Food: Eating and Taste in England and France from the Middle Ages to the Present*, 2nd ed. (Urbana, IL, 1996), 50–51.

in a published work, *A Proper Newe Booke of Cokerye,* in 1545, with a recipe
for a tart made "after the Frenche Fashyan."[8] The publication of La
Varenne's *Cuisinier François* in 1651 was followed two years later by an
English translation, *The French Cook,* arguably the first rendition of a
French cookbook into English. *The French Cook* included French terms
such as *à la daube* and *à la mode,* suggesting that Anglophones were adopting a new vocabulary along with new techniques.[9] The second half of
the seventeenth century saw the translation of more French cookbooks.
Samuel Pepys, among others, was known to prefer French cuisine, but
English-language commentaries on French foods were not always favor-
able.[10] Three English "gentlemen" who traveled in France in September 1701, for instance, complained that breakfast "à la Française" was
merely "a crust of bread and a glass of wine."[11]

An emerging eighteenth-century fashion for French foods among
the urban affluent in the Anglophone countries was combined with an
occasional preference expressed for "the roast beef of old England."
This was especially marked during the revolutionary period with scorn-
ful references to France's onions, snails, and watery *soupe maigre.* The
London-based *Gentlemen's Magazine* responded to the increase in Parisian restaurants in the 1790s by grumbling that "a French cook can disguise his manufacture so artfully, that it is sometimes impossible to
conjecture what the raw material could be."[12]

In 1825 Jean-Anthelme Brillat-Savarin published his *Physiologie du
goût,* which spurred interest in gastronomy as a science and increased
France's culinary reputation. At the time the concept of the restaurant
as a public dining place of value equal to or greater than a private salon
was only just emerging.[13] An article published three years later noted
the increase in the numbers of French chefs coming to work in England,

8 Catherine Frances Frere, ed., *A Proper Newe Booke of Cokerye* (Cambridge, 1913), 45, quoted
in Roy Schreiber, "Samuel Pepys and His Cookbooks," *Art and Food,* www.londonfoodfilmfiesta
.co.uk/Literature%20Main/Pepys.htm (accessed Sept. 10, 2013). A digitized version of *A Proper
Newe Booke of Cokerye* is available on www.uni-giessen.de/gloning/tx/bookecok.htm (accessed Sept.
10, 2013).

9 "Continental Cookery," in *Recipes for Domesticity: Cookery, Household Management, and the
Notion of Expertise,* in Web Exhibits—Special Collections Research Center, University of Chicago
Library, www.lib.uchicago.edu/e/webexhibits/recipes/continentalcookery.html (accessed Sept.
10, 2013). See also Peter Brears et al., *A Taste of History: 10,000 Years of Food in Britain* (London,
1993), 183.

10 Mennell, *All Manners of Food,* 89. For English ambivalence about French haute cuisine,
see also Amy B. Trubek, *Haute Cuisine: How the French Invented the Culinary Profession* (Philadelphia,
2000), 60–63. For Pepys, see Schreiber, "Samuel Pepys and His Cookbooks."

11 "Descriptive Journal of a Tour Taken by Three Gentlemen in the Last Year of the Reign
of King William III. (1701), from London to Paris, by Way of Calais, and Back through Normandy
and Dieppe," *Gentleman's Magazine,* Jan. 1819, 29.

12 "A Trip to Paris," *Gentleman's Magazine,* Nov. 1797, 909–10.

13 See Honoré Blanc, *Le guide des dineurs ou statistique des principaux restaurans de Paris* (1815;
repr. Paris, 1985).

a sign of the rising prestige of French cuisine.[14] Similarly, French chefs won influential positions in the United States, as exemplified by the establishment of Delmonico's restaurant in New York in 1833. Menus from leading American hotel restaurants during the first half of the nineteenth century, such as the Tremont House in Boston, also show the increased prestige of French gastronomy. With technological developments lowering the cost of printing, the restaurant menu itself had become a souvenir, often a way to remember a special night out.[15] By the early twentieth century the French government also intervened to promote French food through the *appellation d'origine contrôlée*, as in the case of Roquefort cheese in 1925.

From the late nineteenth century through the 1970s, French culinary preeminence in the Anglophone world surfaced in the writings of M. F. K. Fisher, Samuel Chamberlain, A. J. Liebling, André Simon, and many others, along with Julia Child's popularization of French food in the United States. The appearance of French culinary terms in American articles listed in the *Reader's Guide to Periodical Literature* shows the impact of the automobile in making French regions more accessible to American tourists. Brittany appears in the title of a culinary article in 1926, Normandy in 1933, Provence in 1950, Alsace and "Bordelaise" in 1957, and the Basques in 1959. *Cassoulet* first appears in a title in 1961; Marseilles, with respect to *bouillabaisse*, in 1962; and *quiche Lorraine* in 1964.

There is a dramatic increase in *Reader's Guide* listings for French under "cookery" in the 1950s and early 1960s that corresponds to the appearance of the jumbo jet and increased tourism, including the university junior year abroad, with peaks in the 1970s. A relative decline in the 1980s and thereafter indicates shifts toward other cuisines, notably a *nouvelle* or California-Mediterranean style, illustrated in books such as Patric Kuh's *Last Days of Haute Cuisine: The Coming of Age of American Restaurants* (2001) and Michael Steinberger's *Au Revoir to All That: Food, Wine, and the End of France* (2009). This new culinary approach still uses French terms, as exemplified in the name *nouvelle cuisine* itself.[16] Cover images of French food items for *Gourmet Magazine*, from its inception in 1941 through its demise in 2009, peaked in the 1960s, and the magazine's proportion of French restaurant reviews declined in the 1980s. In 1991 a *Newsweek* article by Laura Shapiro, "An American Revolution,"

---

14 "Gastronomy. — Ude, Jarrin, Mrs Glasse," *Blackwood's Magazine*, Jan.–June 1828, 589.

15 The New York Public Library had an estimated twenty-five thousand to fifty thousand menus in its collection in 1986. See Bertram M. Gordon, "Researching Popular Culture — Archival Sources in Europe and America: An Address to the First International Working Conference on Resources for Culinary Research at the New York Public Library," Mar. 8, 1986.

16 See R. A. de Groot, "French Cooking Is Dead — the New French Cooking Is Born," *Esquire*, June 1975, 131; and Jacques Pepin, "La Nouvelle Cuisine: Is It Truly New?," *House Beautiful*, Jan. 1976, 66.

argued that "our love affair with French food is over, done in by new passion for our own chefs and ingredients." Shapiro added, however, that for "the animated faces, the buzz of conversation, the clusters of friends lingering for hours," one still had to go to Paris to dine.[17]

The intensity of that "love affair" may have ended, but the effects linger on. As Priscilla Parkhurst Ferguson has shown, French promoters have argued persuasively that "French cuisine and culture are central to what it means to be civilized" and that the French have a particular talent for taking everyone else's ingredients and dishes and transforming them "into an unquestionably French product."[18] Even as today's food world pays less attention to French haute cuisine, the history of French food is still a prominent field in food studies. Scholars continue to debate whether the country's Catholicism made food more sacred by analogy with ingestion of the host along with the blessing of an indulgent clergy (as suggested by Jean-Pierre Poulain and Jean-Robert Pitte) or whether French secularism encouraged the rise of gastronomy and culinary sensualism, as Ferguson argues. Most researchers see the French state playing a key role, protecting and promoting French food products in Europe and around the world.[19]

Food history, as is evident from studies of France and elsewhere, lets scholars explore large historical questions from a perspective that is immediate and personal for the actors involved. People's hunger for any kind of food under conditions of deprivation or for more appetizing dishes when times are better provides a new angle from which to view questions of nationalism, global networks, gender, race, ethnicity, and class. Food history also throws a new light on historians' standard periodization, as people's dietary options and preferences change on a different time scale than do political regimes.[20] Each article in this special issue illuminates these sorts of questions.

Julia Landweber's article on the French adoption of coffee as a beverage and ingredient sets out the fascinating story of how seventeenth-century French consumers began to learn about and appreciate this new taste. In so doing, she provides a wealth of insight into European attitudes toward the Ottoman Empire, French willful ignorance about

17 Laura Shapiro, "An American Revolution," *Newsweek*, Dec. 16, 1991, 54–56.

18 Priscilla Parkhurst Ferguson, *Word of Mouth: What We Talk about When We Talk about Food* (Berkeley, CA, 2014), 6–7.

19 Jean-Pierre Poulain, "French Gastronomy, French Gastronomies," in *Culinary Cultures of Europe: Identity, Diversity, and Dialogue*, ed. Darra Goldstein and Kathrin Merkle (Strasbourg, 2005), 157–70; Jean-Robert Pitte, "Is Gourmandism a Sin in France?," in *French Gastronomy: The History and Geography of a Passion* (New York, 2002), 33–68; Ferguson, *Word of Mouth*, 12–13.

20 Peter Scholliers, "Twenty-Five Years of Studying *un Phénomène Social Total*: Food History Writing on Europe in the Nineteenth and Twentieth Centuries," *Food, Culture and Society* 10, no. 3 (2007): 461.

products coming from their own slave colonies, and changing attitudes toward alcohol in society. Landweber's article also teases out the interplay between embracing one's coffee-fueled sexuality and displacing one's sexual desire onto racialized others. When a French woman lounged in Turkish robes, sipping her coffee, was she displaying her sexual nature or only playing at being sexual by dressing up in a harem costume, or was she precariously balanced between those positions?

Philippe Meyzie's careful analysis of the early promotion of *terroir* in the eighteenth century shows how producers, consumers, and distributors began to associate a food product's provenance with its quality. Here we see how commercial interests fanned early signs of interest in a region's reputation into more than a passing fashion. Rather than assume in a nostalgic vein that the foods we now connect with a particular region have remained the same for centuries, Meyzie historicizes the process of the identification of product with place. Consumers' insecurity over the distances food traveled via the country's developing infrastructure (long before the eras of the railroad or the airplane) led to a desire for reassurance about the food's quality. Beyond providing a historical perspective on the highly valorized and marketed term *terroir*, Meyzie reveals the social aspirations of an emerging bourgeoisie. These rising elites found *terroir* a straightforward guide to imitating aristocratic taste in gifts and hospitality. The standard periodization of French history also comes into question: from the perspective of commercial networks, the French Revolution no longer seems like a bright line separating the ancien régime from modern France.

The rise of restaurants for workers in turn-of-the-twentieth-century Paris is addressed from two different angles in this collection. Martin Bruegel compares French rhetoric about a *repas normal* with the more affordable but barely adequate lunches workers often consumed. Bruegel's work allows the reader to see not a monolithic working class but, rather, gradations: an older male artisan enjoying several courses at a *restaurant à prix fixe*; a younger man making do with just a hearty soup at a *bouillon* establishment; a seamstress having a thin soup, bread, and cheese at a *crèmerie*; or poor workers of either sex trying to satisfy their hunger with fried tripe, fried potatoes, or a bowl of soup from a street vendor.

Patricia Tilburg looks at cultural attitudes toward *midinettes*, the working women who survived on street food for lunch or sometimes had a minimal restaurant meal when times were better. Tilburg shows that French popular culture romanticized these women and their meager meals, reading a modern sense of sophistication into those small portions. At the same time, popular representations suggested that these women could be tempted by better food into a dalliance with a man

from a higher social class, shedding their limited expectations along the way and, they hoped, raising their social status. Both Tilburg and Bruegel highlight moments when workers were perceived as choosing pleasure over austere adherence to factory discipline. Pastries, cherries, pickles, or fries—these foods were for fun, not just sustenance. Tilburg stresses that the *midinette* was imagined to be poor but not interested in politics. Indeed, popular images of these working women did not necessarily correspond to reality. The imagined *midinette* character was content with the world as it was, while actual garment workers turned to strike actions to increase their wages. The lunch world of Parisian workers was clearly far removed from the post–Brillat-Savarin restaurants that so influenced the Anglophone idea of French restaurants.[21]

Kenneth Mouré's article on black market restaurants in Paris during the Second World War demonstrates how people of different social situations experienced wartime food shortages in occupied France. The Pétain government had to struggle to maintain its legitimacy, given the evidence of extreme inequities. German forces and wealthy French businessmen and war profiteers ate luxurious restaurant meals, even as most Parisians had to stand in long lines for inadequate rations. Food studies offer an excellent opportunity to analyze the politics behind wartime deprivation, as well as provide a clear picture of how much less the wealthy may be impacted by a country's hard times. Mouré also problematizes the usual periodization of the war, since rationing and price controls put in place under the German occupation continued after the Liberation.

All the articles also ground our understanding of France's place in the world. Coffee became one of the products the French brought to other countries, such as Vietnam, where a French-inspired coffee culture is one of the few positive associations with the colonial period. Likewise, *terroir* may have started as a promotional tool within France, but before long French wine, cheeses, and foie gras were marketed abroad with the same earthy rhetoric. Since the 1970s the promotional language of *terroir* has even been adopted by farmers outside France. Turn-of-the-twentieth-century worker restaurants represented a different side of Paris from fine dining establishments, but by the interwar period Anglophone travelers found the prix fixe menus appealing. The "bouillon restaurant" opened by Frédéric and Camille Chartier in 1896 was classified as a *monument historique* in 1989; it now boasts a website in English and long lines of tourists waiting to get in. At the other end of the dining spectrum, access to Paris's most exclusive restau-

---

21 Rebecca L. Spang, *The Invention of the Restaurant: Paris and Modern Gastronomic Culture* (Cambridge, MA, 2000), 219–26, 242.

rants became a trophy first seized by German forces in 1940 and then claimed by the Americans in 1944. The view from outside France shines a light refracting the history of French cuisine and revealing new facets.

Awareness of the many ways in which culinary history opens deeper understandings of social and cultural history, shown in the growing number of academic programs, courses, and writings on the subject, is also evidenced by the decision of *French Historical Studies* to devote a special issue to food. The five articles published here were selected from more than two dozen submissions. Chronologically, most of the original submissions focused on the modern period, defined as starting at the end of the Middle Ages. Using the periodization that *French Historical Studies* employs for its Recent Articles on French History listings, three of the submissions could be classified under "General and Miscellaneous," two under "Ancient and Medieval," seven under "1500–1774," one under "Revolutionary Period and Napoléon," eight under "Third Republic," and six under "1940 to the Present." Food studies sometimes challenge these standard divisions of research and may suggest broad issues that mattered more than politics for ordinary people. Thematically, the articles submitted and published represent a view of French food history that extends far beyond haute cuisine. The editors appreciate the good work of all the authors and hope that this special issue will open the door to heightened discussion of how food history elucidates French history in future pages of *French Historical Studies.*

"This Marvelous Bean": Adopting Coffee into Old Regime French Culture and Diet

Julia Landweber

Abstract   *This article examines coffee's adoption into French culture and diet between 1644 and 1788, empha-sizing the period 1670–1730. In these sixty years, a beverage initially mistrusted by the French (for its bitterness, health risks, and associations with the Ottoman Empire) became a beloved beverage, gave its name to the new space of the café, and attracted a burgeoning culture of consumers interested in exotic novelties. Through a focus on coffee, we gain fresh insights into a number of disparate subjects, including the evolving cultural relationship between France and the Ottoman Empire; shifts in the sociability structures of the urban middling classes, from socializing around alcohol to the promotion of sobering stimulants; the developing role of merchants, physicians, and pharmacists in assessing the safety of new foodstuffs; the rise of* cuisine moderne, *with its openness to new ingredients; and the birth of a global French coffee trade in the eighteenth century.*

Keywords   *coffee, consumer revolution, cuisine,* turquerie

In the sixteenth and seventeenth centuries, the world's great trio of caffeinated beverages—chocolate, tea, and coffee—began to enter the European consciousness, first as exotic curiosities circulating far from Europe's shores and eventually as lucrative commodities imported for consumption in the home countries. Of these three drinks, coffee would become by far the most successful import to France, easily out-stripping interest in tea and, to a lesser extent, chocolate in the first 150 years after its arrival on French soil in the mid-seventeenth cen-tury. The history of coffee's adoption into Old Regime French culture and diet is still surprisingly underresearched, especially compared with its well-documented history in early modern England.[1] From our mod-

Julia Landweber is assistant professor of history at Montclair State University. She has published essays in the *Journal of Ottoman Studies,* the *International History Review,* and elsewhere.
    The author thanks Thomas Brennan, Hernán Cortés, Tabetha Ewing, W. Scott Haine, Katharine J. Hamerton, Elizabeth Hyde, Craig Koslofsky, Gayle Levy, Lynn Mollenauer, Preston M. Perluss, Erica J. Peters, Thierry Rigogne, Alyssa Sepinwall, and the editors and anonymous review-ers of *French Historical Studies* for their helpful comments and advice. Portions of this material were originally presented at conferences of the Western Society for French History and the Society for French Historical Studies. The phrase quoted in the title derives from coffee's description as "cette merveilleuse feve" in the dedication to Philippe Sylvestre Dufour, *De l'usage du caphé, du thé, et du chocolate* (Lyon, 1671).

[1] See S. D. Smith, "Accounting for Taste: British Coffee Consumption in Historical Perspec-tive," *Journal of Interdisciplinary History* 27, no. 2 (1996): 183–214; and Brian Cowan, *The Social Life of Coffee: The Emergence of the British Coffeehouse* (New Haven, CT, 2005). However, the history of the

ern vantage point, it might seem strange that people had to learn to drink coffee; in the twenty-first century coffee has been so thoroughly adopted around the globe that we nearly take it for granted. Moreover, France, long heralded as the birthplace of the café, quintessential locus of the Enlightenment and the public sphere, is inextricably linked in the modern popular imagination with a love of coffee. But historically societies had to learn to like coffee, which for many was no easy thing. In the case of France, three barriers of varying significance blocked coffee's entry into the general diet. The first problem was its bitter taste, which repelled many; the second was its astronomical price, which put it beyond the reach of most consumers. Third, commercially grown coffee came initially only from Yemen, via Ottoman middlemen, which gave it uncomfortably alien associations with Islam and the Ottoman Empire. Nonetheless, within fifty years of coffee's arrival in France, the French people moved from complete indifference, if not outright dislike, toward it to marked fascination with the bean, the drink, and the flavor. As familiarity with coffee developed in France, coffee helped make French society more cosmopolitan even while coffee itself began to seem "French."

This article reconstructs this remarkable about-face, which raises the question of explaining a dramatic shift in a given society's culinary tastes and cultural habits. Having begun by rejecting it, why and how did the French then rapidly adopt coffee between the late seventeenth and mid-eighteenth centuries? When did coffee change, for the French, from a peculiar novelty to an item of cultural consequence? For centuries, both antiquarians and historians have recycled what Thierry Rigogne rightly decries as "myths and legends" about the arrival of coffee in France and the origins of the café.[2] An envoy from the Ottoman Empire named Suleiman Aga is said to have first introduced coffee to France in 1669, and another foreigner, the Sicilian Francesco Procopio Cutò, supposedly invented the café in 1686. Between the exotic attractions of the first and the elegant interior decorating schemes of the second, the French were smitten and, seemingly overnight, became coffee drinkers. This is clearly too simplistic an explanation, yet it has been repeated without question in popular histories, guidebooks, and cookbooks from the seventeenth century to the present.

Moving away from the "great man" theory of consumer innova-

Old Regime French café, as a key site for drinking coffee, is gaining interest among researchers, including works recently published or in progress by Hernán Cortés, Tabetha Ewing, W. Scott Haine, Craig Koslofsky, Preston M. Perluss, and Thierry Rigogne.

2 Thierry Rigogne, "Entre histoire et mythes: Le premier siècle des cafés à Paris (1670–1789)," in *Les histoires de Paris (XVIe–XVIIIe siècle)*, ed. Thierry Belleguic and Laurent Turcot, 2 vols. (Paris, 2013), 2:163.

tion, some have suggested that caffeine's sheer addictiveness, or selective taxation that artificially lowered the price of coffee while elevating that of competing goods, was all it took to persuade European societies to drink coffee.[3] But in France, as elsewhere, coffee's domestication was accomplished only gradually and by a remarkably diverse collection of people. Understanding how this worked requires a more complex historical analysis, such as Ralph S. Hattox and Brian Cowan offer in their studies of coffee's adoption into late medieval Near East and seventeenth-century English societies. Hattox demonstrates that the Near East, cradle of both coffee cultivation and the coffeehouse, also pioneered a pattern for coffee adoption that would be repeated across Europe: initial usage by the intellectually curious, followed by the foundation of public coffeehouses, which in turn provoked attempts at government regulation.[4] By the mid-sixteenth century coffee had become established within Arab, Egyptian, and Ottoman society. European visitors took notice and, within a few decades, started bringing beans home. Cowan begins here, with the English virtuosi, or gentlemen scholars, who first observed coffee's potential as a medically and commercially valuable commodity. Although coffee arrived earlier in Venice and the Netherlands, and barely later in France, England's unique "combination of genteel curiosity, mercantile commerce, and metropolitan civil society" caused the English to take up coffee drinking sooner and with greater intensity than anywhere else in seventeenth-century Europe.[5] Yet after the pleasures and dangers of coffee were vigorously debated, and hundreds of coffeehouses were founded in London, that focus withered almost as rapidly as it had started. In the 1720s, exactly when the French were quickening their own interest in coffee, the English transferred their attention to the Asian tea trade, ultimately becoming a nation of tea drinkers and leaving coffee to the Continent.

Historians are finally focusing similarly analytic attention on the history of coffee adoption in France. Emma Spary devotes two chapters to coffee in *Eating the Enlightenment*, her study of food and science in Old Regime Paris. Applying a sociological model, Spary divides the many French individuals who promoted coffee into Oriental, Indian, and American networks of information exchange. Members of these networks possessed different sorts of expertise—Orientalist scholar-

3 William G. Clarence-Smith, "The Global Consumption of Hot Beverages, c. 1500 to c. 1900," in *Food and Globalization: Consumption, Markets, and Politics in the Modern World*, ed. Alexander Nützenadel and Frank Trentmann (Oxford, 2008), 37–49.

4 Ralph S. Hattox, *Coffee and Coffeehouses: The Origins of a Social Beverage in the Medieval Near East* (Seattle, WA, 1985).

5 Cowan, *Social Life of Coffee*, 30. For a very different history, examining how neighboring German and Jewish communities fought over whether to welcome or reject coffee, see Robert Liberles, *Jews Welcome Coffee: Tradition and Innovation in Early Modern Germany* (Waltham, MA, 2012).

ship, maritime trade, or botanical science. Each in turn was applied to coffee in an effort to understand its properties or promote its use. What united these experts, claims Spary, was a desire to deploy their particular skills to simultaneously serve the Crown and prove themselves bona fide members of the Republic of Letters as scholars of coffee. She concludes that coffee consumption in Paris, especially during the crucial years of 1670–1715, when these networks were most active, was primarily "a way of displaying fashionable familiarity with the cutting edge of academic scholarship."[6] French coffee consumption in this period was indeed about fashion, but not, I will argue, of the academic variety. Many early coffee promoters did have academic associations or literary aspirations, but most drinkers were responding to a different lure. Alongside Spary's networks need to be added the trendsetters who established other kinds of high fashion during the reign of Louis XIV; the merchants, artisans, and colonists seeking to profit from these new fashions; and the doctors, pharmacologists, theologians, and cooks who contested coffee's merits in public debates. In the late seventeenth century medical studies and commercial interests intersected with a new taste for *turquerie* to set the stage for a wider adoption of coffee drinking in France during the following century. Ultimately these groups were as significant as Spary's networks to the project of transforming coffee from an exotic Arab/Ottoman good into a "French" commodity.

This article takes a two-part approach to the history of coffee's adoption in France. I address first why the French decided to drink coffee and then how they determined to think about the substance. To understand why and how a society develops new collective habits, it may be useful to ask a related question: how can preferences in drink, like food, be used to express personal identity? "Consumption clusters" (as Jan de Vries calls unexpected combinations of goods bundled together in a socially meaningful way) can lend social distinction to their users.[7] The bundling of coffee with sugar (in England) and milk (in France) was one such combination; Woodruff D. Smith believes that sugar consumption actually drove rising coffee consumption in both countries, by linking coffee to the virtuous respectability associated with sugar usage.[8] I argue that another combination of goods was even more significant than milk or sugar for making coffee appealing in the

---

[6] Emma Spary, *Eating the Enlightenment: Food and the Sciences in Paris, 1670–1760* (Chicago, 2012), 68. For another approach, see Ina B. McCabe, *Orientalism in Early Modern France: Eurasian Trade, Exoticism, and the Ancien Régime* (Oxford, 2008), 163–203.

[7] Jan de Vries, *The Industrious Revolution: Consumer Behavior and the Household Economy, 1650 to the Present* (Cambridge, 2008), 31.

[8] Woodruff D. Smith, *Consumption and the Making of Respectability, 1600–1800* (New York, 2002), 121–30.

first place. Twenty or thirty years after coffee had arrived in France very quietly, in the 1680s its social value rose dramatically when fashion purveyors began to link coffee's consumption to an emerging trade in Eastern-themed luxury goods manufactured in France. Formerly overlooked by most, it now became widely desired. Coffee's early connection with costly visions of high fashion and Oriental exoticism would persist through the eighteenth century, even as its price dropped, familiarity with it spread through different levels of society, and it increasingly came from the Caribbean and Java instead of from Arabia.

Jordan Goodman argues that coffee and other new pharmacologically active imports, such as tobacco and tea, underwent a "Europeanization" process of appropriation in the eighteenth century. New social rituals that legitimated their consumption were in turn "used to proclaim a powerful ideology of sobriety and respectability."[9] Goodman's argument is persuasive, but how Europeanization happened is not yet well understood for some quite basic commodities, coffee among them. In France, innovative uses for coffee developed in a relatively smooth sequence: first coffee was introduced as a medical marvel; then it became a familiar beverage; lastly, chefs discovered its utility in flavoring desserts. While the problem of cost excluded all but the well-to-do from accessing coffee until well into the eighteenth century, by then cookbooks reveal that those who could afford to had moved beyond consuming coffee solely as a beverage to completely integrating it into their cuisines. When the price dropped, coffee was positioned to become a flavor attractive to all, available in multiple forms.

Over the past thirty years a rich historiography has explored the European consumer revolution in the latter part of the early modern period, especially in France and England. Long before the industrial revolution, individuals of ordinary means began to adopt patterns of conspicuous consumption formerly limited to the elite, by buying goods in new ways that both shaped and announced the buyer's identity. Initially historians—notably John Brewer and Neil McKendrick for England and Daniel Roche for France—studied changes in material culture and the circulation of goods.[10] Under the influence of Jennifer Jones, Colin Jones, Natacha Coquery, Maxine Berg, and Helen Clifford, scholarly attention turned to the birth of advertising, which intro-

9 Jordan Goodman, "Excitantia; or, How Enlightenment Europe Took to Soft Drugs," in *Consuming Habits: Drugs in History and Anthropology*, ed. Jordan Goodman, Paul E. Lovejoy, and Andrew Sherratt (London, 1995), 127.

10 Among their many works, see esp. John Brewer, Neil McKendrick, and J. H. Plumb, *The Birth of a Consumer Society: The Commercialization of Eighteenth-Century England* (Bloomington, IN, 1982); and Daniel Roche, *L'histoire des choses banales* (Paris, 1997), translated by Brian Pearce as *A History of Everyday Things: The Birth of Consumption in France, 1600–1800* (Cambridge, 2000).

duced things previously unknown or unwanted to new categories of shoppers.[11] It is now clear that what began as a limited market in luxury goods for mid-seventeenth-century aristocrats had mutated by century's end into a rising demand among the middling classes, the various social strata between the wealthy elites and the poor, for novelties and imported goods, especially for items from Asia. During the eighteenth century, thanks to the growing purchasing power of most households and to innovative marketing techniques, consumerism spread throughout society, reaching even the working classes.

Among historians of consumerism, Mimi Hellman proposes an idea particularly significant for this study: purchased goods "conveyed meaning not simply through possession but also through usage."[12] It is worth remembering that, unlike many status-carrying objects, food and drink were consumed literally: not only used but used up. Thanks to the consumer revolution, commodities (such as sugar, coffee, tea, and chocolate) and practices (including the idea of fashion cycles in clothing and furnishings), formerly considered luxuries for the elite, were gradually perceived as necessities for the many.[13] Coffee was at the center of these developments. It was a new Asian foodstuff that arrived in Europe complete with rituals of preparation and consumption, as well as with particular spaces and material goods in which and with which to consume it. The coffeehouse and café, far from being English and French creations, were at heart an import from Mecca, Cairo, and Constantinople. And the practices of serving coffee with delicate porcelain cups, saucers, and trays and with fine embroidered napkins were similarly imported Ottoman customs. The exotic combination of these practices and things doubly taught the French to desire coffee, by first appealing to an elite audience and then spreading to a wider swath of society desiring to imitate aristocratic modes of con-

[11] Jennifer Jones, "Repackaging Rousseau: Femininity and Fashion in Old Regime France," *French Historical Studies* 18, no. 4 (1994): 939–67; Colin Jones, "The Great Chain of Buying: Medical Advertisement, the Bourgeois Public Sphere, and the Origins of the French Revolution," *American Historical Review* 101, no. 1 (1996): 13–40; Natacha Coquery, "The Language of Success: Marketing and Distributing Semi-luxury Goods in Eighteenth-Century Paris," *Journal of Design History* 17, no. 1 (2004): 71–89; Maxine Berg and Helen Clifford, "Selling Consumption in the Eighteenth Century: Advertising and the Trade Card in Britain and France," *Cultural and Social History* 4, no. 2 (2007): 145–70.

[12] Mimi Hellman, "Furniture, Sociability, and the Work of Leisure in Eighteenth-Century France," *Eighteenth-Century Studies* 32, no. 4 (1999): 417.

[13] Coquery, "Language of Success," 72–76. See also Cissie Fairchilds, "The Production and Marketing of Populuxe Goods in Eighteenth-Century Paris," in *Consumption and the World of Goods*, ed. John Brewer and Roy Porter (London, 1993), 228–48; Colin Jones and Rebecca Spang, "Sansculottes, *sans Café, sans Tabac*: Shifting Realms of Necessity and Luxury in Eighteenth-Century France," in *Consumers and Luxury: Consumer Culture in Europe, 1650–1850*, ed. Maxine Berg and Helen Clifford (Manchester, 1999), 37–62; and Michael Kwass, "Ordering the World of Goods: Consumer Revolution and the Classification of Objects in Eighteenth-Century France," *Representations*, no. 82 (2003): 87–116.

sumption. Within this history, one consumption cluster led to another very different one. The first bundling that made coffee socially interesting was entirely centered on Asian goods and fashions imported from the Eastern Mediterranean and the Indian Ocean: Arabian coffee, Ottoman sultana dresses, Armenian and Indian dressing gowns, and Ottoman and Chinese porcelain. In the eighteenth century this was replaced with a vastly more global and cheaper cluster of goods, which mixed genuine imports (coffee from Arabia, Java, or the West Indies; sugar from the West Indies) with domestically produced goods. Some of the latter were frankly local (milk), while others retained an exotic patina, such as *turquerie*- and *chinoiserie*-influenced porcelain, silver, pewter, or faience services and décor *à la turque* in the cafés of Paris and the homes of the wealthy.

The history of coffee's adoption thus has additional value to students of French history: it offers a different way to integrate France into larger narratives of early modern world history. A perpetual import that developed strong domestic associations, coffee offers a lens through which we can broaden our view of French history to encompass an interconnected global perspective. Although far less psychotropically powerful than other popular drugs, such as cannabis or nicotine, caffeine is a profoundly addictive substance that has driven world-historical events. Historians are more aware of sugar's potential to turn worlds upside down than of coffee's, but colonial European coffee growers similarly depended on slave labor in the West Indies and completely disrupted native societies in eighteenth-century Java to undersell coffee from Mocha. Through the history of coffee's adoption into French culture and diet, the global exchanges underlying the Old Regime's world of goods can be viewed in a fresh light.

Coffee Enters France

Through the seventeenth century, commercially grown coffee came exclusively from Yemen in southern Arabia. Arab and Indian merchants handled most exports, and the bulk of their cargo went north to Cairo, Constantinople, and other parts of the Islamic world, where coffee had been a staple beverage since the mid-sixteenth century.[14] Coffee allegedly first reached France in 1644, when the merchant Pierre de La Roque carried beans and roasting implements home from Constantinople to Marseille.[15] But coffee may have shown up even earlier;

14 Hattox, *Coffee and Coffeehouses*, 28.

15 This claim, like many regarding the murky origins of coffee in France, is problematic. Its only source is a history published by Pierre's son seventy years later. Jean de La Roque, a coffee merchant operating during a period of great interest in coffee, would have had personal reasons

a claim exists that Cardinal Mazarin imported a trained coffee maker (and presumably beans) from Italy, conceivably as early as 1642.[16] Sounder evidence of the first French awareness about coffee comes from the records of the English East India Company, whose agents in 1647 found a French pirate ship in the Persian Gulf with a cargo of coffee it had taken from another ship.[17] Coffee's first confirmed appearance in France dates to 1657, when the Orientalist scholar Jean de Thévenot brought some to Paris on returning from his travels in the Ottoman Empire. While a precise dating of coffee's real entry to France will likely never be determined, it is clear that most early coffee consumers were associated by travel experience, profession, or birth with the Ottoman world of the eastern Mediterranean, including French, Armenian, and Jewish merchants; diplomats and Orientalist scholars; sailors; knights of Malta; and Turkish galley slaves.[18] Only travelers like these had had the prior exposure to the taste and culture of coffee necessary to persuade them to seek it out in France. In 1660 coffee began to attract a small but loyal coterie of customers in Marseille, soon copied by nearby Lyon, with distant Paris following more slowly.[19] In response, a few Armenian entrepreneurs experimented with selling brewed coffee in coffeehouses and as street vendors. Their ventures, catering mostly to these foreigners, flourished in Marseille as early as 1671, but according to Jean de La Roque, in Paris they could not at first attract enough local customers to survive.[20] Coffee had arrived, but few knew or cared.

Most histories of coffee's adoption in France — indeed, in continental Europe — claim that the turning point for coffee's popularity came in 1669, when Suleiman Aga, a diplomatic envoy sent to Louis XIV from the Ottoman sultan Mehmed IV, abruptly made coffee fashionable with the royal court at Versailles and elite society in Paris. Numerous aristocratic women, drawn by curiosity, called on him to see his temporary residence, sumptuously decorated with Turkish accessories, and to be served exotic Turkish coffee. Noting their inability to finish the bitter

---

for crediting his father with originating the idea of importing coffee to France. La Roque, *Voyage de l'Arabie heureuse . . . fait par les Français pour la première fois, dans les années 1708, 1709 et 1710. Avec . . . un traité historique de l'origine et du progrès du café, de son introduction en France et de l'établissement de son usage à Paris,* 2nd ed. (Paris, 1716), 363–65, 372.

16 François Audiger, *La maison réglée, et l'art de diriger la maison d'un grand seigneur* (Paris, 1692), 166–69. According to Audiger, Mazarin's coffee brewer was named "More"; could he mean Moro/ Moor (a Muslim from North Africa)? Audiger also tells us that More trained *him*—the third man in France "to make coffee-drinking fashionable"—in the "science" of coffee making, rendering this claim for priority both plausible and as suspect as La Roque's, for nearly the same reasons.

17 Cowan, *Social Life of Coffee,* 60.

18 Hélène Desmet-Grégoire, *Le* divan *magique: L'Orient turc en France au XVIIIe siècle* (Paris, 1980), 76–77.

19 Michel Tuchscherer, "Café et cafés dans l'Egypte ottoman, XVIe–XVIIe siècles," in *Cafés d'Orient revisités,* ed. Hélène Desmet-Grégoire and François Georgeon (Paris, 1997), 101.

20 La Roque, *Voyage de l'Arabie heureuse,* 364–80.

drink, the diplomat added sugar to make it more palatable. *Et voilà!* A French taste for coffee was born.[21] Yet crediting Suleiman Aga with single-handedly making coffee fashionable in France becomes untenable on closer examination. Clearly he did not introduce coffee to the royal court, as it had been available to the discerning and the curious for over a decade. Craig Koslofsky has recently shown that coffeehouses kept by Englishmen for their compatriots thrived in Paris as early as 1664 and found evidence that French customers came there at least occasionally; Louis XIV himself is also, probably not coincidentally, said to have first tasted coffee that same year.[22] Suleiman Aga was by all accounts a taciturn and difficult diplomatic guest who famously insulted the king to his face, was poorly received at court, and became the butt of satire in Molière's 1670 comedy of identities, *Le bourgeois gentilhomme.* How much of a trendsetter could he really have been? But more problematic is the ten- to fifteen-year time lag between when Suleiman Aga served coffee to a few aristocratic guests in 1669 and the richly documented emergence across France of medical, fashionable, and commercial interest in coffee during the 1680s and 1690s.

One reason for the slow spread of coffee was that its original black Turkish form did not appeal to seventeenth-century French palates. A French traveler in the Levant earlier in the century found that Turkish coffee had "not an agreeable taste, but rather bitter."[23] Despite the tales told about Suleiman Aga's visitors, coffee with just sugar added did little better initially among the French.[24] It took assurances from physicians that coffee had serious curative powers, especially when combined with milk, to establish coffee's popularity in France with doctors and women, from whom it passed gradually into wider usage. Philippe Sylvestre Dufour, a medically trained Lyonnais spice merchant, authored the two earliest French treatises on coffee. The first

21 This tale is alive and well, as evident in Spary, *Eating the Enlightenment*, 55–61. The legend dates to the eighteenth century: see La Roque, *Voyage de l'Arabie heureuse*, 373–74; and Jean-Baptiste Legrand d'Aussy, *Histoire de la vie privée des Français*, 3 vols. (Paris, 1782), 3:109–11. It was later picked up by Alfred Franklin, *Le café, le thé et le chocolat*, vol. 13 of *La vie privée d'autrefois* (Paris, 1893), 36; and repeated by (among others) Jean Leclant, "Le café et les cafés à Paris (1644–1693)," *Annales: Economies, sociétés, civilisations* 6, no. 1 (1951): 3–4; and Bennett Alan Weinberg and Bonnie K. Bealer, *The World of Caffeine: The Science and Culture of the World's Most Popular Drug* (New York, 2001), 68–71.

22 Craig Koslofsky, "Parisian Cafés in European Perspective: Gender, Smoke, and Clientele, 1660–1750" (paper presented at the Society for French Historical Studies, Cambridge, MA, Apr. 2013); Edélestan Jardin, *Le caféier et le café* (Paris, 1895), 23.

23 Quoted in Jacob Spon [more probably Philippe Sylvestre Dufour], *The Manner of Making of Coffee, Tea and Chocolate, as It Is Used in Most Parts of Europe, Asia, Africa, and America, with Their Virtues*, trans. John Chamberlain (London, 1685), 33; see also Cowan, *Social Life of Coffee*, 17–25.

24 Susan Pinkard, *A Revolution in Taste: The Rise of French Cuisine* (New York, 2009), 125. However, by the 1680s sugared coffee was so popular in Paris that some were chastised for turning their coffee into "black syrup": Sabine Coron, *Livres en bouche: Cinq siècles d'art culinaire français* (Paris, 2001), 153.

recorded mention of café au lait appears in his initial work, *De l'usage du caphé, du thé, et du chocolate* (1671).[25] He devoted an entire chapter to the effects of combining milk and coffee in his next study, *Traitez nouveaux et curieux du café, du thé et du chocolate* (1685), which despite the title focuses overwhelmingly on coffee. Dufour attributed the invention of café au lait to a German doctor as a medical remedy for chest complaints, and the testing of its efficacy to a French doctor of Grenoble who had prescribed it to patients since about 1680. He also suggested a reason why café au lait would please when black coffee did not: "When [ground] coffee is boiled in milk, and a little thickened, it approaches the flavor of chocolate, which nearly everyone finds good."[26] The consumption of drinking chocolate had reached northern Europe nearly half a century before coffee began to catch on in France and may have given the French the ability to appreciate another hot bitter stimulant drink that resembled chocolate enough to be somewhat familiar.[27] Coffee began to sell well in France only during the mid-1680s, exactly when Dufour publicized the café au lait as a tonic and described how to make it.[28]

Along with elevating coffee's health benefits and improving its taste and appearance, adding French milk de-emphasized the alien quality of a drink strongly associated with Islam, Arabia, and the Ottoman Empire. Milk was one of the most local of all provisions in the premodern world. Even Parisians, who depended on food often imported from very distant regions, produced their own milk. Milk was also widely celebrated in this period for its embodiment of womanly fertility and pastoral health and virtue, making milk products especially appealing to aristocratic and royal women.[29] The marquise de Sévigné, who for over twenty years recorded her nervous approach to coffee according to whether others she knew were drinking it and what doctors had to say about its safety, was rapturous when royal physicians approved coffee with milk as a tonic. In the late 1680s, after a decade of abstention, she began to take it again and soon ascribed her good health to it. Dur-

25 Dufour, *De l'usage du caphé*, 143.

26 Philippe Sylvestre Dufour, *Traitez nouveaux et curieux du café, du thé et du chocolate* (Lyon, 1685, 1688; repr. The Hague, 1693), 152.

27 Marcy Norton, *Sacred Gifts, Profane Pleasures: A History of Tobacco and Chocolate in the Atlantic World* (Ithaca, NY, 2008), 260–62. The early history of chocolate in France overlaps that of coffee more closely than is generally understood. Chocolate seems to have entered French consciousness between 1643 and 1659 and became popular following the 1660 wedding of Louis XIV to the Spanish infanta Maria-Theresa: Bertram M. Gordon, "Chocolate in France: Evolution of a Luxury Product," in *Chocolate: History, Culture, and Heritage*, ed. Louis Evan Grivetti and Howard Yana Shapiro (New York, 2009), 570.

28 Dufour, *Traitez nouveaux*, 148, 151.

29 Reynald Abad, *Le Grand Marché: L'approvisionnement alimentaire de Paris sous l'Ancien Régime* (Paris, 2002); McCabe, *Orientalism in Early Modern France*, 179; Meredith Martin, *Dairy Queens: The Politics of Pastoral Architecture from Catherine de' Medici to Marie-Antoinette* (Cambridge, MA, 2011), 4–5; Anne Mendelson, *Milk: The Surprising Story of Milk through the Ages* (New York, 2008), 26–27.

ing a 1690 country retreat she wrote to her daughter: "All my ridiculous little ailments have disappeared. . . . We have here good milk and good cows; we've taken it into our heads to skim the cream . . . and mix it with sugar and good coffee: my dear child, it's the loveliest thing. [Doctor] Du Bois approves it for the chest, and for a cold; in a word, it's the 'coffee'd milk' or 'milky coffee' of our friend [Doctor] Aliot."[30]

The other development that made coffee not just drinkable but outright fashionable—the must-have commodity among the elite of French society—was the birth of a taste for *turquerie*. This passion for all things Turkish is generally perceived as an eighteenth-century phenomenon. In 1721 and 1742 two Ottoman ambassadors made dramatic state visits to the court of Louis XV. Corresponding closely to these events, beginning in the 1720s and peaking from the 1740s to the 1760s, a strong interest in *turquerie* arose in both the fine and decorative arts, as well as in stylish clothing, music, theater, and literature. However, this taste for Turkishness turns out to have had a precursor in the French luxury trade of the 1680s and 1690s. Because these fashions have never been linked to larger political events, historians of *turquerie* have paid them almost no attention.[31] There was the 1669 Ottoman envoy who inspired the famous Turkish masquerade in *Le bourgeois gentilhomme*. But Suleiman Aga's sour visit faded from popular memory so quickly that he can no more have influenced fashionable clothing of the 1680s than he can have taught the French court to like coffee. If, however, we consider these unusual new styles alongside the early history of coffee's penetration into Parisian and court culture, the supporting influence of each on the other becomes evident.

Writing about the emergence of early modern consumer interest in novelty goods, Jan de Vries theorizes that "goods in combination may possess characteristics different from those pertaining to the same goods consumed separately. . . . Moreover, when bundled, consumer goods can acquire nontangible qualities that affect their utility to the consumer."[32] In the 1680s coffee was joined, in the minds of consumers, with an even newer trade in French-manufactured luxury goods with Eastern associations, such as "Armenian" and "Indian" dressing gowns, "Turkish" sofas, and "sultana" dresses, the latter two directly inspired

---

30 Madame de Sévigné to Madame de Grignan, Jan. 29, 1690, in Marie de Rabutin-Chantal, marquise de Sévigné, *Lettres*, ed. Emile Gérard-Gailly, 3 vols. (Paris, 1960), 3:664. The term *café au lait* had not yet been settled on.

31 Nebahat Avcıoğlu, *Turquerie and the Politics of Representation, 1728–1876* (Farnham, 2011); Julia Landweber, "Turkish Delight: The Eighteenth-Century Market in *Turqueries* and the Commercialization of Identity in France," *Proceedings of the Western Society for French History* 30 (2004): 202–11; Perrin Stein, "Exoticism as Metaphor: *Turquerie* in Eighteenth-Century French Art" (PhD diss., New York University, 1997).

32 De Vries, *Industrious Revolution*, 31, 33.

by Ottoman furniture and costume.[33] Combining coffee with fresh milk turned a Turkish drink into a French one; sipping that same aromatically steaming beverage while wearing a *sultane* or dressing gown, or while lounging on a sofa with a turbaned Moorish attendant at hand, ushered the French consumer into an elegant fantasy of *turquerie*.

Much of *turquerie*'s attraction had to do with sensual pleasure. The novel taste of coffee, the *commodité* of Turkish robes and furniture, and the way both hinted at sexual adventure made *turquerie* highly tempting to elite French consumers. Fashion plates began to depict aristocrats displaying their fine clothes while sitting on sofa-like chairs and drinking coffee. Men appear to have been the first object of this trend. In 1674, when coffee was still a rarity reserved for only the most curious of epicures, a plate of a gentleman decreeing "the coffee of the Levant" a "necessary extravagance" specifically connected drinking it with dressing stylishly (fig. 1). By the 1680s the focus of *turquerie* in fashion plates had shifted to women. Fashionable women were depicted rising from their beds in Turkish undress, receiving lovers' letters while reclining on Turkish sofas in sometimes sexualized poses, and taking coffee.[34] Coffee's growing reputation for producing insomnia could also be useful in the boudoir, as several prints of 1688 make clear. In one, a maid warns her mistress even while pouring her a cup of coffee, "Madame, put down that coffee given to you, if you want to sleep a little tonight." Another shows a gentlewoman lifting a coffee cup and advising the viewer, "This drink's peculiar taste can be bitter in the mouth, but very sweet to the heart." In a third, a lady smiles serenely while announcing that her *sultane* dress is just the thing "for the practices of the harem."[35]

Although much about these images was fantasy, some apparently took them literally. A 1695 fashion plate depicts the princesse de Bournonville wearing a Turkish robe and turban, with a steaming cup of coffee at her right elbow, and a young Moorish servant, also dressed in Turkish robe and turban, at her left hand (fig. 2). Several years later Charlotte-Elisabeth, duchesse d'Orléans, described another noblewoman who might have learned her habits from Madame de Bournonville: "The duchesse de Lesdiguières . . . has a strange temperament. All day long she does nothing but drink coffee or tea. . . . When she takes coffee, her chambermaids and herself must be dressed in the Turkish

33 Madeleine Dobie, *Foreign Bodies: Gender, Language, and Culture in French Orientalism* (Stanford, CA, 2001), 91–96.

34 E.g., N. Arnoult, *Madame la Duchesse de Boüillon en deshabillé negligé sur un Sopha*, n.d., Bibliothèque Nationale de France, Cabinet des Estampes (hereafter BNF and Est., respectively), Oa 52.

35 P. Talleran, *Dame prenant du caffé*, 1688, BNF, Département des Manuscrits, Man. coll. Clairembault, "Mémoires, notes et gravures sur le cacao et l'usage du café, du chocolat et du sucre"; R. Bonnart, *Dame qui prend du café*, 1688, BNF, Est., Oa 20 fol.; and H. Bonnart, *Dame vestue à la sultane*, Feb. 1688, BNF, Est., Oa 51 pet. fol.

Homme de qualité

C'est peu que je me rasasie   Ie fais encor' cas du Café de Leuant
De ce que mon pais a de plus excellent   Et trouue des raisons à cette fantaisie
Chez Bonnart vis avis les Mathurins au Coq avec priuil. 1674.

Figure 1 Henri Bonnart, *Homme de qualité buvant du café* (Paris, 1674). Image courtesy of the Bibliothèque Nationale de France, Département Estampes et Photographie, Oa 62 pet. fol. p. 15960

Madame la Princesse de Bournonville

les portraits de la Cour se trouuent chez N.Bonnart, ruë S.ᵗ Iaques à l'aigle auec priuil.

Figure 2 Nicolas Bonnart, *Madame la Princesse de Bournonville, en pied* (Paris, 1694). Image courtesy of the Bibliothèque Nationale de France, Département Estampes et Photographie, Reserve FOL-QB-201 (69)

manner; when she takes tea, the servants who bring it must be dressed in the Indian manner. The chambermaids often weep bitter tears that they must change their clothes two or three times a day."[36] Invoking de Vries again, such "consumer clusters . . . acquire the marking functions that supply social distinction."[37] These images of aristocratic society were selling a concept of elegant living as much as they were promoting new kinds of clothing, new beverages, and new furniture. These symbolic relationships persisted through the eighteenth century. The most striking image linking an avatar of high fashion with coffee and intimacy is Carle Vanloo's famous 1755 portrait of Madame de Pompadour as a sultana being served coffee.[38] What makes this painting remarkable is its double evocation of actual Ottoman customs and the established tradition of French fashion plates associating expensive taste, undress, and coffee.[39] Fashion plates continued the theme even as late as 1780, when showing a man in an Oriental dressing gown holding a cup of coffee, and showing a woman in dishabille reclining on a sofa in a sexualized pose, remained natural associations.[40]

The preceding evidence would suggest that coffee was originally an object of domestic consumption among the French. The purveyors of such imagery envisioned a domestic gender divide, with men drinking coffee for themselves and women drinking it in preparation to receive a lover. Whatever their supposed motives, these aristocrats enjoying coffee alongside their fashionable furnishings and clothing were clearly drinking it at home. But from the outset coffee was also consumed in public establishments. Just as the producers of fashion plates associated the new clothing *à la turque* with coffee and sofas, so too at some point coffee merchants in France began to attract customers by associating the beverage with elements of *turquerie*. Most histories of the café, beginning with Jean de La Roque's mythmaking narrative work,

36 Charlotte-Elisabeth, duchesse d'Orléans, letter of Mar. 8, 1699, in *A Woman's Life in the Court of the Sun King: Letters of Liselotte von der Pfalz, 1652–1722*, trans. Elborg Forster (Baltimore, MD, 1984), 111.

37 De Vries, *Industrious Revolution*, 33.

38 Carle Vanloo, *Sultan's Wife Drinking Coffee* (1755), in the collection of the State Hermitage Museum, tinyurl.com/n26qele; Perrin Stein, "Amédée Van Loo's *Costume Turc*: The French Sultana," *Art Bulletin* 78, no. 3 (1996): 427.

39 See "Fille turque prenant le caffé sur le sopha," in Jean Baptiste Vanmour, *Receuil de cent estampes représentant différentes nations du Levant* (Paris, 1712), pl. 48; and Seth Gopin and Eveline Sint Nicolaas, *Jean Baptiste Vanmour, peintre de la sublime porte, 1671–1737* (Bayeux, 2009), 159–62. Since the 1680s Dufour and others had purposely emphasized coffee's Ottoman associations with honor and status to market coffee to the French as a refined drink, worthy of being drunk by the most elegant consumers: Alexander Bevilacqua and Helen Pfeifer, "*Turquerie*: Culture in Motion, 1650–1750," *Past and Present*, no. 222 (2013): 95.

40 "Homme de qualité en robe de chambre" (1780) and "Femme en deshabillé du matin" (1780), repr. in *Eighteenth-Century French Fashion in Full Color: 64 Engravings from the "Galerie des Modes," 1778–1787*, ed. Stella Blum (New York, 1982), 8, 34.

date the first café in Paris to a stand at the Saint-Germain fair run by
an Armenian named Pascal in 1672 and claim that no café before Procopio's was successful at attracting a clientele. In fact, sit-down establishments selling coffee already existed in Paris before 1669, only they
were not yet called cafés, and for the most part they did not yet claim
any Ottoman associations.[41] These drinks shops were run by *limonadiers*
(makers and sellers of soft drinks and spirits). They sold a wide range
of drinks, hard and soft, hot and cold, including coffee, chocolate, and
tea as each became available. These shops' very ubiquity and familiarity
meant that Parisians paid little attention when *limonadiers* added coffee
to the other drinks for sale. Coffee was just one more item on a long
menu. Tellingly, the first to notice coffee for sale in Paris were not the
French but English, Dutch, and German travelers, whose longing for
the coffeehouses of home caused them to seek out and report on coffee
for sale wherever they found it.[42]

In the 1670s coffee sellers began to emphasize Ottoman connections, real or borrowed. Seventeenth-century coffee sellers in France
had always included Armenians and Jews from the Ottoman and Persian
Empires; La Roque's history suggests that Pascal earned his erroneous
identification as founder of the café concept because his Armenian
robes distinguished him from the French competition. Even Procopio
supposedly learned his craft by apprenticing under Pascal, giving him
too a gloss of Armenian heritage. The generation of *limonadiers*, including Procopio, who opened new establishments in the 1680s did seem to
be consciously trying something new. However, their chief innovation
had nothing to do with *turquerie*. Rather, they altered expectations about
what the interior of a coffeehouse should be like by elevating the luxury quotient of their business over the humbler English and Ottoman
predecessors. They added marble tables, large mirrors, and fancy chan-
deliers, and they mostly banned tobacco and smoking (staples of the
Ottoman, English, Dutch, and German coffeehouses).[43] In the 1690s
these fancier establishments became linked with coffee more than previous lemonade shops had been, earning them the name *café*—which
itself provided yet another link to an "Armenian, Turkish, and Persian

---

41 However, one of the first known coffeehouses in Paris sold coffee "at the sign of the
Grand Turk." See Francis Petersen, *De potu coffi* (Frankfurt am Main, 1666), fol. B3r. I thank Craig
Koslofsky for bringing this work to my attention.

42 Thomas Brennan, *Public Drinking and Popular Culture in Eighteenth-Century Paris* (Princeton,
NJ, 1988), 85–87; Spary, *Eating the Enlightenment*, 104.

43 La Roque, *Voyage de l'Arabie heureuse*, 378–79, and Joachim Christoph Nemeitz, *Sejour de
Paris, c'est-à-dire, instructions fidéles, pour les voiageurs de condition* (Frankfurt am Main, 1718; French
trans. Leiden, 1727), 110–14, document the disappearance of smoking in the first French cafés.
Seventeenth-century smoking involved a surprising amount of coughing and spitting, making it
"anything but dainty" and unappealing in an environment designed to attract respectable society:
Jordan Goodman, *Tobacco in History: The Cultures of Dependence* (New York, 1993), 82–83.

Orient."[44] Additionally, many early French cafés kept servers dressed like Armenians and Turks.[45] By 1716 over three hundred cafés were flourishing; by the 1780s that number would reach nearly two thousand. Even though coffee in France by then was mostly imported from the Antilles and the café had become thoroughly domesticated as a French institution, some of the grandest Parisian cafés of the late eighteenth century still featured Turkish décor; one was even named the Café Turc.[46]

Combining luxurious interiors with an interactive experience of *turquerie* touched every fashionable nerve. Was this sufficient enticement for women to enter these establishments? Historians acquainted with England's male-only coffeehouses have long assumed that respectable women did not patronize eighteenth-century cafés.[47] Scattered evidence occasionally places women in French cafés as customers, but most women documented there were proprietors, servers, or prostitute companions of male customers.[48] While men of many classes flocked to cafés, well-to-do women more often restricted their coffee usage to domestic settings, consuming it at breakfast with family, in the afternoon with female friends, or as a conclusion to evening banquets with guests.[49] Coffee did not become less fashionable to women for developing into an emblem of the emerging public sphere, but women's usage more often happened in contexts of domestic sociability or medicinal utility.

Wherever imbibed, coffee required a new panoply of accoutrements: roaster, grinder, coffeepot, cups, saucers, serving trays. For roasting and grinding the beans, tools already present in most French kitchens sufficed. Brewing and serving coffee correctly was a different matter, and owning the right objects became another opportunity for conspicuous consumption of Asian-themed goods. The earliest coffee connoisseurs, such as Jean de Thévenot, imported authentic *ibriks*

---

44 Rigogne, "Entre histoire et mythes," 167, 175.

45 See the frontispiece to Louis de Mailly, *Les entretiens des cafés de Paris, et les deferens qui y surviennent* (Trévoux, 1702).

46 La Roque, *Voyage de l'Arabie heureuse*, 373–83; Jardin, *Le caféier et le café*, 23–24; Robert Isherwood, *Farce and Fantasy: Popular Entertainment in Eighteenth-Century Paris* (Oxford, 1986), 57–59, 165; Brennan, *Public Drinking and Popular Culture*, 86–87.

47 Cowan, *Social Life of Coffee*, 229–46.

48 La Roque, *Voyage de l'Arabie heureuse*, 381; Mailly, *Les entretiens*; and Jacques Savary des Brûlons and Philemon-Louis Savary, *Dictionnaire universel de commerce*, 4 vols. (Amsterdam, 1726–32), 1:506, depict women of quality as café patrons in the first quarter of the eighteenth century. But we lack evidence of respectable women in Paris cafés for most of the midcentury (Tabetha Ewing, Hernán Cortés, and the author, pers. comm., July 11, 2014).

49 One way for a woman to bypass any restrictions on her gender in the café space, while still reaping the benefits of a *limonadier*'s expertise, was to have brewed coffee delivered to her home. Louis-Sébastien Mercier describes this morning custom in "The Hours of the Day," in *Tableau de Paris*, 4 vols. (Amsterdam, 1782), 4:146–47.

(special wide-bellied narrow-necked copper pots with high spouts used in the Ottoman Empire both to prepare and serve coffee). In France, domestically manufactured versions were renamed *cafetières*, sometimes with the appendage "du Levant," "de Constantinople," or "à la Turque," to emphasize their exotic association. Whether made of silver, copper, tin, porcelain, or glazed ceramic, they retained the basic shape of the *ibrik* well into the eighteenth century.[50]

An expensive and hot beverage brewed in tiny quantities, coffee also required little heat-resistant cups for drinkers not to injure themselves. Coincident with rising interest in coffee and other Oriental goods, in the 1670s French potters began to imitate Chinese porcelain, then a much-sought-after rarity in France. Their invention was called "soft-paste" porcelain because it was a notably different product than true "hard-paste" porcelain from China. It became commercially viable in the 1690s and joined the parade of faux-Oriental goods produced in France for the discriminating consumer.[51] For manufacturers of French porcelain and its older relative faience (tin-glazed earthenware), producing complete coffee, tea, and chocolate services was excellent business. According to Christine A. Jones, these artisan-inventors made a conscious effort to "cast their innovative porcelain body not as mere imitation [of Chinese porcelain] but as a symbol of fashionability."[52] By choosing delicate porcelain cups for serving coffee, French fashion leaders merged a love of *turquerie* with another budding fashion for Eastern things, *chinoiserie*. In 1699 Antoine Galland published a detailed account of how coffee was served among Ottoman grandees. His description affirmed the new usage of porcelain on French tables while applauding the French for outdoing the original master coffee drinkers: in Constantinople "the servant brings in a tray of silver or of painted wood, [holding] cups of porcelain *rather less grand than those which are used here* [in France]." After the recipients spread napkins across their knees to protect from spills, the servant poured out the near-boiling beverage, "never filling cups to the rim" to prevent guests from burning their fingers or lips.[53] In France, by contrast, creative pot-

---

50 Hélène Desmet-Grégoire, *Les objets du café dans les sociétés du Proche-Orient et de la Méditerranée* (Paris, 1989), 58–69.

51 Julie Emerson, *Coffee, Tea, and Chocolate Wares in the Collection of the Seattle Art Museum* (Seattle, WA, 1991), 2–3, 23–25; Meredith Chilton, "The Pleasures of Life: Ceramics in Seventeenth- and Eighteenth-Century France," in *Daily Pleasures: French Ceramics from the MaryLou Boone Collection*, ed. Elizabeth A. Williams (Los Angeles, 2012), 23–24, 32–37; Stéphane Castelluccio, *Collecting Chinese and Japanese Porcelain in Pre-revolutionary Paris*, trans. Sharon Grevet (Los Angeles, 2013), 50–52, 60.

52 Christine A. Jones, *Shapely Bodies: The Image of Porcelain in Eighteenth-Century France* (Newark, DE, 2013), 4–5.

53 Antoine Galland, *De l'origine et du progrès du café* (Caen, 1699), 69–74. Emphasis mine.

ters had already invented the porcelain saucer as a superior method for preventing spills and holding a hot cup.[54]

From Medical Marvel to Cultivated Commodity

Once rendered palatable with sugar and milk, coffee was increasingly hailed as tasty; in short order, its associations with *turquerie* and *chinoiserie* made it fashionable. Indeed, the French themselves were startled by the rapidity of its adoption. But making coffee an intellectually palatable element of the French diet took far longer than adopting it as a consumable good. The mystery of coffee (was it a drug? a drink? a food? was it healthful or harmful? moral or immoral?) inspired numerous examinations by medical experts, theologians, chefs, and others from the 1670s through the 1790s. By the late 1680s it was clear that coffee held great potential as a profit maker for both individuals and the government. However, coffee's druglike qualities also alarmed many. It was a new substance with obvious but unmapped powers to affect the human body. Proponents needed to situate it firmly within established European ideas about the natural world and about human health and diet, while detractors sought to prove it unsuitable for common consumption, or at least immoral for Christians to use. Supporters would have to overcome their opponents' concerns before coffee could become an acceptable part of French life. The intellectual domestication of coffee in France may best be explained through a set of rubrics established by Louis, chevalier de Jaucourt, in the 1750s. In a set of interrelated entries on food and cooking composed for Diderot's *Encyclopedia*, Jaucourt identified three ways of comprehending the culinary realm: through classification, though a religious-moral tradition, and through medical-dietetic knowledge.[55] Reading the early French discourse on coffee through Jaucourt's interpretive lenses reveals how various experts collectively made coffee part of French culinary habits.

Early modern knowledge acquisition began with a desire to organize and classify the things of this world. Jaucourt believed that while it was possible to describe and catalog visible facts about food, one should not attempt to classify the world of flavors that depended entirely on individual experience. Likewise with coffee: merchants, physicians, and pharmacists all felt a primary duty to describe the plant using both

54 Nicolas de Blégny, *Le bon usage du thé, du caffé et du chocolat pour la préservation et pour la guerison des maladies* (Paris, 1687), 168. Handles on coffee cups became common only in the 1730s: see Emerson, *Coffee, Tea, and Chocolate Wares*, 25.

55 Jean-Claude Bonnet, "The Culinary System in the *Encyclopédie*," in *Food and Drink in History*, ed. Robert Forster and Orest Ranum, trans. Elborg Forster and Patricia Ranum (Baltimore, MD, 1979), 142.

words and images and to inventory knowledge about the bean, its uses, and its effects. But they stopped short of describing the taste of coffee, beyond noting its bitterness. These were the first steps in the messy process of transforming coffee from a mysterious Oriental import into a familiar domestic commodity. Sylvestre Dufour was the perfect man to launch this project: a university-educated and medically trained spice merchant connected to the Levantine trade, he was interested in promoting coffee and well qualified to vouch for coffee's health benefits. Dufour's most influential work, the 1684 *Traitez nouveaux et curieux du café, du thé et du chocolate,* opens with a botanical description richly indicative of the uncertainties then surrounding Western knowledge of coffee: "Coffee is a type of legume, or seed, about the size of our littlest *haricots.* . . . Earlier authors classified coffee among the beans, owing to their seeming affinity. Only twenty-five years ago coffee was so little known in France, that some called it a mulberry [*meure*]." Dufour was referring to a handbill that had circulated in Paris circa 1664, advertising coffee for sale at a *limonadier*'s shop in the Rue des Boucheries, faubourg Saint-Germain.[56]

Nicolas de Blégny, a Paris doctor with royal connections, also produced two coffee studies. In *Le bon usage du thé, du caffé et du chocolat* (1687), Blégny tries to describe coffee in terms that would make sense to someone who had never seen the plant—which included himself. His text, printed alongside an illustration of a coffee tree's branch, betrays his own lack of knowledge: "Its leaves somewhat resemble those of a cherry tree. . . . The body is like one of our domestic beanstalks. Its fruit, which has the texture of our field beans, holds two seeds in a little pod, which is why in Europe the fruit is identified as a kind of Indian bean. Whatever it is most like, you should decide for yourself after inspecting the illustration printed here."[57] Important cultural information was also transmitted through these books' illustrations. Seventeenth-century French coffee merchants needed to teach professional *limonadiers* and potential consumers everything about coffee, including how to prepare and serve it as a drink. In an attempt to render the hidden visible and the strange familiar, both Dufour and Blégny showed the plant and its beans, the implements for roasting the beans, the accoutrements for making and serving the drink, and even representative Turks enjoying a cup.[58]

The difficulty was that prior to the eighteenth century coffee was strictly a Yemeni import. Apart from an intrepid traveler or two, no

---

56 Dufour, *Traitez nouveaux,* 5, 7; "Les tres-excellentes vertus de la Meure appellée Coffe," repr. in Petersen, *De potu coffi,* fols. B2v–3r.
57 Blégny, *Le bon usage . . . du caffé,* 88–89.
58 Dufour, *De l'usage du caphé,* 4–7; Blégny, *Le bon usage . . . du caffé,* 105–6.

Frenchman had ever reached the port of Mocha to see the great coffee markets or seen the plant that produced coffee beans, let alone ventured into the hinterlands to witness its cultivation and production. In 1696 the Dutch (who, with the English, had been trading at Mocha since the early seventeenth century) began to establish coffee plantations in Java; within a decade they would have the first commercial coffee harvest to be produced outside Yemen. At this point, navy minister Jérôme de Pontchartrain decided France should enter the coffee trade at its source. He gave this right to an ambitious company of Breton merchants from Saint-Malo, which in 1707 funded the first of many French voyages to Mocha. These voyages reached public attention in 1715, when Jean de La Roque published his account of the Malouins' first two voyages and their observations of coffee production in Yemen.[59] In this same period, Antoine de Jussieu, professor of botany at the Jardin du Roi, Paris's royal natural history garden, received both a coffee plant and, separately, some coffee seeds that he was able to sprout. The first plant died, but Jussieu was able to replace it with a full-grown coffee plant sent by the burgomaster of Amsterdam in 1714. The new plant soon flowered and fruited at the Jardin du Roi, making it the first coffee plant to reach maturity on French soil. Between 1713 and 1716 Jussieu prepared several reports on these plants for the Académie Royale des Sciences and defended coffee's health benefits before the Paris medical faculty.[60]

La Roque and Jussieu each published illustrations of coffee plants drawn from life: a first for French studies of coffee. Alongside this knowledge gain, the Arabian import was acquiring a new identity. What made a plant French? In the late seventeenth century botanists at the Jardin du Roi decided that imported specimens that reproduced on French soil "were now French plants" because they had been naturalized into French agriculture and gardening.[61] If coffee could flower and reproduce in Paris, and those seeds could in turn reproduce under French cultivation, in what sense were their offspring still Arabian? Between 1716 and 1725 the Jardin du Roi and the Académie Royale des Sciences sent clippings and seeds from these Paris plants to overseas

59 Spary, *Eating the Enlightenment*, 70–71; La Roque, *Voyage de l'Arabie heureuse*. Although unreliable on the history of coffee and cafés, La Roque may be trusted for contemporaneous events such as the voyages to Mocha. His descriptions of the Mocha expeditions were based on interviews with, and the papers of, the ship captain and head of the expedition, and also the ship's surgeon. See Jean-Pierre Brown, *Les corsaires sur la route du café* (Saint-Malo, 2006).

60 Report of Antoine de Jussieu, presented Nov. 18, 1713, Archives de l'Académie des Sciences, Paris, "Procès-verbaux," fol. 339v; Jussieu, "Mémoires," in *Histoire de l'Académie des Sciences* (Paris, 1716), 291–98.

61 Chandra Mukerji, "Dominion, Demonstration, and Domination: Religious Doctrine, Territorial Politics, and French Plant Collection," in *Colonial Botany: Science, Commerce, and Politics in the Early Modern World*, ed. Londa Schiebinger and Claudia Swan (Philadelphia, 2005), 30.

French colonies. Soon coffee plantations were established in Bourbon in the Indian Ocean and Martinique in the West Indies. This project succeeded best in Saint-Domingue, which by the 1780s would become the world leader in coffee production, even exporting coffee back to Mocha itself.[62] Not all those plants actually trace their ancestry to Jussieu's plants at the Jardin du Roi (although that claim is frequently repeated in popular histories of coffee). But the link was strong enough to make coffee, once an exotic specimen associated with elegant *turqueries*, transform during the eighteenth century into a thoroughly domesticated (if colonial) French commodity.

Establishing the nature of coffee through attempts at classification was a straightforward process of positive investigation, initiated by medical and pharmacological experts in the seventeenth century and then taken over by botanists in the eighteenth century. Returning to the first decades of coffee usage, we find a different set of concerns applied to determining how coffee fit into the religious-moral traditions of Old Regime France. Most French scholars of coffee found it a beneficial drink, but some vehemently disagreed. In 1679 Claude Colomb, a medical student in Marseille, publicly attacked coffee.[63] In a thesis presented for his degree, he ascribed to coffee "tyrannical" qualities that made it impossible to stop drinking. He feared that such attributes would encourage gluttony and corrupt drinkers. Persuaded, the Marseille city leaders promptly banned the importation and sale of coffee and burned what beans they had. While economic jealousy against Armenian merchants, a rival group of foreigners then dominating the fledgling business of coffee importation to France, may have spurred their actions, others gradually adopted the idea that coffee possessed a dangerous side.[64] In 1705 Daniel Duncan, a doctor from Montpellier, invoked God to chastise the "abuse" of overdrinking coffee.[65] The *Traité des dispenses du carême*, first published in 1709 by doctor and theologian Philippe Hecquet, applied Colomb's and Duncan's observations to the Christian tradition of religious fasts. Hecquet agreed that coffee was "highly seductive, and so able to corrupt the palate that, once tried, it is forever desired." Worse, it was "voluptuous," which made it

62 Holden Furber, *Rival Empires of Trade in the Orient, 1600–1800* (Minneapolis, MN, 1976), 253–55; Alan K. Smith, *Creating a World Economy: Merchant Capital, Colonialism, and World Trade, 1400–1825* (Boulder, CO, 1991), 140; Philip Boucher, "The French and Dutch Caribbean, 1600–1800," in *The Caribbean: A History of the Region and Its Peoples*, ed. Stephan Palmié and Francisco A. Scarano (Chicago, 2011), 218–19.

63 *Question de médecine proposée par Messieurs Castillons et Fouqué, docteurs de la faculté d'Aix, à Monsieur Colomb, pour son agrégaton au collège des médecins de Marseille* (Feb. 27, 1679), BNF, Département des Manuscrits.

64 McCabe, *Orientalism in Early Modern France*, 177.

65 Daniel Duncan, *Avis salutaire contre l'abus du café, du chocolat, et du thé* (Rotterdam, 1705), 6–7.

contrary to penitence.[66] He concluded that coffee was not acceptable for Christians during fasts, and maybe not ever. Nicolas Andry de Boisregard disagreed. In his 1713 *Traité des alimens de caresme*, he cited a Persian legend as proof that coffee cooled sexual ardor, leading to chaste marriages focused less on bodily lust and more on spiritual union. Coffee, theorized Andry de Boisregard, could actually improve average Christians by "making marriages more holy."[67]

Despite its association with sexual chastity, coffee still threatened to fill consumers with lust, a sin widely understood in the seventeenth and eighteenth centuries to include such forbidden enjoyments as pleasures of the palate. Many philosophers of the table perceived a moral dichotomy between foodstuffs and condiments. They tried to distinguish between a simple diet of roasted or boiled foods, considered saintly and healthful, and one that involved culinary activities catering to pleasure, such as combining several foods to make a sauce (*ragoût*) or seasoning foods to improve or alter their taste.[68] Where did coffee fit into this worldview? At its most basic, the coffee drink was a simple preparation derived from boiling ground beans. But when condiments such as sugar and milk were added, the palate risked being catered to unduly. With the invention of the café au lait we arrive at the true source of coffee's seductiveness, according to Duncan, and the reason that coffee was originally not a dangerous drink in the Ottoman Empire, where it was drunk black and bitter.[69]

The sin of lust also encompassed the desire for luxury. Histories of coffee normally associate its adoption with an eighteenth-century turn toward the bourgeois values of moderation, sobriety, and self-conscious rationality. Coffee would become *the* drink of the nonintoxicated intellectual world of the Enlightenment. Before the 1730s, however, the consumption of coffee in France principally provided opportunities for display and excess. Into the first quarter of the eighteenth century coffee remained a very expensive import, mostly because the French lagged far behind the English and Dutch in tapping into the coffee trade at its source. For decades in France coffee was chiefly available only to the wealthy, and a pound of beans went for eighty livres, almost four thousand dollars in today's money.[70] The price began to drop in the 1720s but remained out of reach for all but the well-to-do until the following decade. Fashion plates from these same years, discussed

---

66 Philippe Hecquet, *Traité des dispenses du carême*, 2 vols. (Paris, 1709–10), 2:417–18.
67 Nicolas Andry de Boisregard, *Traité des alimens de caresme*, 2 vols. (Paris, 1713), 2:378–79.
68 Bonnet, "Culinary System in the *Encyclopédie*," 142–43, 148.
69 Duncan, *Avis salutaire*, 11; Andry de Boisregard, *Traité des alimens de caresme*, 2:370.
70 Joan DeJean, *The Essence of Style: How the French Invented High Fashion, Fine Food, Chic Cafés, Style, Sophistication, and Glamour* (New York, 2005), 135, 147.

above, demonstrate coffee's reputation as a rare luxury. The coffee drinkers in the prints were always described as "ladies" and "men of quality," when not identified by actual titles such as the princesse de Bournonville, and they were always portrayed in the most elegant settings and latest fashions in lace, jewels, and clothing. These individuals would have had no qualms about their entitlement to luxuries like coffee, and moralists' concerns would have little effect on consumers seeking to emulate such plates. In addition, the quickly proliferating cafés, far from encouraging aristocratic Parisians to adopt the bourgeois values of thrift and sensible hours, instead taught bourgeois customers about the aristocratic consumption of time. Their late hours, which soon required police regulation, were better suited to display and excess than to early bedtimes.[71]

The question of whether to consider coffee more properly as a natural foodstuff or as something corrupted by condiments allows us to revisit the question of how coffee was classified while also moving into the area of medicine and dietetics. In this way we may connect all three of Jaucourt's rubrics for interpreting coffee's domestication in the French culinary universe. Inducting coffee into European schemata for understanding the natural and edible world required determining its effects on the body and establishing the degree to which these were beneficial or dangerous. Between the 1670s and the 1780s medical experts subjected coffee to numerous analyses. The pre-1666 circular was the first text in French to declare coffee a wonder drug, claiming that it "dries up cold and wet humors . . . fortifies the liver . . . refreshes the heart . . . and soothes those with stomach troubles"; even the steam emanating from coffee "is good for eye problems, for ringing in the ears, for colds which attack the lungs," and so on.[72] Dufour, basing his 1671 treatise partly on Francis Petersen's 1666 *De potu coffi*, agreed that "coffee helps digestion, dries the humidities under the skin, and gives an excellent smell to all the Body."[73] Both authors invoked humoral theory, the ancient medical belief that human health depended on keeping the body's four humors (blood, bile, phlegm, and choler) in balance, to regulate a person's temperature and degree of dryness or moistness. Good health varied by an individual's age, sex, and constitution: men were expected to be hotter and drier, and women colder

---

[71] In the late 1710s some Paris cafés were caught serving customers as late as three in the morning, despite laws against all-night establishments: *Sentence qui enjoint à tous limonadiers, vendeurs de caffé, d'avoir leurs Boutiques fermées à huit heures du soir en hiver, et à dix en eté* (Paris, Dec. 17, 1720); Craig Koslofsky, *Evening's Empire: A History of the Night in Early Modern Europe* (Cambridge, 2011), 176.

[72] Petersen, *De potu coffi*, fol. B2v.

[73] Dufour, *De l'usage du caphé*, 4–7; quoted from the English translation, *Manner of Making of Coffee, Tea and Chocolate*, 3–4, 7.

and moister, relative to one another. After Colomb's attack, many questioned coffee's safety for health reasons as much as for moral ones. Madame de Sévigné had been an early adopter, recording casual coffee usage by 1672. Devoted equally to following trends in medical advice and to guiding her children's health, however, she warned her grown daughter in late 1679: "Dr. Duchesne . . . believes that coffee is bad for you: it quickens and heats your blood; it may be good for those without bad chests, but it is not recommended for people in your poor state of health." A few months later she fretted about the contradictory views in circulation:

> Duchesne still abhors coffee, while his brother believes nothing wrong about it. . . . My daughter, what should I say? Sometimes one blames what is good, one chooses what is bad. . . . My heart knows that coffee has never done you good in all the time you've used it. Should it be taken only as a medicine? [Dr.] Caderousse sings its praises. Coffee fattens one person and weakens another. I don't believe that one should talk so positively about a thing when there are so many contrary examples.[74]

Madame de Sévigné feared that coffee, with its reputation as an overly hot and dry substance, could endanger her daughter, perhaps even render her barren.[75]

Such confusions persuaded Dufour to investigate coffee's unusual powers more seriously. His first book contained 47 pages on coffee, largely based on others' work; by contrast, the 1684 study devoted 216 pages to coffee, much of it original. In 1683 his editor announced to readers of the forthcoming *Traitez nouveaux*:

> No matter what approval is daily granted to coffee, there are still doctors who believe its usage is pernicious. The pains Monsieur Dufour has [now] taken to explain its properties, the analysis he has made of this bean, and the explanations he provides for the different effects it can produce will disabuse the most prejudiced and will instruct those who continue to question whether coffee heats or cools the body.[76]

The increasing popularity of coffee in the 1680s caught the king's attention as well. In 1687 Louis XIV commanded Blégny to scientifically analyze coffee's properties. Blégny agreed with Dufour that coffee was highly beneficial when used correctly but then detoured into entrepreneurial quackery by promoting his own invented coffee extract syrup as

---

[74] Madame de Sévigné to Madame de Grignan, Nov. 8, 1679; Sévigné to Grignan, Feb. 16, 1680, *Lettres*, 2:497–98, 610.

[75] Cowan, *Social Life of Coffee*, 41.

[76] Falconet fils, "Attestation pour le Livre . . . par le Sieur Dufour," in Dufour, *Traitez nouveaux*, n.p.

a tonic superior to regular brewed coffee. Worse, he questioned *limona-diers*' ability to safely prepare coffee. He argued that only experts with medical training (such as he) should dispense coffee, a serious drug that "could prevent apoplexy, palsy, lethargy, . . . calm agitated spirits that prevent sleep, and dissipate the vapors that interrupt the function-ing of a sensitive spirit."[77] Blégny claimed that problems with coffee derived from improper preparation, such as using adulterated coffee, overboiling, or reusing old grinds. Moralists stubbornly remained more concerned by coffee's addictive qualities than by how it was prepared. In 1713 Andry de Boisregard warned: "Those who take too much coffee rarely enjoy good health. We observe that vapors are never more com-mon than after too frequent usage of this drink."[78]

Nonetheless, in the cafés and grand kitchens of Paris, coffee was finding a niche. The surest proof that coffee was becoming part of the French alimentary lexicon can be traced through its passage from medi-cal treatises in the 1680s to books on drinks in the 1690s and finally into cookbooks in the 1730s. Decades after coffee's introduction to the French market, apothecaries still envisioned the coffee bean exclusively as a drug and beverage. Pierre Pomet decreed, in his authoritative *His-toire générale des drogues* (1695), that coffee "has no other use than . . . as a drink made with sugar and water," while also upholding coffee's medi-cal reputation: it "is a powerful remedy against . . . chest ailments and loss of appetite and is esteemed for curing headache."[79] Professional *limonadiers* also approached coffee exclusively as a drink, although not necessarily as a drug. François Audiger, one of the earliest Frenchmen to become a formally trained coffee brewer, was the first in France to publish a book entirely about drinks, in 1692. Others had described the coffee-brewing process, but nothing previously published approached Audiger's recipe. He detailed the accoutrements for roasting, grind-ing, brewing, and serving; described how the beans should look after roasting ("blacken[ed] evenly to the color of iron . . . neither burned nor reduced to charcoal"); gave exact measurements for all ingredi-ents and precise boiling techniques for brewing; and concluded with presentation instructions ("Let it rest until clear, then serve in porce-lain cups with powdered sugar to add as desired").[80] François Massia-lot and Pierre Masson, who followed Audiger's book with two more on drinks, in 1692 and 1705, respectively, both included similarly detailed

77 Blégny, *Le bon usage . . . du caffé*, 175–77, 180, quotation on 190; Blégny and Léonard Biet, *Le bon usage du chocolat dégraissé* [. . . *et du*] *caffé volatile* (Paris, n.d. [ca. 1687–1700]), n.p.

78 Andry de Boisregard, *Traité des alimens de caresme*, 2:369.

79 Pierre Pomet, *Le marchand sincère, ou . . . Histoire générale des drogues*, and appendix, "Remarques très-curieuses sur plusieurs Vegetaux" (Paris, 1695), 205 and 7.

80 Audiger, *La maison réglée*, bk. 4, 295–96.

coffee-making recipes. Oddly, Massialot prefaced his recipe by remarking that few would need it: "Coffee is in such common usage today, that almost no one is ignorant of how to prepare it."[81] Simply by instructing readers how to brew coffee without analyzing its curative properties, these three men paved the way for coffee's move "from medical literature into the realm of savoir-faire for cooking professionals."[82]

In the 1730s French cookbook authors adopted a new approach to food and cooking, called *cuisine moderne*. Jennifer J. Davis argues that these authors and their readers, as much as culinary guilds, actively set standards for prepared food in the eighteenth century. Consulting the text of a cookbook was as much a path to good taste as any other form of education in social customs.[83] While recognizing that coffee's appeal to clients continued to reside chiefly in its exotic quality as a drink from the Ottoman Empire, professional chefs seeking to radically alter French cooking practices began to consider its potential to flavor other foods. In his groundbreaking 1735 cookbook *Le cuisinier moderne*, Vincent La Chapelle published a recipe for chicken gizzards in a coffee cream sauce—the first recorded use in Europe for coffee other than as a drink. However, this savory dish was an aberration. Four years later coffee moved to the realm of sweets when the first record of a coffee-flavored dessert appeared in François Marin's equally groundbreaking cookbook, *Les dons de Comus*.[84]

With no visible debate, sweet immediately triumphed over savory uses for coffee in food. A host of inventive pastry chefs embraced coffee in the burgeoning French dessert repertoire. The eighteenth-century dessert craze achieved full glory with the publication of Joseph Gilliers's *Cannameliste français* (1751) and Emy's *L'art de bien faire les glaces d'office* (1768), definitive guides to confectionary and ice cream, respectively. Both featured coffee in numerous recipes.[85] More so even than Gilliers and Emy, leading experts of the *office* (a dedicated room in grand kitchens for producing pastries, preserves, and ice cream), chef-author Menon may deserve the most credit for establishing coffee in the world of sweets. All his very successful cookbooks included coffee-based desserts; for example, the *Science du maître d'hôtel confiseur*

81 François Massialot, *Nouvelle instruction pour les confitures, les liqueurs, et les fruits* (Paris, 1692), 267; Pierre Masson, *Le parfait limonadier, ou la manière de préparer le thé, le café, et le chocolat, et autre liqueurs chaudes et froides* (Paris, 1705).

82 Coron, *Livres en bouche*, 153.

83 Jennifer J. Davis, *Defining Culinary Authority: The Transformation of Cooking in France, 1650–1830* (Baton Rouge, LA, 2013), 86–87.

84 Vincent La Chapelle, *Le cuisinier moderne*, 3 vols. (The Hague, 1735), 3:258–60; François Marin, *Les dons de Comus, ou les délices de la table*, 4 vols. (Paris, 1739), 4:225.

85 Joseph Gilliers, *Le cannameliste français* (Nancy, 1751), 19, 58, 94, 154; Emy, *L'art de bien faire les glaces d'office* (Paris, 1768), 178–81, 197–98, 231–32.

(1749–50), written for the elegant tables of the great houses and their well-trained kitchen staff, included no fewer than eight coffee-flavored desserts—and should be remembered eternally for recording the first recipe for coffee ice cream.[86]

Menon's greatest publishing success, the *Cuisinière bourgeoise* (1746), provides especially invaluable evidence about the spread of coffee's use in France beyond the great houses to the more modest homes of the middling classes. According to Daniel Roche, this best-selling and frequently plagiarized cookbook was equally likely to be found "in the servants' quarters, in the living-room and in the dining-room of both aristocratic and plebeian houses."[87] While it contains only two recipes involving coffee (one for a cream custard and another for a jamlike spread), Menon's instructions presume that the reader owns a *cafetière* (coffee pot) and has easy access to ground coffee. All the same Menon makes no assumptions that his reader actually knows how to use her coffee pot; the first step of the recipe for *crème au caffé* consists of precise instructions for brewing coffee.[88] For the 1760s Roche has found *cafetières* listed in almost 40 percent of homes inventoried in the bourgeois Paris neighborhoods of Saint-Sulpice and Saint-Germain-l'Auxerrois, and even in 20 percent of the lower-class households in the faubourgs to the east.[89] These inventories, coupled with the runaway publishing success of the *Cuisinière bourgeoise,* offer the soundest proof yet that by midcentury coffee was no longer just the province of cafés and grand kitchens; increasingly it was an ingredient known inside private homes at most social levels.[90]

[86] Menon, *Science du maître d'hôtel confiseur,* 2 vols. (Paris, 1749–50). Menon (whose first name is lost to history) was more innovative in his use of coffee than in his selection of desserts. Fifty years earlier Massialot had published many similar recipes. Notably, in 1692 ice cream entered cookbooks (although not Massialot's, who only offered recipes for coarsely textured frozen ices). The Neapolitan Antonio Latini is widely credited with the first published recipe for a milk sorbet (in *Lo scalco alla moderna* [Naples, 1692]), and Audiger with the first true *crème glacée.* The first published English recipe for ice cream appeared in *Mrs. Mary Eales' Receipts* (London, 1718). However, neither Latini, Audiger, Massialot, nor Eales suggested coffee to flavor anything. See Michael Krondl, *Sweet Invention: A History of Dessert* (Chicago, 2011), 157–60; and Jeri Quinzio, *Of Sugar and Snow: A History of Ice Cream Making* (Berkeley, CA, 2009), 9–25, 42–43.

[87] Roche, *History of Everyday Things,* 248.

[88] Menon, *La cuisinière bourgeoise: Suivie de l'office, à l'usage de tous ceux qui se mêlent de dépenses de maisons* (Paris, 1746), 324, 437. On Menon's belief that a sizable percentage of the *Cuisinière bourgeoise* readership lacked understanding of basic kitchen knowledge, see Davis, *Defining Culinary Authority,* 82.

[89] Roche, *History of Everyday Things,* 246.

[90] This pattern had parallels elsewhere in northwestern Europe, such as the Netherlands, where the specialized accoutrements for coffee (pots, cups, saucers), nonexistent or restricted to the very wealthy homes in probate inventories before 1700, were by 1740 widespread in the inventories of working-class households in both urban and rural communities. Anne E. C. McCants, "Porcelain for the Poor: The Material Culture of Tea and Coffee Consumption in Eighteenth-Century Amsterdam," in *Early Modern Things: Objects and Their Histories, 1500–1800,* ed. Paula Findlen (New York, 2013), 320–22.

Menon was also representative of, if not responsible for, a less tangible aspect of midcentury French thinking about coffee. In his fourth and best-known cookbook, *Les soupers de la Cour* (1755), he strategically reminded readers of coffee's Eastern origins. "The best [beans] come from Mocha," he asserted, several decades after colonially produced beans had stripped coffee of most of its Arabian connection.[91] This comment echoed Gilliers, who showed even greater disregard for the French Caribbean plantations by asserting that coffee "only grows in Arabia and in the East Indies," by 1751 a blatant untruth.[92] Madeleine Dobie suggests why: in eighteenth-century France, the Caribbean provenance of many newly mass-produced crops was often ignored as a way to "turn a blind eye to slavery along with other vicissitudes of plantation agriculture."[93] Such claims were further abetted by metropolitan coffee traders, who, unlike their English counterparts, did not yet adorn their advertisements with colonial imagery, and by literary titans, including Voltaire, who inserted a plug for Mocha coffee "unadulterated with the bad coffee of Batavia or the American islands" into the conclusion of *Candide* (1759).[94] A counterclaim from a Caribbean planter that coffee from Martinique "is the equal of Mocha" was unlikely to garner much attention in the face of such willful negativity.[95] Worldwide, coffee production was increasingly dominated by the French Antilles colonies, yet customers in thrall to a fresh wave of *turquerie* (which peaked in French literature, art, music, and fashion between the 1740s and the 1760s) preferred to imagine that their cups, cakes, and ices tasted of the East.

Private cooks' embrace of coffee, whatever its provenance, did little to quell old debates over its healthfulness. Coffee had by now spread to the provinces, where it was advertised as a tonic, yet doctors and even some food experts in the larger cities continued to worry about its misuse. The 1767 *Dictionnaire portative de cuisine*, a reference work of food, diet, and health intended for both bourgeois and elite kitchens, described how to brew coffee and provided recipes for coffee custard, coffee mousse, and coffee ice cream. But under "Medicinal Observations," the authors warned that "daily use of coffee is a habit

91 Menon, *Science du maître d'hôtel confiseur*, 2:171–72, 175–76, 185, 191, 397–400, and *Les soupers de la Cour, ou l'art de travailler toutes sortes d'alimens . . . suivant les quatre saisons*, 4 vols. (Paris, 1755), 4:6, 301–4, quotation on 331.

92 Gilliers, *Cannameliste français*, 24.

93 Madeleine Dobie, "Orientalism, Colonialism, and Furniture in Eighteenth-Century France," in *Furnishing the Eighteenth Century: What Furniture Can Tell Us about the European and American Past*, ed. Dena Goodman and Kathryn Norberg (New York, 2011), 32.

94 Berg and Clifford, "Selling Consumption," 146, 160; Voltaire, *Candide, or Optimism*, trans. Daniel Gordon (New York, 1999), 118.

95 Elie Monnereau, *Le parfait indigotier . . . [avec] un traité sur la culture du café* (Amsterdam, 1765), 139.

that can shorten one's life and cause serious illnesses; consult your doctor before taking it."[96] The author of the *Discours familier sur le danger de l'usage habituel du café* (1774) agreed. This treatise pushed the contradictions in Blégny's and Andry de Boisregard's views to their logical conclusion, noting that if coffee was universally dangerous, it would never have been so widely adopted, but if coffee was universally safe, it would never have inspired so many doctors and even coffee "partisans" to warn against its use. "This conflict in opinions . . . demonstrates that coffee cannot be classified as an indifferent thing." How should coffee be used? Who could safely consume it? The author determined that it was at best a corrupting influence: "Coffee considered solely as a simple beverage is safe for corpulent people . . . accustomed to regular exposure at good tables, with a robust constitution . . . able to withstand the shock of irritating seasonings." But for the general population, coffee was so risky that it should be "banished from classification as a foodstuff, and relegated to the class of drugs" available only by special prescription.[97]

A mere fifteen years later, such worries suddenly appeared antiquated. A much soberer and more soundly scientific analysis of coffee was the order of the day, represented by André-Antoine-Pierre Le Gentil's 1787 *Dissertation sur le caffé*. Le Gentil was a retired member of the University of Paris medical faculty, as well as a retired army doctor. He took a sensible line on the preceding century of debates about coffee. Along with a thorough chemical analysis of coffee, a botanical history of the plant, and a series of closely reported medical observations on fourteen patients who took a medicinal preparation derived from coffee, he made the simple though counterintuitive pitch that "there are many ways to prepare coffee, but the commonest practice is usually not the best." He advised using "methodically roasted coffee," paying careful attention to the infusion process, and warned strenuously against "coffee prepared without method"—meaning, do not overboil it.[98]

Pierre-Joseph Buc'hoz, doctor to Louis XVI's brother Monsieur, cataloged the final prerevolutionary word on coffee's healthfulness, as well as on its adoption by cooks and consumers alike. His 1788 *Dissertations sur le tabac, le café, le cacao et le thé*, although not a cookbook, includes detailed instructions for making five preparations as a drink,

96 François-Alexandre Aubert de La Chesnaye des Bois, Jean Goulin, and Auguste Roux, *Dictionnaire portative de cuisine, d'office et de distillation* (Paris, 1767), 101–4. "Café de santé" was advertised for sale in Toulouse in the 1770s: Jones, "Great Chain of Buying," 28.

97 [Jean-François Bastien], *Discours familier sur le danger de l'usage habituel du café* (Amsterdam, 1774), 8, 12–13, 56.

98 André-Antoine-Pierre Le Gentil, *Dissertation sur le caffé et sur les moyens propres à prevenir les effets qui résultent de sa preparation communément vicieuse* (Paris, 1787), 3, 8, 65.

La Chapelle's savory cream, and six coffee-based desserts. Buc'hoz was attempting to say everything possible about coffee: its history of discovery and cultivation, its botanical and medical properties, its place in the kitchen, and its modern value in France. "One needs coffee today more than ever to calm the surprising vapors afflicting both men and women . . . excited by all the newly invented liqueurs. Coffee is good for everyone," he declared, even though many doctors in the preceding century had leveled the same accusations against coffee itself.[99] All agreed with the new verdict, from the king on down the social ladder: by then, "no bourgeois house fails to offer coffee at dinner; no shop girl, no cook, no chambermaid breakfasts without her café au lait."[100]

The spread of coffee cultivation around the world, spearheaded separately by the Dutch in Java and the French in Saint-Domingue, dropped the price of a cup so rapidly that by the mid-eighteenth century coffee had become a staple drink of most urbanites in France, whatever their social status or income level. Coffee would become a leading commodity of prerevolutionary French global trade and, along with sugar, would make Saint-Domingue the most profitable of all France's colonies. By 1789 coffee was considered an essentially French product, and the café a Parisian institution, not an import from Mecca, Cairo, or Constantinople. Yet when we try to understand the origin of coffee's success in France, we find that its appeal lay as much in its exotic Arabian and Ottoman associations during a cultural era marked by successive waves of *turquerie* as in anything connected with scholarship, health, or commerce. The allures of being tasty, fashionable, and eventually cheap enabled coffee proponents to trump the skeptics and made coffee a staple part of French life. An astonishing array of people developed vested interests in promoting coffee in seventeenth- and eighteenth-century France. In doing so, they transformed an exclusively wine-drinking society into one that was also caffeinated. Coffee had joined the French gustatory mainstream, and it has never left.

99 Pierre-Joseph Buc'hoz, *Dissertations sur le tabac, le café, le cacao et le thé* (Paris, 1788), 69.
100 Legrand d'Aussy, *Histoire de la vie privée*, 3:125.

La construction de la renommée des produits des terroirs : Acteurs et enjeux d'un marché de la gourmandise en France (XVIIe–début XIXe siècle)

Philippe Meyzie

Précis   *La valorisation de l'origine géographique des produits alimentaires se construit durablement en France au cours du XVIIIe siècle. Pour les marchands, les consommateurs et les amateurs éclairés (voyageurs, gastronomes), l'identification à une ville ou une province est un signe de qualité sur ce marché singulier et bien structuré de l'alimentation qui se rapproche de celui du luxe par le poids de la demande et sa dimension socioculturelle. Tout à la fois ancrées dans les usages de la société d'Ancien Régime et sensibles aux innovations commerciales, la circulation et la consommation de ces denrées représentent un marché alimentaire original qui témoigne de la promotion des produits des terroirs provinciaux dans l'imaginaire gourmand du début du XIXe siècle. En étudiant la manière dont se construit la renommée de ces produits localisés, cet article met en évidence les acteurs et les enjeux de ce marché français de la gourmandise.*

> C'est principalement des consommations de la Capitale que les Provinces tirent l'argent qui doit remplacer ce qu'elles payent annuellement de taille, de sel, de dixième, etc. [. . .] Plus l'imposition augmente et plus la consommation devient nécessaire. [. . .] Les étoffes d'or de Lyon, les vins de Bourgogne et de Champagne, les volailles de Normandie et du Maine, les perdrix et les truffes du Périgord payent les tributs de ces provinces. Le vulgaire ignorant s'irrite de ces folles dépenses et l'homme d'Etat les regarde comme un effet désirable.
>
> Jean-François Melon, *Essai politique sur le commerce*

Dans son *Essai politique sur le commerce* publié en 1734, Jean-François Melon intègre ainsi les produits des terroirs dans le champ de la réflexion économique et leur confère une place de choix sur le marché du luxe. Mercantiliste et défenseur du luxe, Melon rend ici compte de l'existence en France d'un marché différencié pour ces produits alimentaires associés aux provinces. La demande[1], notamment urbaine, pour

Philippe Meyzie est maître de conférences en histoire moderne à l'Université Bordeaux-Montaigne et membre junior de l'Institut Universitaire de France. Il a publié *La table du Sud-Ouest et l'émergence des cuisines régionales (1700–1850)* (2007) et une *Histoire de l'alimentation en Europe à l'époque moderne* (2010). Ses recherches actuelles portent sur la consommation et le commerce des produits alimentaires des terroirs en France et en Europe du XVIIe au XIXe siècle.

  [1] Cette question de la demande et des consommations occupe aujourd'hui une place importante dans les réflexions des historiens sur l'économie préindustrielle ; voir notamment Jean-Yves

French Historical Studies, Vol. 38, No. 2 (April 2015)   DOI 10.1215/00161071-2842554

ces denrées et ces boissons bien identifiées à un territoire (provinces, villes) comme les truffes du Périgord, les volailles du pays de Caux ou les vins de Champagne, joue un rôle moteur essentiel et fait une partie de la richesse de ces provinces. L'origine du produit n'est alors plus considérée comme une simple provenance mais représente une plus-value et un gage de qualité aux yeux des consommateurs-connaisseurs. Dans la pensée économique du XVIIIe siècle, la notion d'espace est de plus en plus prise en compte par des auteurs tels Richard Cantillon dans son œuvre posthume *Essai sur la nature du commerce en général* (1755), contribuant à l'émergence d'une « économie différenciée des lieux »[2]. La croissance des campagnes s'appuie en effet selon lui largement sur une demande urbaine qui favorise les progrès de l'agriculture. Cette perception nouvelle de l'espace et des territoires par certains économistes de la seconde moitié du XVIIIe siècle s'accompagne d'une valorisation grandissante de l'origine des produits. Si le mot de « terroir » a conservé pendant longtemps un sens négatif associé au goût désagréable de la terre, sa définition commence à évoluer vers un sens plus positif dans la seconde moitié du XVIIIe siècle et occupe encore aujourd'hui une place originale dans la culture alimentaire française[3]. Sous la plume de l'abbé Rozier dans son *Cours complet d'agriculture* (1796), le terroir confère une qualité particulière à un produit et le distingue des autres[4]. Face à l'essor et à la libéralisation des marchés au cours du XVIIIe siècle, l'identification des produits devient de plus en plus nécessaire et favorise les échanges[5]. Les références à une produc-

---

Grenier, « Travailler plus pour consommer plus : Désir de consommer et essor du capitalisme du XVIIe siècle à nos jours », *Annales : Histoire, sciences sociales* 65, n°3 (2010) : 787–98 ; Jan de Vries, *The Industrious Revolution : Consumer Behavior and the Household Economy* (Cambridge, 2008) ; Maxine Berg et Elizabeth Eger, dirs., *Luxury in the Eighteenth Century : Debates, Desires, and Delectable Goods* (New York, 2003) ; Patrick Verley, *L'échelle du monde : Essai sur l'industrialisation de l'Occident* (Paris, 1997) ; et Maxine Berg et Helen Clifford, dirs., *Consumers and Luxury : Consumer Culture in Europe, 1650–1850* (Manchester, 1999).

2 Jean-Marie Baldner et Anne Conchon, « Les territoires de l'économie : Lectures croisées de Montchrestien et Cantillon », dans *Monchrestien et Cantillon : Le commerce et l'émergence d'une pensée économique*, dir. Alain Guery (Paris, 2011), 258–301.

3 Serge Wolikow et Olivier Jacquet, *Territoires et terroirs du vin du XVIIIe au XXIe siècles : Approche internationale d'une construction historique* (Dijon, 2011) ; Florent Quellier, « Le discours sur la richesse des terroirs au XVIIe siècle et les prémices de la gastronomie française », *XVIIe siècle*, n°254 (2012) : 141–54. Sur l'importance en France de la notion de terroir, voir Amy B. Trubek, *The Taste of Place : A Cultural Journey into Terroir* (Los Angeles, 2008).

4 « Terroir : Terre considérée par rapport aux produits en agriculture ; mais ce mot terroir s'applique plus particulièrement à la qualité de ces produits », abbé Rozier, *Cours complet d'agriculture théorique, pratique, économique et de médecine rurale et vétérinaire ; suivi d'une méthode pour étudier l'agriculture par principes, ou Dictionnaire universel d'agriculture* (Paris, 1796).

5 Jean-Yves Grenier, « Une économie de l'identification : Juste prix et ordres des marchandises dans l'Ancien Régime », dans *La qualité des produits en France (XVIIIe–XXe siècles)*, dir. Alessandro Stanziani (Paris, 2003), 25–53 ; Anne Cochon et Dominique Margairaz, « De l'idiome mercantiliste à l'idiome libéral : Classement, déclassement, reclassement des produits (XVIIIe–début XIXe siècles) », dans *Classement, déclassement, reclassement de l'antiquité à nos jours*, dir. Gilles Chabaud (Limoges, 2011), 337–62 ; Michael Kwass, « Ordering the World of Goods: Consumer

tion localisée dans le cas de la manufacture de Birmingham au XVIIIe siècle analysée par Philippe Minard ou celles au « Made in Italy » et à la Renaissance à partir du XIXe siècle comme outils de promotion de la mode italienne sur les marchés internationaux étudiés par Marco Belfanti servent à asseoir des réputations dans le secteur de l'industrie et à fonder des images de marque[6]. Notre propos consiste à comprendre comment l'origine géographique devient de plus en plus valorisée dans un autre secteur, celui des marchés de l'alimentation en France de la fin du XVIIe au début du XIXe siècle. Il s'agit d'analyser de quelle manière les produits des terroirs deviennent des produits alimentaires de luxe, prisés et recherchés par des consommateurs avertis qui perçoivent dans leur origine géographique un signe de qualité[7].

Dans le champ de l'histoire de l'alimentation, l'étude à partir des produits offre des perspectives nouvelles à la croisée de l'histoire des consommations et de l'histoire économique[8]. En effet, l'historiographie française sous l'égide notamment de Jean-Louis Flandrin à partir des années 1980 s'est beaucoup intéressée aux goûts et à la diversité sociale des consommations[9]. Le succès de l'histoire des mentalités n'a alors guère laissé de place à l'histoire économique de l'alimentation ; ces approches ont cependant permis de mieux comprendre la cuisine, les consommations et la culture alimentaire de l'époque moderne, cadre nécessaire à l'étude des produits. Les interrogations actuelles sur le terroir, l'authenticité, la typicité ou la qualité des produits conduisent aujourd'hui l'historien à s'intéresser plus en détail à l'évolution de ces notions et à mobiliser les problématiques de l'histoire économique pour mieux en appréhender le sens[10]. Pour l'époque contempo-

---

Revolution and the Classification of Objects in Eighteenth-Century France », *Representations*, n°82 (2003) : 87–116.

6 Carlo Marco Belfanti, « Renaissance et Made in Italy : L'invention d'une identité culturelle pour l'industrie de la mode », dans *La gloire de l'industrie, XVIIe–XIXe siècle : Faire de l'histoire avec Gérard Gayot*, dir. Corinne Maitte, Philippe Minard et Matthieu de Oliveira (Rennes, 2012), 145–62 ; Philippe Minard, « Le bureau d'essai de Birmingham ou la fabrique de la réputation au XVIIIe siècle », *Annales : Histoire, sciences sociales* 65, n°5 (2010) : 1117–46.

7 Les historiens n'ont guère jusqu'à présent abordé cette question du lien entre qualité, territoire et produit alimentaire alors que les géographes et les ethnologues ont mené de nombreuses études dans cette perspective depuis une quinzaine d'années ; voir, par exemple, Claire Delfosse, « Noms de pays et produits de terroir ou les enjeux des dénominations géographiques », *L'espace géographique*, n°4 (1997) : 220–30 ; « Local Foods », numéro spécial de la revue en ligne *Anthropology of Food*, n°4 (2005) ; et Claire Delfosse, dir., *La mode du terroir et des produits alimentaires* (Paris 2011).

8 Franck Trentmann, *The Oxford Handbook of the History of Consumption* (Oxford, 2012) ; Philippe Meyzie, *L'alimentation en Europe à l'époque moderne* (Paris, 2010).

9 Odile Redon, Line Sallmann et Sylvie Steinberg, dirs., *Le désir et le goût : Une autre histoire, XIIIe – XVIIIe siècles* (Saint-Denis, 2005) ; Florent Quellier, « L'après Jean-Louis Flandrin, une décennie d'histoire de l'alimentation en France (XVe–XIXe siècles) », *Food and History* 10, n°2 (2012) : 89–102.

10 Parmi les travaux des historiens, on peut citer notamment les publications récentes de Giovanni Ceccarelli, Alberto Grandi et Stefano Magagnoli, dirs., *Typicality in History : Tradition,*

raine, les réflexions initiées par Alessandro Stanziani sur la qualité alimentaire, objet historique à part entière, proposent un certain nombre de clefs pour comprendre la valorisation des produits des terroirs en soulignant notamment que l'Ancien Régime ne se soucie pas uniquement de l'alimentation d'un point de vue quantitatif, mais prend aussi en considération la qualité des denrées[11]. Les orientations nouvelles de l'histoire économique abordent l'histoire des produits en les mettant en relation avec les cultures de la consommation[12]. Les théories du marché des singularités développées par le socio-économiste Lucien Karpik ou celles plus anciennes de Karl Polanyi sur l'encastrement de l'économie dans la culture et la société sont des outils d'analyse repris par les historiens de l'économie préindustrielle, qui peuvent également nourrir la réflexion des historiens de l'alimentation car, en se détachant du modèle classique de décryptage de l'économie, ils permettent de comprendre comment les marchés et les consommations des produits des terroirs s'insèrent dans les mécanismes de l'économie et de la société d'Ancien Régime tout en rendant compte de sa modernisation notamment dans la seconde moitié du XVIIIe siècle[13]. La notion de réputation est très présente dans les transactions commerciales sous l'Ancien Régime[14] ; elle représente donc selon nous une perspective d'analyse pertinente pour essayer de saisir l'émergence et le fonctionnement de ce marché des produits des terroirs en France à partir de la fin du XVIIe siècle. En 1721, dans le *Dictionnaire de Trévoux*, la réputation est un « bruit avantageux, opinion que les hommes ont des choses ou des personnes. [. . .] Les vins de Champagne, les melons de Langeais, les jambons de Mayence sont en réputation », emploi qui atteste d'un lien étroit entre réputation et nourriture[15] ; les dictionnaires de commerce à partir de Savary des Bruslons mobilisent d'ailleurs cette notion fréquemment, évoquant des produits alimentaires « renommés », « réputés » ou « estimés ». Les récentes études

---

Innovation, and Terroir (Bruxelles, 2013) et « The Taste of Typicality », *Food and History* 8, n°2 (2010) : 45–76.

[11] Alessandro Stanziani, dir., *La qualité des produits en France (XVIIIe–XXe siècles)* (Paris, 2003) ; Stanziani, *Histoire de la qualité alimentaire, XIXe–XXe siècle* (Paris, 2005).

[12] « Comme le comportement du consommateur est bien loin de se ramener exclusivement à sa capacité de choisir, sous la contrainte du revenu disponible, les biens les plus capables de satisfaire à ses besoins dont l'utilité serait la seule mesure, il faut tenir compte des facteurs sociaux, culturels ou symboliques qui le déterminent et des processus qui le façonnent. C'est dire que, au bout du chemin, on devrait rencontrer les cultures de la consommation qui sont historiquement très différenciées, et, en tout cas, existent bien avant la " société de consommation " », selon Jean-Claude Daumas, *Faire de l'histoire économique aujourd'hui* (Dijon, 2013), 180–81.

[13] Lucien Karpik, *L'économie des singularités* (Paris, 2007) ; Karl Polanyi, *La grande transformation : Aux origines politiques et économiques de notre temps* (Paris, 1983) ; Dominique Margairaz et Philippe Minard, « Le marché dans son histoire », *Revue de synthèse* 127, n°2 (2006) : 241–52.

[14] Philip T. Hoffman et Jean-Laurent Rosenthal, « New Work in French Economic History », *French Historical Studies* 3, n°3 (2000) : 439–53.

[15] *Dictionnaire universel françois et latin vulgairement appelé dictionnaire de Trévoux* (Paris, 1721).

de Natacha Coquery sur le monde parisien de la boutique confirment l'importance de la réputation dans l'économie d'Ancien Régime et l'identification du « remarquable »[16]. Intégrée de plus en plus dans le champ de réflexion de l'histoire économique[17], la réputation constitue une information qui favorise l'échange et la confiance entre les acteurs économiques[18] ; elle demeure une forme de qualification importante, pour les hommes comme pour les biens, dans la logique de la société d'Ancien Régime. Au XVIIIe siècle, la renommée s'affirme donc comme un critère de différenciation entre les producteurs et entre les produits auquel les denrées n'échappent pas. Le secteur de l'alimentation occupe même une place centrale dans ce processus de distinction où l'origine géographique fonctionne comme un critère de hiérarchisation pour tous les acteurs économiques, du producteur aux consommateurs.

Comment l'origine géographique et l'association avec un « terroir » deviennent-elles un signe de qualité ? pourquoi se développe-t-il au XVIIIe siècle, particulièrement en France, ce goût pour les produits des terroirs[19] ? de quelle manière la construction de la réputation de certains d'entre eux relève-t-elle à la fois du maintien d'usages anciens et de la mise en place de marchés alimentaires singuliers et novateurs[20] ? Ces multiples questions doivent permettre de mieux comprendre la construction de la réputation des produits des terroirs en France du XVIIe au XIXe siècle, d'en saisir les sources, les enjeux et les mécanismes en présentant un schéma d'analyse appuyé sur quelques exemples significatifs de ce processus révélateur du fonctionnement de l'économie d'Ancien Régime et de la place de la gastronomie en France.

Usages et goûts de l'Ancien Régime

A partir de la fin du Moyen Age, certains produits localisés[21] ont déjà acquis une réputation sur le marché parisien[22]. La réputation de cer-

---

16 Natacha Coquery, *Tenir boutique à Paris au XVIIIe siècle : Luxe et demi-luxe* (Paris, 2011).

17 C'est notamment le cas dans le domaine du vin et des produits de luxe. Voir, par exemple, Pierre-Marie Chauvin, *Le marché des réputations : Une sociologie du monde des vins de Bordeaux* (Bordeaux, 2010).

18 Alessandro Stanziani, « Les signes de qualité : Normes, réputation et confiance (XIXe–XXe siècles) », *Revue de synthèse* 127, n°2 (2006) : 329–58.

19 L'origine géographique comme signe de qualité continue encore aujourd'hui d'occuper une place à part en France sur le marché du luxe alimentaire ; voir Vincent Marcilhac, *Le luxe alimentaire : Une singularité française* (Rennes, 2012).

20 Cette double tendance a été soulignée à propos du marché de l'alimentation par Alessandro Stanziani, « Social Inequalities and Product Identification in Food Markets : A Critique of Modernization and Globalization Paradigms », *Food and History* 10, n°1 (2012) : 13–45.

21 Selon les ethnologues Laurence Bérard et Philippe Marchenay, *Produits du terroir : Comprendre et agir* (Bourg-en-Bresse, 2007), les produits localisés se caractérisent par leur inscription en un lieu, l'ancrage historique et des savoir-faire partagés.

22 Bruno Laurioux, « " Il n'est de bon bec qu'à Paris " : La naissance d'une capitale gastro-

taines spécialités culinaires n'est donc pas une nouveauté, mais à partir de la seconde moitié du XVIIe siècle, le goût pour ces produits provinciaux ainsi que leur identification se renforcent assez nettement et la gamme des produits concernés s'élargit. La demande de ces consommateurs avertis devient alors un moteur essentiel dans la construction et la diffusion de leur renommée.

Les produits des terroirs prennent en effet une place grandissante dans les consommations des élites comme en témoignent livres de dépenses de bouche et repas. Au XVIIIe siècle, les menus des repas servis à Louis XV à Choisy mentionnent du veau de Pontoise, des poules de Caux, des cailles de Saintonge ou des canetons de Rouen[23]. La précision donnée aux convives sur l'origine géographique de ces mets suggère que celle-ci est bien alors un signe de qualité distinctif. A la veille de la Révolution, les jambons de Bayonne et les fromages de Roquefort font partie des consommations courantes de la reine Marie-Antoinette selon le journal de sa femme de chambre[24]. Les grandes familles parisiennes apprécient également ces denrées venues des quatre coins du royaume. En 1782 et 1783, le comte d'Artois achète à plusieurs reprises des canetons de Rouen, des marrons de Lyon, des mauviettes (alouettes) de Chartres, des poules de Caux ou du beurre de Vanves, autant de produits nommément rattachés à un lieu dans ses dépenses de bouche[25]. Il en est de même pour des aristocrates européens installés en France comme le duc de Saxe qui accorde une place de choix à ces produits localisés lors des repas servis dans son hôtel parisien ou dans son château de Pont-sur-Seine. Les livres de dépenses de bouche extrêmement détaillés tenus par son homme d'affaires entre 1778 et 1786 comprennent, à plusieurs reprises, des achats de pâtés de Périgueux, de veau de Pontoise, de fromage de Brie, de pain d'épices de Reims ou de jambons de Bayonne[26]. Si, dans l'aristocratie, ce goût des produits venus des provinces est manifeste, il s'exprime également à des niveaux plus modestes du monde des élites comme à la table des magistrats municipaux. Dans plusieurs villes de province en effet, même si les repas sont dominés par les produits locaux, les édiles (magistrats, marchands) se font servir du jambon de Bayonne, du fro-

---

nomique à la fin du Moyen Age », dans *Etre parisien*, dir. Claude Gauvard et Jean-Louis Robert (Paris, 2005), 209–28.

[23] Marie-France Noël, « La table de Louis XV au château de Choisy », *Lumières*, n° 11 (2008) : 95–103.

[24] Danielle Gallet, dir., *Dans l'ombre de Marie-Antoinette : Le Journal de Madame Brunyer, 1783–1792* (Paris, 2003).

[25] Archives Nationales (désormais AN), R 1/250, dépenses extraordinaires du comte d'Artois.

[26] Archives départementales de l'Aude (désormais ADA), EE 3134–36, livre de dépenses de bouche, 1778–86.

mage de Roquefort et de Brie, du beurre d'Isigny ou des chapons de Barbezieux, clairement identifiés dans les factures des traiteurs[27].

Au-delà de cette simple présence dans leur alimentation, on constate une attention toute particulière des élites, des plus riches aux plus modestes, pour ces produits clairement distingués des autres. Ainsi, le duc de Saxe, dans sa correspondance avec son secrétaire, évoque à plusieurs reprises l'achat de pâtés de Périgueux ; le prince se soucie de savoir si les pâtés seront disponibles et bien acheminés alors qu'il ne s'intéresse guère aux autres fournitures alimentaires[28]. L'intérêt suscité par ces produits jugés exceptionnels montre bien que l'origine leur confère une place à part dans les consommations des élites et leur donne un statut d'objet de luxe digne de l'attention de ces grands personnages. Mais, si ces aliments ont du succès auprès des élites du temps, c'est également parce qu'ils correspondent parfaitement à une culture alimentaire du bon goût partagée par tous. Parmi ces produits appréciés figurent en bonne place les volailles, les gibiers à plumes, les charcuteries et les pâtisseries, mets fortement valorisés par les élites nobiliaires et la grande cuisine française[29]. Certains produits du terroir ne gagnent ainsi leurs lettres de noblesse que lorsque les goûts des élites leur accordent une place de choix. Les truffes, par exemple, furent au Moyen Age et jusqu'au XVIIe siècle dédaignées par la cuisine de cour et réservées aux consommations paysannes, voire à la nourriture des animaux. Aliment souterrain, mystérieux, associé à la sorcellerie et suspect aux yeux de l'Eglise, la truffe n'apparaît guère alors à la table des élites. A partir du XVIIe siècle, les champignons en général et la truffe en particulier sont réhabilités et ne sont plus perçus comme des aliments néfastes[30]. Dès lors, la truffe devient un mets recherché des élites et les truffes noires du Périgord voient leur réputation grandir grâce à cette nouvelle orientation de la haute cuisine. Chaque année en janvier et février, le contrôleur général des finances Calonne fait ainsi acheminer à Paris et à Versailles des paniers contenant plusieurs livres de truffes du Périgord pour des sommes pouvant aller jusqu'à une centaine de livres[31]. Il devient alors assez courant de trouver trace dans les correspondances officielles ou privées de ces expéditions de

---

27 Lyon, archives municipales, CC 3324 ; Agen, archives municipales, CC 429 et 444 ; Angers, archives municipales, 8 Mi 10 et 12 ; Bayonne, archives municipales, CC 321 et 328.

28 ADA, EE 16655/3, correspondance de M. Silvestre, secrétaire du duc de Saxe, 1776.

29 Susan Pinkard, *A Revolution in Taste : The Rise of French Cuisine, 1650–1800* (Cambridge, 2009) ; Priscilla Parkhurst Ferguson, *Accounting for Taste : The Triumph of French Cuisine* (Chicago, 2004) ; Meyzie, *L'alimentation en Europe*, en particulier 143–68.

30 Jean-Louis Flandrin et Massimo Montanari, dirs., *Histoire de l'alimentation* (Paris, 1996), 562.

31 AN, T 261/1-4, livres de cuisine de Calonne.

paniers de truffes vers Paris[32]. La noblesse et l'aristocratie apparaissent comme des meneurs d'opinion et des prescripteurs de goûts qui, par leur demande et leur prestige social, construisent la renommée de certains produits des terroirs[33].

L'action du monde des élites et du pouvoir se manifeste également au niveau de la circulation de ces produits. Au-delà des circuits commerciaux traditionnels, leur diffusion s'appuie en effet largement sur l'usage du don très présent dans une France d'Ancien Régime où les relations sociales ou politiques sont régies par les préséances[34]. Les produits des terroirs figurent couramment parmi ces cadeaux tant dans le cadre privé que dans le domaine public[35]. Les sommes consacrées par les autorités municipales des grandes capitales provinciales à cette pratique s'avèrent importantes : chaque année, les capitouls de Toulouse investissent plusieurs centaines de livres pour offrir des fromages de Roquefort et des jambons ; en 1757, les édiles de Lyon dépensent 10 000 livres pour ces présents de bouche et ils décident en 1779 de fixer la somme à 20 000 livres[36]. Même pour des villes plus modestes comme Angers, les dépenses pour offrir des denrées à ses protecteurs ne sont pas négligeables ; en 1775, par exemple, 1 084 livres sont employées pour des présents de gibiers et de poissons, ce qui peut représenter certaines années jusqu'à 13 pour cent des dépenses de l'échevinage[37]. En aucun cas, il ne s'agit donc de cadeaux anecdotiques, mais au contraire d'un usage bien établi et reconnu. La plupart des villes du royaume entretiennent ainsi des réseaux de protecteurs et d'intermédiaires parmi les puissants, mais ces présents participent dans le même temps à la valorisation des produits des terroirs et à leur identification. Mis en œuvre également par les Etats provinciaux, ces cadeaux contribuent largement à renforcer le lien entre une spécialité culinaire et une ville. Angers offre du gibier ou des volailles, Brive des truffes, Troyes des andouilles, Toulouse des pâtés et des fromages de Roquefort, et ainsi de suite[38]. La distribution de ces présents est très bien organisée

32 Par exemple, Brive, archives municipales, 5 S 1345 ; Archives départementales du Puy-de-Dôme, 1 C 7410 ; Archives départementales du Lot, 23 J 36.

33 Le rôle de médiateur de cette clientèle de prestige est l'une des caractéristiques du marché du luxe ; Louis Bergeron, *Les industries du luxe en France* (Paris, 1998), 29 ; Vincent Marcilhac, *Le luxe alimentaire : Une singularité française* (Rennes, 2012). Le statut de l'aliment découle du statut social du consommateur.

34 Natalie Zemon Davis, *The Gift in Sixteenth-Century France* (Madison, WI, 2000), trad. française *Essai sur le don dans la France du XVIe siècle* (Paris, 2003).

35 Philippe Meyzie, « Les cadeaux alimentaires dans la Guyenne du XVIIIe siècle : Sociabilité, pouvoirs et gastronomie », *Histoire, économie, société* 25, n°1 (2006) : 33–50.

36 Toulouse, archives municipales, CC 2775 ; Archives départementales de la Gironde (désormais ADG), C 1065 ; Lyon, archives municipales, CC 3353 et 3587.

37 Angers, archives municipales, CC 214 ; Jacques Maillard, *Le pouvoir municipal à Angers de 1657 à 1789* (Angers, 1984), 28.

38 Angers, archives municipales, CC 34, 44 et 214 ; Troyes, archives municipales, AA 45 et

et se pratique à l'échelle du royaume. Le chargé d'affaires des Etats de Béarn, par son action, montre bien comment certaines spécialités culinaires assoient leur renommée en devenant des outils politiques. Lors d'une affaire concernant la création en Béarn d'une maîtrise des Eaux-et-Forêts en 1750, Domec est chargé de distribuer des jambons et du vin aux ministres et à leur entourage afin d'obtenir leur soutien ; il a pour mission tout d'abord de sonder « adroitement » M. Laporte, premier commis et de tâcher de découvrir si « un présent en jambons et en vin du pays lui serait agréable » avant de lui offrir, quelques jours plus tard, vins et jambons « pour le prier de rendre de bons offices à la province »[39]. Plusieurs ministres ou personnages influents à Versailles reçoivent ainsi régulièrement et en quantité les spécialités culinaires des provinces. Le comte de Saint-Florentin, secrétaire d'Etat à la Maison du Roi au milieu du XVIIIe siècle bénéficie amplement de ces largesses puisqu'il reçoit, entre autres, des cuisses d'oie et des jambons de la Jurade bordelaise, des truffes venues du Périgord, des jambons et des fromages de Roquefort expédiés par les capitouls de Toulouse, et ainsi de suite[40]. Ces dons alimentaires sont très appréciés de ces grands personnages qui assurent sans doute leur promotion à Versailles et à Paris. D'autres réseaux sont également mobilisés. A l'instar de la famille de Taillefer, la noblesse du Périgord contribue largement à la renommée des produits locaux (truffes, pâtés, volailles truffées). Cette noblesse possessionnée crée un lien direct entre la province et la cour par l'intermédiaire notamment de réseaux familiaux et de clientèle ; les envois de pâtés de Périgueux ou de dindes truffées émaillent leurs correspondances et leurs livres de comptes[41]. Ces relais amicaux ou politiques servent la renommée des produits des terroirs en France au XVIIIe siècle ; ils leur permettent surtout de se faire connaître dans la capitale et de prendre place à la table des élites. La circulation de ces produits à différentes échelles tire ainsi parfaitement profit des réseaux de clientèle et des usages politiques de l'Ancien Régime.

Pour les élites gourmandes du XVIIIe siècle composées aussi bien de la noblesse que des élites bourgeoises en pleine ascension qui cherchent à imiter les goûts de l'aristocratie, l'origine géographique

46 ; Toulouse, archives municipales, CC 2775, 2802 et 2807 ; Albert Babeau, *La ville sous l'Ancien Régime* (Paris, 1884).

39 Archives départementales des Pyrénées-Atlantiques (désormais ADPA), C 1294, correspondance de Domec, agent des Etats de Béarn à Paris.

40 Toulouse, archives municipales, CC 2775 ; Archives départementales de la Gironde, C 1050.

41 Archives départementales de la Dordogne (désormais ADD), 12 J 73, envois de pâtés de perdrix par le marquis d'Abzac de la Douze, 1771–72 ; ADD, 23 J 90, livre journal de M. de Montancieux, 1748–76 ; ADD, 2 E 1835 (99), envois de dindes truffées à Paris par le marquis d'Arlot de la Roque ; ADD, 2 E 1812 (38), facture du 13 mai 1788 pour l'envoi de dindes truffées à Paris par le chevalier de Cablan ; Joseph Durieux, « Un mémoire du traiteur Courtois », *Bulletin de la Société historique et archéologique du Périgord* (1922) : 142.

des produits est un signe de qualité auquel ils prêtent une attention croissante. A la veille de la Révolution, Louis-Sébastien Mercier rend compte de cette perception de plus en plus nette dans son portrait du gourmand parisien :

> S'il vous parle, il ne vous entretient que des dindes aux truffes du Périgord, des pâtés de foie gras de Toulouse, des pâtés de thon frais de Toulon, des terrines de perdrix rouges de Nérac, des mauviettes de Petiviers, et des hures cuites de Troyes ; il ne connaît, il n'estime les différentes provinces que par leur volaille ou par leur poisson ; il vous annonce qu'il arrive de Strasbourg une carpe de la plus belle grosseur ; il ira à sa rencontre à l'hôtel des diligences ; là, selon lui, on devrait doubler les postes pour amener plus vite les bartavelles des montagnes, les bécassons et les coqs vierges de Caux[42].

Même si, comme souvent sous la plume de Mercier, cette description est empreinte d'ironie, elle atteste de l'intérêt porté à ces produits des terroirs dont la renommée semble bien établie et dont l'attrait s'exerce alors de plus en plus nettement sur les élites roturières urbaines offrant ainsi à ces spécialités un marché élargi dans la seconde moitié du XVIIIe siècle. Pour les habitants de ces régions comme pour les consommateurs étrangers, il semble aussi que l'identification entre un produit et un territoire soit bien perçue et que la qualité associée à l'origine soit aussi de leur côté tout à fait consciente. En 1751, le chevalier d'Aydie, noble périgourdin, dans une lettre qui accompagne un présent expédié à Paris à son amie la marquise de Créquiy, précise : « J'ai l'honneur, Madame, de vous adresser un pâté de Périgueux. C'est le seul hommage matériel que puisse offrir un Périgourdin. Je souhaite donc qu'il soit de votre goût »[43]. Dans une lettre du 14 juillet 1771, le président au parlement de Bordeaux, de Lalanne, s'adresse à M. de Savornin de Saint-Jean installé à Apt en Provence pour le remercier de l'envoi d'huile, d'anchois et d'olives en soulignant « c'étoit un composé de tout ce que votre païs produit de meilleur et de plus friand : des olives farcies de plusieurs manières, des saucissons d'Arles, du vin muscat de Toulon, des prunes et des figues confites, etc. »[44].

La renommée des produits des terroirs s'appuie donc largement sur les usages de la société d'Ancien Régime mais aussi sur l'émergence de nouveaux groupes fortunés. La demande croissante d'élites gourmandes amatrices éclairées des spécialités culinaires provinciales participe à la « désirabilité » de ces produits. Les présents culinaires assoient leur notoriété notamment à Paris et favorisent leur diffusion ;

---

42 Louis-Sébastien Mercier, *Tableau de Paris* (Paris, 1990), 346.
43 Emile Dusolier, *Un gentilhomme périgourdin du XVIIIe siècle : La vie passionnée et calme du chevalier d'Aydie* (Bordeaux, 1935), 14.
44 *Archives historiques du département de la Gironde*, t. 45 (Bordeaux, 1910), 459.

cette économie du don fait partie intégrante du marché des produits des terroirs[45]. Leur circulation semble de mieux en mieux structurée dans la seconde moitié du XVIIIe siècle et leur consommation s'étend à de nouvelles catégories sociales (marchands, magistrats, professions libérales)[46]. Au sein du commerce alimentaire, un marché des produits des terroirs va progressivement se développer pour satisfaire aux goûts de cette clientèle d'amateurs. La valorisation de ces produits par les réseaux commerciaux renforce alors leur réputation.

Le développement d'un marché des produits des terroirs

La renommée des produits des terroirs ne saurait en effet s'établir sans l'appui de circuits commerciaux efficaces[47]. Ce marché gourmand réservé la plupart du temps aux élites, se démarque assez nettement des marchés alimentaires plus ordinaires comme ceux des céréales et de la viande de boucherie bien connus grâce aux travaux de Steven Kaplan ou de Sydney Watts[48]. Les produits des terroirs ne font pas partie du marché des subsistances et le fonctionnement économique de ce marché s'apparente plus aux mécanismes du secteur du luxe. Différenciation des produits, influence de la demande, soin de la qualité, innovations commerciales, effets de mode, forte dimension sociale sont autant de caractéristiques communes avec le marché des cosmétiques ou celui des objets d'art[49].

A partir de la fin du XVIIe siècle, les dictionnaires de commerce mettent en place des classifications des produits dans lesquels ces denrées sont bien représentées[50]. En 1692, *Le livre commode des adresses de Paris* d'Abraham du Pradel mentionne langues de porc venues de Troyes, fromage de Brie ou de Marolles, beurre d'Isigny ou confitures

45 Carlo Ginzburg, « Don et reconnaissance : Lecture de Mauss », *Annales : Histoire, sciences sociales* 65, n°6 (2010) : 1303–20 ; James G. Garrier, *Gifts and Commodities : Exchange and Western Capitalism since 1700* (Londres, 1995).

46 L'élargissement de cette consommation des produits des terroirs vers des catégories intermédiaires par émulation correspond assez bien à ce qui a pu être observé, par exemple, sur le marché des perruques ; Michael Kwass, « Big Hair : A Wig History of Consumption in Eighteenth-Century France », *American Historical Review* 111, n°3 (2006) : 631–59.

47 Sur les réseaux du commerce de l'alimentation, voir Anne Radeff, « Food Systems : Central-Decentral Networks », in *A Cultural History of Food in the Early Modern Age*, dir. Beat Kümin (New York, 2012), 29–46.

48 Steven Kaplan, *Provisioning Paris : Merchants and Millers in the Grain and Flour Trade during the Eighteenth Century* (Londres, 1984) ; Sydney Watts, *Meat Matters: Butchers, Politics, and Market Culture in Eighteenth-Century Paris* (New York, 2006).

49 Charlotte Guichard, *Les amateurs d'art à Paris au XVIIIe siècle* (Paris, 2008) ; Catherine Lanoë, *La poudre et le fard : Une histoire des cosmétiques de la Renaissance aux Lumières* (Paris, 2008).

50 Jean-Claude Perrot, « Les dictionnaires de commerce au XVIIIe siècle », *Revue d'histoire moderne et contemporaine* 28 (1981) : 36–67 ; Jochen Hoock, « Discours commercial et économie politique en France au XVIIIe siècle : L'échec d'une synthèse », *Revue de synthèse* 108, n°1 (1987) : 57–73.

de Dijon[51]. L'étude de ces dictionnaires[52], outils pratiques du monde du commerce mais aussi lectures de l'aristocratie, révèle que l'origine géographique est un critère important de hiérarchisation des aliments. Les dénominations faisant référence à un lieu se fixent durablement d'un dictionnaire à l'autre. Ainsi, dans le cas des jambons, l'appellation jambon de Bayonne s'installe alors que les autres appellations comme jambons des Basques, de Lahontan ou du Béarn qui avaient pendant longtemps cohabiter les unes avec les autres tendent à disparaître. Les dictionnaires de commerce contribuent ainsi à fixer une nomenclature basée sur l'origine géographique qui, en distinguant les qualités, doit favoriser la circulation des produits. Quels sont les produits des terroirs identifiés dans cette littérature commerciale ? Les produits à la réputation bien établie sont sensiblement les mêmes que ceux qui servent aux présents de bouche. Le *Dictionnaire universel de commerce* de Jacques Savary des Bruslons en fournit une bonne illustration : andouilles de Troyes, prunes de Brignoles, dragée de Verdun, jambon de Bayonne ou huile d'olive d'Aix y sont distingués des productions ordinaires.

Plusieurs catégories émergent assez nettement dans la littérature commerciale du siècle des Lumières : outre les boissons (vins, liqueurs et eaux-de-vie), les fromages, les viandes de conserve (charcuteries, viandes confites) et les confiseries (bonbons, confitures, pâtés de fruits) sont les mieux représentés. Les fromages font certainement partie des premiers produits à être clairement identifiés et valorisés selon leur origine ; on les retrouve aussi couramment distingués dans les livres de comptes et les correspondances commerciales. Les produits des terroirs en France au XVIIIe siècle ne sont donc pas des produits frais, mais, dans la plupart des cas, des produits de conserve adaptés à la commercialisation sur de grandes distances et à une consommation différée. Pour un même produit émergent alors des qualités différentes selon leur origine. Le marché des prunes en fournit une bonne illustration. Plusieurs prunes sont mentionnées régulièrement dans les dictionnaires de commerce, mais elles semblent correspondre à des marchés différents. La prune de Brignoles présentée comme l'une des plus renommées prend place sur le créneau du luxe avec une production restreinte et une clientèle limitée. En 1761, le *Dictionnaire portatif de*

---

[51] Abraham du Pradel, *Le livre commode contenant les adresses de la ville de Paris, et le trésor des almanachs pour l'année bissextile 1692, avec les séances et les vacations des tribunaux, l'ordre et la discipline des exercices publics, le prix des matériaux et des ouvrages d'architecture, le tarif des nouvelles monnoyes, le départ des courriers. . .* (Paris, 1692).

[52] *Dictionnaire universel de commerce* (Amsterdam, 1726) ; *Dictionnaire universel de commerce* (Genève, 1742) ; *Dictionnaire portatif de commerce* (Copenhague, 1761) ; *Dictionnaire du citoyen, ou abrégé historique, théorique et pratique du commerce* (Amsterdam, 1762) ; *Almanach général des marchands* (Paris, 1778) ; *Dictionnaire géographique et universel des postes et du commerce* (Paris, 1782) ; *La parfaite intelligence du commerce* (Paris, 1785) ; *Almanach du commerce de Paris* (Paris, 1811).

commerce les présente comme les meilleures et précise que ces prunes sèches sont expédiées dans des petites caisses ou des boîtes à confiture, indice de leur valeur[53]. La prune de Tours, elle aussi fort estimée, s'apparente à un marché de haut de gamme avec un produit de qualité destiné principalement au marché parisien. La prune de Guyenne, en revanche, ne bénéficie pas du même prestige et n'est guère identifiée comme un produit d'exception dans les dictionnaires. Production destinée principalement aux colonies, aux expéditions vers le nord de l'Europe et à l'avitaillement des navires, l'origine géographique de cette prune n'est guère considérée comme un critère distinctif jusqu'au XIXe siècle[54]. La réputation sert donc à la différenciation entre les produits et, en fonction de leur origine, ils s'insèrent dans des marchés et des cultures de consommation différents.

La renommée de la plupart de ces denrées se construit dans le cadre de marchés restreints, des marchés de niches, mais très bien structurés. Les marchands et les métiers de bouche y font notamment preuve d'une grande adaptation à la demande tout en s'appuyant sur des savoir-faire traditionnels. Les réseaux commerciaux assurent des liens efficaces entre les producteurs en province et les consommateurs très souvent parisiens ou installés dans les capitales provinciales. Les progrès des transports par voie d'eau (canaux) et surtout par la route, en matière de vitesse et de régularité, favorisent la circulation de ces productions de territoire jusqu'alors bien souvent en marge des principales voies de communication. Cette réduction de l'espace-temps dans la seconde moitié du XVIIIe siècle est indispensable au développement d'un marché national structuré de ces produits de terroir qui doivent être acheminés en petites quantités et avec rapidité le plus souvent par diligence[55]. Comme a pu le montrer Reynald Abad dans *Le grand marché*, Paris fait appel à l'ensemble du royaume pour assurer son approvisionnement au XVIIIe siècle[56]. La capitale joue un rôle centralisateur pour tous ces produits des terroirs qui acquièrent en partie leur renommée grâce au marché parisien. Parmi les marchands du XVIIIe siècle, les épiciers occupent une place majeure dans leur commercialisation ; les livres de comptes des épiciers parisiens ou versaillais identifient en effet clairement certains d'entre eux : le livre d'achats de l'épicier Martiner fait ainsi état en octobre 1771 de la fourniture de

---

53 *Dictionnaire portatif de commerce.*

54 Jean-Pierre Williot, « Une revendication territoriale mise en concurrence : Le pruneau d'Agen au début du XXe siècle », dans *Les produits de terroirs aquitains*, dir. Corinne Marache (Agen, 2010), 267–81.

55 Guy Arbellot, « La grande mutation des routes de France au milieu du XVIIIe siècle », *Annales : Economies, sociétés, civilisations* 28, n°3 (1973) : 765–91 ; Verley, *L'échelle du monde*, 246–47.

56 Reynald Abad, *Le grand marché : L'approvisionnement alimentaire de Paris sous l'Ancien Régime* (Paris, 2002).

quatre pots de beurre d'Isigny ; l'épicier Lebrun propose du fromage de Roquefort et compte dans sa clientèle des personnages de haut-rang comme la maison du Roi ou le duc de Fronsac[57]. On les retrouve également à Bordeaux. Plusieurs livres de comptes et correspondances d'épiciers de cette ville portuaire en plein essor au siècle des Lumières mentionnent des fromages d'Auvergne ou de Roquefort, des sardines fines de Concarneau ou des prunes de Brignoles[58]. A Lyon, les marchands diffusent les produits du Midi comme les olives de Provence, les châtaignes du Vivarais ou les truffes du Dauphiné[59]. A partir de la fin du XVIIIe siècle et surtout au XIXe siècle, le développement des magasins de comestibles représente un nouveau relais dans la diffusion de ces denrées. A Paris, l'Hôtel des Américains abrite l'une de ces boutiques où sont proposées les meilleures et les plus renommées des denrées des provinces. Installé rue Saint-Honoré, il propose ainsi à la vente auprès d'une clientèle fortunée bon nombre de spécialités culinaires comme en témoignent les annonces parues dans divers journaux tels les *Annonces, affiches et avis divers de l'Orléanois* en 1783 :

> On trouvera au dépôt de Provence & du comestible, rue St Honoré, à l'hôtel des Américains, à Paris, les articles suivants : bœuf fumé de Hambourg, la livre, 30 sols ; mortadelles de Bologne cuites, 3 liv, anchois à l'huile, sans écailles, pour être mangés tels qu'ils sont, 3 liv ; olives farcies aux anchois & aux câpres 3 liv. ; moutarde aux anchois, 48 sols ; nougat blanc, 3 liv ; gelée de pommes de Rouen, le pot 45 sols ; pâtés de veau de rivière de Rouen, l'un 6 liv. ; cuisses d'oie marinées, le baril de 12 liv 21 liv ; enfin toutes sortes d'épiceries.[60]

D'autres magasins de comestibles (Corcellet, Mme Chevet), situés au Palais-Royal dans l'un des quartiers les plus prestigieux de la capitale, concourent également à la renommée des produits des terroirs[61].

De manière assez novatrice, tous ces professionnels cherchent à faire connaître ces spécialités estimées grâce à la presse commerciale. Ainsi le *Journal de commerce* publié à Bruxelles en 1760 évoque les prunes de Brignoles, le miel de Morlaix ou l'huile fine d'Aix comme des productions distinguées des autres[62]. L'innovation sur ce marché du luxe alimentaire passe également par la mise en place du système de dépôts-vente associés à des journaux. En 1767, le *Gazetin du comestible* permet aux gourmands parisiens de se fournir en spécialités culinaires des pro-

---

57 Archives de la ville de Paris, D5B6 (2318), livre d'achats de l'épicier Martinet (1771) ; D5B6 (799), livre de comptes de l'épicier Lebrun (1777–78).

58 ADG, 7 B 2261, 7 B 3055, 7 B 1392.

59 Pierre Léon, dir., *Papiers d'industriels et de commerçants lyonnais : Lyon et le grand commerce au XVIIIe siècle* (Lyon, 1976), 365.

60 *Annonces, affiches et avis divers de l'Orléanois*, 27 juin 1783.

61 Jean-Paul Aron, *Essai sur la sensibilité alimentaire à Paris au 19e siècle* (Paris, 1967).

62 *Journal de commerce* (Bruxelles, 1760).

vinces[63]. Ce mensuel, vendu par correspondance avec un abonnement de six livres à l'année, n'est pas simplement le recensement des « spécialités » régionales disponibles dans la capitale, mais il a aussi pour vocation de faciliter l'approvisionnement de ces produits de luxe destinés aux tables des élites : « ces gazetins indiqueront tout ce qu'il y de plus renommée & de plus rare, en tout Genres de Comestibles, naturels & factices »[64]. Sous forme de tableaux y sont proposés des pâtés de perdrix rouges aux truffes de Nérac, des andouilles de Troyes, du cotignac d'Orléans ou des pâtes d'abricot de Clermont. Les lecteurs peuvent faire appel au *Gazetin du comestible* pour commander les différents produits auprès des fournisseurs provinciaux. Le bureau du Comestible, situé rue du Mail, reçoit ainsi, par messagerie, jambons, pâtés et autres spécialités. Stimulé par la demande parisienne, ce marché a donc une dimension nationale caractéristique des marchés du luxe qui se construit progressivement à partir des années 1750–60, mais il a aussi un impact économique local parfois fort notamment comme facteur de spécialisation[65].

Au XVIIIe siècle, par exemple, le pays d'Isigny produit ainsi des beurres de qualité destinés aux marchés parisiens, ce qui permet une spécialisation agricole dans l'élevage laitier[66]. Le pays de Bray connaît lui aussi une croissance économique grâce à la demande parisienne comme le souligne en 1787 le subdélégué de Gournay-en-Bray : « Dans toute cette contrée, on s'occupe principalement du commerce du beurre. Cette denrée, que la nature du sol donne en excellence, est portée chaque semaine, avec le plus grand soin, à Paris, où elle est justement tant estimée, tant recherchée »[67]. Le terroir, la qualité et la renommée sont ici perçus comme les bases des progrès agricoles. L'inspecteur des manufactures François de Paule Latapie mesure bien lors de l'une de ses tournées en Guyenne l'importance du commerce des terrines de perdrix pour la petite ville de Nérac : « les conserves du sieur Taverne, aubergiste à Nérac, sont devenues très fameuses. Ce sont des pâtés de perdrix confites dans du saindoux et garnis de truffes. Ils se conservent des années entières sans se gâter. On en transporte non

---

63 Philip Hyman et Mary Hyman, « *Le Gazetin du comestible* », dans *Livres en bouche : Cinq siècles d'art culinaire français* (Paris, 2001), 189–91 ; François Moureau, « Gazetin du comestible », dans *Dictionnaire des journaux, 1600–1789*, dir. Jean Sgard (Paris, 1991), 441–42.

64 Philippe Meyzie, « La gourmandise des provinces au siècle des Lumières », *Lumières*, n°11 (2008) : 105–22.

65 Il conviendrait de mesurer avec plus de précision cet impact de la production et du commerce des produits des terroirs sur l'économie locale en multipliant les études de cas.

66 Fabrice Poncet, « Eleveurs et marchands de beurre à Isigny de la fin du XVIIe siècle à 1840 », *Annales de Normandie* 50, n°2 (2000) : 267–96.

67 Archives départementales de la Seine-Maritime, C 185, Observations du subdélégué de Gournay-en-Bray, 29 août 1787, publiées par Michel de Boüard, dir., *Documents de l'histoire de la Normandie* (Toulouse, 1972), 230–31.

seulement à Bordeaux et à Paris, mais dans le Nord »[68]. Cette impression est confirmée par le subdélégué de Nérac qui indique, dans une lettre à l'intendant de Guyenne en 1769 qu'« il ne peut trouver assés de perdrix dans la province pour remplir ses commissions » et il ajoute que « si le sieur Taverne trouvoit assés de perdrix, il debiteroit plus de 1 000 terrines »[69]. La réputation de ces pâtés et de leur producteur dynamise leur diffusion commerciale. Au moment de la Révolution dans une délibération municipale, les autorités de Brive s'inquiètent des problèmes de transport qui perturbent les expéditions de truffes, dindes, jambons, marrons et « autres espèces de comestibles » vers Paris ; selon eux, cette situation risque de ruiner un secteur économique considéré ici comme important notamment lors des étrennes de début d'année où ces spécialités servent de cadeaux[70]. A travers ces exemples, on voit bien que ce marché des produits des terroirs témoigne d'un dynamisme des campagnes et des villes moyennes qui parviennent à s'inscrire dans les circuits commerciaux. En entraînant un recul des marchés coloniaux et internationaux, la Révolution française favorise la promotion de ces produits qui sont alors de plus en plus perçus comme les symboles de la diversité et de la complémentarité des départements qui fondent la nation[71]. Plusieurs voyageurs indiquent que ce commerce gastronomique participe à la richesse de certaines provinces au début du XIXe siècle. Lorsqu'en 1841 Victor-Adolphe Malte-Brun évoque dans son guide la ville de Périgueux, il souligne l'importance économique de ces spécialités culinaires estimées au même titre que d'autres productions industrielles : « Aujourd'hui la principale source de ses richesses est son commerce de dindes, de pâtés truffés, de liqueurs, de papiers et de lainage »[72]. Des capitales provinciales comme Bordeaux et Lyon (pour les produits méditerranéens) sont les principaux relais des produits des terroirs à l'échelle nationale notamment vers Paris, mais des petites villes et leurs campagnes environnantes par leur insertion dans les réseaux commerciaux bénéficient également de cette stimulation de la demande.

Dans les correspondances commerciales, la question de la qualité occupe une place essentielle lorsque sont évoquées ces denrées d'exception. Les travaux d'Alessandro Stanziani ont bien montré que la

68 « Journal de tournée de François de Paule Latapie, inspecteur des manufactures en 1778 », dans *Archives historiques du département de la Gironde*, t. 38 (Paris, 1903), 319.

69 ADG, C 613.

70 Brive, archives municipales, 1D1/5, délibération de la municipalité du 15 déc. 1794.

71 Gérard Béaur et Philippe Minard, *Atlas de la Révolution française*, t. 10 (Paris, 1997) ; Julia Csergo, « L'émergence des cuisines régionales », dans Flandrin et Montanari, *Histoire de l'alimentation*, 823–41.

72 Victor-Adolphe Malte-Brun, *Les jeunes voyageurs en France ou description pittoresque du sol et des curiosités de ce pays, avec l'esquisse des mœurs de chaque province*, t. 1 (Paris, 1841), 161.

qualité alimentaire est un objet historique à la définition variable selon les époques, bien présente avec le XIXe siècle et irréductible à un seul critère[73]. Sur ce marché des produits des terroirs, la qualité est une convention partagée entre les différents acteurs qui assure la pérennité des réputations. Du côté des producteurs, une attention toute particulière est accordée à la fabrication de ces produits. Pour préserver leur réputation, ils doivent proposer un produit à la hauteur des attentes d'une clientèle exigeante. Un pâtissier de Périgueux, fournisseur habituel du duc de Saxe en pâtés de Périgueux, refuse ainsi en 1788 de lui expédier les fameuses terrines de perdrix aux truffes car il considère que les perdrix ne sont pas alors d'une qualité satisfaisante[74]. La lutte contre la contrefaçon s'inscrit aussi dans cette volonté de veiller à la qualité et à l'authenticité de ces produits. Pour identifier l'origine de leurs terrines et garantir leur qualité, certains pâtissiers vont même jusqu'à fournir un certificat :

> M. Charles Lafon, l'ainé, Maître Pâtissier à Périgueux, près la Manufacture, & vis-à-vis le marché, prévient qu'il est seul possesseur de secret du célèbre M. Villereynier son oncle, pour la composition des pâtés de perdrix truffées. Il garantit les siens pendant un an dans tous les pays, sur mer comme sur terre, & s'oblige à rendre le prix & les dépenses occasionnées par le transport, par un acte en bonne forme : précaution qu'il croit nécessaire pour éviter les contrefactions & ranimer la confiance publique ; prix de chaque pâté, 10 l par perdrix, franc de port pour tout le royaume, & 15 l. pour le pays étranger, rendu à Bordeaux. On peut également s'adresser audit Sieur pour les dindes aux truffes[75].

Ce lien entre qualité alimentaire et origine est également manifeste dans les dictionnaires de commerce. Dans l'article « Miel » du *Dictionnaire universel de commerce*, par exemple, il est précisé que « le meilleur miel blanc est celui de Narbonne, qu'on tire principalement du petit bourg de Corbière à trois lieux de la ville. Le véritable Corbière doit être nouveau, épais, grenu, d'un goût doux & piquant, d'une odeur douce & un peu aromatique, assez semblable à l'œil au sucre royal »[76]. L'authenticité du produit ne peut être ici attestée que par une analyse sensorielle dont ce dictionnaire d'usage pratique fournit les éléments[77]. Si l'attention porte sur l'origine et les qualités gustatives du produit, il est également pris grand soin de veiller à l'emballage et à la rapidité du

---

[73] Stanziani, *Histoire de la qualité alimentaire*, 9.

[74] ADA, E 1822/1, lettre du 22 févr. 1788.

[75] *Journal de Guyenne*, 23 déc. 1784.

[76] Savary des Bruslons, *Dictionnaire universel de commerce*, t. 2 (Genève, 1742).

[77] La référence à un lieu sert à la fois de garantie de qualité et d'argument de vente, Rolande Bonnain-Dulon et Aline Brochot, « De l'authenticité des produits alimentaires », *Ruralia*, n°14 (2004) : 2–19.

transport. Les pâtés de Périgueux sont ainsi placés dans des terrines vernissées portant le nom du pâtissier. La plupart de ces envois se font par la route et sont accompagnés de lettres de voiture qui assurent un suivi de la marchandise. Pour ces produits à la notoriété bien établie, le coût du transport ne représente d'ailleurs jamais un problème ; au contraire, un prix élevé renforce leur statut de produit de qualité aux yeux de consommateurs aisés. Un avis des messageries royales paru en 1786 dans les *Annonces, affiches et avis divers de la ville de Troyes* montre que la circulation de ces denrées tient une place importante dans l'économie locale et que le transport des langues de mouton, des hures de porc et des andouilles fréquemment expédiées vers Paris fait l'objet des plus grands soins :

> Comme il est souvent arrivé des inconvéniens dans l'envoi des volailles, du gibier & d'autres comestibles, que l'on fait passer à paris, faute d'avoir pris les précautions nécessaires ; on prévient le Public d'avoir l'attention de les mettre dans des paniers ou boëtes bien conditionnés, de fournir une déclaration signée, qui contiendra les noms, qualités & demeures des personnes auxquelles on fait des envois, la quantité de pièces & leur nature, & de mettre deux adresses bien lisibles, l'une sur les paniers ou boëtes, & l'autre en dedans, afin de faciliter la remise des articles, dans le cas où celles mises en dehors seroient perdues ou effacées.
>
> Les particuliers privilégié sont priés de faire suivre exactement leurs envois, d'un certificat dans la forme usitée, pour éviter les retards que leurs articles pourroient éprouver à la Douanne[78].

Tous ces dispositifs visent à renforcer la confiance entre les acteurs et témoignent de la modernité de ce secteur économique[79]. L'origine géographique y apparaît de plus en plus au cours du XVIIIe siècle comme un signe de qualité qui favorise la circulation de ces produits dont la réputation est établie tout à la fois sur des hiérarchies commerciales et sur le prestige social de leurs consommateurs. Dès le milieu du XVIIIe siècle, un réseau commercial efficace, principalement centré sur Paris et sur quelques capitales provinciales comme Bordeaux et Lyon, assure la diffusion de ces spécialités locales appréciées des gourmands.

---

78 *Annonces, affiches et avis divers de la ville de Troyes*, 19 avr. 1786.
79 Lucien Karpik, « L'économie de la qualité », *Revue française de sociologie* 30, n°2 (1989) : 187–210 ; Egizio Valceschini, « La valorisation économique des terroirs sur les marchés alimentaires », postface à Claire Delfosse, dir., *La mode du terroir et des produits alimentaires* (Paris, 2011), 347–54.

La reconnaissance des produits des terroirs
et la valorisation de l'origine

Si les produits des terroirs parviennent au XVIIIe siècle à circuler et à être bien identifiés grâce à la mise en place de réseaux privés, politiques et commerciaux, ils ont besoin de se faire connaître pour entériner leur renommée. La valorisation de l'origine va s'insérer dans des dispositifs de jugements qui permettent d'élargir la reconnaissance de ces denrées sur les marchés et légitimer les hiérarchies. En les mettant en avant, ils contribuent aussi à la fin du XVIIIe siècle et surtout dans les premières décennies du XIXe siècle à façonner, en France et en Europe, un imaginaire gourmand de la France incarné par quelques produits phares dont l'authenticité s'appuie sur l'origine affirmée. Des guides de voyage à la littérature gastronomique, tous ces amateurs éclairés participent, par leurs discours, à la construction d'une carte gastronomique de la France et à la consolidation d'un marché original des produits des terroirs[80].

La littérature de voyage est un genre en vogue aux XVIIIe et XIXe siècles[81]. Récits, guides ou correspondances de voyageurs sont des lectures très appréciées des élites du temps. Ils participent donc à la construction de cette opinion éclairée. Or, les produits alimentaires localisés occupent une place grandissante sous la plume des voyageurs à partir de la seconde moitié du XVIIIe siècle : les annotations sont alors plus nombreuses, les identifications à un territoire plus précises. Les voyageurs français ou étrangers développent un discours qui met en exergue l'origine comme signe de qualité, ce qui révèle une sensibilité croissante à la réputation de certaines denrées. Marqués par l'esprit encyclopédique des Lumières, les voyageurs et les guides s'emploient quelquefois à établir des hiérarchies en s'appuyant sur le terroir. Il est intéressant de remarquer que les produits les plus évoqués par la littérature de voyage sont assez conformes à ceux que l'on retrouve dans la littérature commerciale. Cette convergence suggère, même si l'analyse devrait être menée plus en profondeur, qu'il existe dès la fin du XVIIIe siècle des « conventions » partagées sur la qualité de ces spécialités culinaires. En 1768, par exemple, le *Guide des chemins de France*, dans sa présentation des « curiosités » de la France, retient le beurre à Isigny, les jambons à Bayonne ou les truffes en Périgord[82]. Au XIXe

---

80 Cette valorisation des produits des terroirs correspond à un processus assez semblable à celui de la naissance du restaurant à la fin de l'Ancien Régime et au développement de son rôle gastronomique au XIXe siècle étudiés par Rebecca L. Spang, *The Invention of the Restaurant : Paris and Modern Gastronomic Culture* (Cambridge, 2000).

81 Daniel Roche, *Humeurs vagabondes : De la circulation des hommes et de l'utilité des voyages* (Paris, 2003).

82 *Guide des chemins de France*, 3e éd. (Paris, 1768).

siècle, le *Guide classique du voyage* de Richard, maintes fois réédité dans
la première moitié du siècle, cite parmi les produits les plus renommés
l'huile d'olive d'Aix, les prunes de Brignoles, le nougat blanc de Montélimar ou le pain d'épices de Reims[83]. Les hiérarchies établies notamment par les marchands sont donc relayées par la littérature de voyage
et s'installent ainsi plus nettement dans l'imaginaire gourmand des
élites du temps, clientèle par excellence de ces produits de luxe. L'origine du produit lui confère une plus-value admise par tous comme en
témoigne fréquemment l'emploi de formules telles « on considère . . .
on juge . . . on estime » et ainsi de suite. Dans son *Itinéraire de Bordeaux
à Tarbes* publié en 1836, Jean-François Samazeuilh note ainsi à propos des terrines de perdrix aux truffes de Nérac en Lot-et-Garonne :
« La réputation des terrines de Nérac est due surtout à la qualité des
truffes que l'on trouve dans son voisinage, et que l'on préfère à celles du
Périgord et du Quercy »[84]. L'origine géographique des produits—leur
« terroir »—concourt alors à distinguer ce pâté des autres.

Ces réputations bien établies ont, en retour, une influence sur le
fonctionnement du marché spécialisé car elles peuvent entraîner des
variations de la demande et des effets de mode. En 1772, l'*Histoire naturelle des végétaux* rappelle ainsi que « la prune de Brignoles l'emporte
par la bonté sur les damas de Tours, autrefois si vantés »[85]. Les effets
de réputation se font ressentir par des baisses de la demande en fonction du goût des consommateurs et du discours qui entoure le produit
dont les voyageurs se font l'écho. A la suite d'un séjour en Provence
dans les années 1780, Bérenger propose à ses lecteurs une réflexion
sur le recul de la réputation des huiles d'Aix dû à des effets de mode :
« Il ne sera pas hors de propos de remarquer, en terminant cet article,
que depuis quelques années les excellentes huiles de *Provence*, connues
sous le nom d'huiles d'*Aix*, sont moins demandées dans le commerce. Il
semble que la mode exerce son influence jusque sur des objets de consommation alimentaire qui devraient être absolument indépendans de
ses caprices ». La cherté du produit ou ses qualités gustatives ne peuvent à ses yeux expliquer cette désaffection, mais elle résulte plus d'un
changement des goûts des consommateurs auquel viennent s'ajouter
des fraudes sur l'origine : « Qu'ils sachent enfin, que s'ils ont reçu des
huiles d'Apt et de Baume, sous le nom de Vitrolle et des Baux, il n'est
pas juste d'envelopper ces dernières dans une même proscription »[86].

83 Richard, *Guide classique du voyageur en France et en Belgique*, 24e éd. (Paris, 1854).
84 Jean-François Samazeuilh, *Itinéraire de Bordeaux à Tarbes* (Auch, 1836).
85 Pierre-Joseph Buch'Hoz., *Histoire naturelle des végétaux considérés relativement aux différens
usages qu'on peut en tirer pour la médecine, et l'économie domestique*, t. 2 (Paris, 1772), 212.
86 *Les soirées provençales ou lettres sur les provinces de Monsieur Bérenger écrites à ses amis pendant ses
voyages dans sa patrie*, 3e éd., t. 2 (Paris, 1786), 234–36.

Les voyageurs eux-mêmes mesurent combien la renommée des produits des terroirs contribue à leur diffusion commerciale à l'échelle nationale et particulièrement dans la capitale. Pour l'abbé de Laporte, auteur du *Voyageur françois*, « les huîtres de Marennes jouissent, depuis longtemps, d'une grande réputation ; il s'en fait un débit considérable ; on les transporte jusqu'à Paris »[87]. La recherche du produit local devient une tendance forte, voire un signe de distinction sociale. La description de tel ou tel produit devient même parfois un passage obligé pour les voyageurs comme on visite un monument célèbre. Jean-Baptiste Joudou lors de son passage à Ruffec en 1818 suggère avec ironie combien les guides de voyage peuvent avoir une influence sur la réputation et le commerce de ces denrées sans lien toujours avec leur qualité :

> On vient nous offrir des fromages que nous achetons, ne trouvant rien de mieux ; un habitant, choqué du peu de prix que nous mettons à cette production si vantée de son pays, s'exprime avec chaleur, et assure qu'on envoie de ces délicieux fromages à Paris, et qu'ils y sont fort estimés ; notre guide de route [. . .] dit de même dans son ouvrage, et voilà que sur la foi du livre et celle de l'habitant de Ruffec, nous commençons à trouver ces fromages excellents ; j'en riais malgré moi, cela me rappelait ces réputations auxquelles on croit sur parole, qui sont l'ouvrage, non de la conviction, mais d'une coterie ; la société exerce une singulière influence à cet égard ; tant de gens n'ont d'opinion que par impulsion[88] !

La mise en avant des produits des terroirs par les voyageurs s'accentue au XIXe siècle au moment où la bonne chère est valorisée par le discours gastronomique et le pittoresque des provinces se construit peu à peu dans de nombreux récits[89]. En 1841, comme d'autres auteurs, Victor-Adolphe Malte-Brun peut ainsi écrire dans *Les jeunes voyageurs en France ou description pittoresque du sol et des curiosités de ce pays, avec l'esquisse des mœurs de chaque province* à propos du Lot-et-Garonne : « importance d'un département, que les truffes, les oies grasses, les prunes d'Agen et les pâtés de perdrix de Nérac, ont rendu cher aux gourmets » et quelques pages plus loin dans sa présentation du Périgord : « Mais ce qui mérite au département l'estime des gastronomes, c'est le vin blanc de Bergerac, c'est la délicatesse de la chair de ses porcs, l'abondance des perdrix rouges, les beaux brochets qui peuplent les étangs, les liqueurs, les dragées fines de Périgueux, et surtout les truffes de son

---

[87] Abbé de Laporte, *Le voyageur françois ou la connaissance de l'ancien et du nouveau monde*, t. 34 (Paris, 1741), 291.

[88] Jean-Baptiste Joudou, *Voyage dans les Pyrénées en 1818* (Paris, 1820), 22.

[89] Jean-Pierre Lethuillier et Odile Parsis-Barubé, dirs., *Le pittoresque : Métamorphoses d'une quête dans l'Europe moderne et contemporaine* (Paris, 2012) ; Julia Csergo et Jean-Pierre Lemasson, dirs., *Voyages en gastronomies : L'invention des capitales et des régions gourmandes* (Paris, 2008).

territoire les plus estimées de France »[90]. Le *Guide classique du voyage* de Richard signale à ses lecteurs que les chapons de Caussade dans le Lot sont « estimés des gourmets » ou que la ville d'Amiens produit d' « excellents pâtés que nous recommandons aux gourmets »[91].

La naissance de la littérature gastronomique au début du XIXe siècle entérine donc le processus de construction des réputations des produits alimentaires déjà initié à la fin du XVIIe siècle[92]. Au XVIIIe siècle, les livres de cuisine évoquent bien ici ou là quelques produits emblématiques : dans la *Cuisine et office de santé propres à ceux qui vivent avec économie et régime,* par exemple, Menon cite les jambons de Bayonne et considère que les truffes du Périgord sont « les meilleur[e]s »[93]. Toutefois, ce genre d'annotation mettant en exergue l'origine géographique comme signe distinctif est la plupart du temps isolé. Les premiers auteurs gastronomes du XIXe siècle comme Grimod de la Reynière et Brillat-Savarin, par leurs écrits, renforcent et généralisent cette différenciation entre les produits notamment par leur origine, mais surtout ils confortent et diffusent des hiérarchies largement partagées et pérennes qui servent de référence au fonctionnement de ce marché. Le gastronome joue alors le rôle d'un expert dont les jugements sont suivis par les consommateurs informés[94]. La publication en 1804 de la première carte gastronomique de la France par Charles-Louis Cadet de Gassicourt, ancien avocat au Parlement de Paris, représente une étape importante dans l'établissement de la réputation culinaire de certains produits. Dans *Les cours gastronomiques ou les dîners de Manant-Ville,* cet auteur s'intéresse à ce qui fait une table de qualité au début du XIXe siècle[95]. Sur cette carte, il représente par des symboles les produits les plus renommés associés à des territoires. Son but est bien de mettre en valeur les richesses gastronomiques des provinces en s'appuyant sur leur renommée puisqu'il écrit dans un chapitre intitulé « Sachons un peu de géographie » : « J'y ai placé avec honneur de modestes villages quand ils se sont fait un nom par leurs productions gastronomiques »[96]. Cette carte témoigne de la mise en place d'une géographie gourmande en France qui correspond parfaitement au marché des produits des terroirs précédemment décrits puisqu'on y retrouve les pâtés

[90] Malte-Brun, *Les jeunes voyageurs,* 102, 154.

[91] Richard, *Guide classique du voyageur,* 9, 294.

[92] Sur la naissance de la littérature gastronomique, voir Pascal Ory, *Le discours gastronomique français des origines à nos jours* (Paris, 1998).

[93] Menon, *Cuisine et office de santé propre à ceux qui vivent avec économie et régime* (Paris, 1758).

[94] Martin Brueguel, dir., *Le choix des aliments : Informations et pratiques alimentaires de la fin du Moyen Age à nos jours* (Rennes, 2010).

[95] Charles-Louis Cadet de Gassicourt, *Cours gastronomiques ou les dîners de Manant-Ville : Ouvrage anecdotique, philosophique et littéraire,* 2e éd. (Paris, 1809).

[96] Ibid., 300.

d'Amiens, les jambons de Bayonne, les chapons de Bourg-en-Bresse, les dindes aux truffes de Périgueux ou les dragées de Verdun. Par la suite, des cartes de la France ancrant ce lien entre réputation, qualité et origine géographique sont couramment présentes dans les œuvres des écrivains gastronomes comme *Le gastronome français ou l'art de bien vivre*, *Le code gourmand, manuel complet de gastronomie* ou le *Nouvel almanach des gourmands servant de guide dans les moyens de faire excellente chère*[97]. Les premiers écrits des gastronomes du XIXe siècle offrent donc une reconnaissance de la renommée de certaines spécialités culinaires locales qui ont construit leur réputation tout au long de l'Ancien Régime. Pour les consommateurs, ces jugements avertis deviennent une référence dans leurs choix. Le prince allemand Hermann Ludwig Heinrich Pückler-Muskau porte ainsi son attention sur les pâtés d'Angoulême car ils ont été évoqués sur la carte gastronomique de la France[98]. En 1824, dans *Les jeunes voyageurs en France ou lettres sur les départements*, Depping faisant référence au périodique de Grimod de la Reynière évoque Nérac, ville fameuse « dans l'almanach des gourmands pour ses pâtés appelés terrines »[99].

L'*Almanach des gourmands* de Grimod de la Reynière représente en effet bien cette conjonction entre faiseurs de goût, marché des produits du luxe alimentaire et une clientèle d'amateurs connaisseurs et fortunés[100]. Le premier numéro de l'*Almanach des gourmands* en 1803 fournit à ses lecteurs un « Itinéraire descriptif ou promenade d'un gourmand dans les divers quartiers de Paris » qui donne des indications sur les magasins de comestibles et les produits des provinces que l'on peut y trouver (mortadelles de Lyon, terrines de Nérac, langues de Troyes, fromages de Marolles, pâtes d'abricot de Clermont, gelée de pommes de Rouen, etc.) Réunissant un jury de dégustateurs, Grimod de la Reynière se propose d'évaluer les denrées qui lui seront soumises sous forme d'échantillons. Selon lui, la réputation de ces produits confirmée et légitimée par les gastronomes stimule leur commerce. Il dévoile ainsi ses ambitions : « Ce journal pourrait devenir un moyen facile de correspondance entre les gourmands de tous les pays. Ils établiraient une communication, désirée depuis longtemps, entre Paris et les provinces, pour tout ce qui est relatif à la bonne chère. Chaque ville déjà connue

---

97 *Nouvel almanach des gourmands servant de guide dans les moyens de faire excellente chère* (Paris, 1826) ; *Le gastronome français ou l'art de bien vivre* (Paris, 1828) ; Horace Raison, *Le code gourmand, manuel complet de gastronomie* (Paris, 1829).

98 Hermann Ludwig Heinrich Pückler-Muskau, *Chroniques, lettres et journal de voyage, extrait des papiers d'un défunt* (Paris, 1836).

99 Georges-Bernard Depping, *Les jeunes voyageurs en France ou lettres sur les départements*, t. 5 (Paris, 1824), 100.

100 Alexandre Balthazar Laurent Grimod de la Reynière, *Almanach des gourmands servant de guide dans les moyens de faire excellente chère, 1803–1812* (Paris, 2012).

par ses produits alimentaires recherchés, ou qui voudrait se faire légitimer sous ce rapport, s'efforcerait d'y mériter une place »[101]. Au fil des numéros, Grimod de la Reynière précise des hiérarchisations appuyées sur l'origine comme pour les fromages et fait l'éloge de produits des terroirs comme les canetons de Rouen, les groseilles de Bar-Le-Duc ou les huîtres de Cancale. Ses écrits illustrent bien le fonctionnement du marché des produits renommés des provinces acheminés dans la capitale où le jugement des experts participe à la définition de la qualité. Dans sa *Physiologie du goût* en 1826, Brillat-Savarin confirme que l'origine est alors considérée comme un signe de qualité pour des produits dont la renommée s'est construite depuis le XVIIe siècle. Lors de son éloge des truffes du Périgord, il évoque ainsi un souper avec une dame de la haute société parisienne à la fin du XVIIIe siècle en reprenant les mots de cette dernière à propos du plat principal : « Notre souper, assez léger d'ailleurs, avait cependant pour base une superbe volaille truffée. Le subdélégué de Périgueux nous l'avait envoyée. En ce temps, c'était un cadeau ; et d'après son origine, vous pensez bien que c'était une perfection »[102]. A propos du gibier, il met aussi en exergue ce lien étroit entre origine géographique et qualité : « Le gibier tire aussi une grande partie de son prix de la nature du sol où il se nourrit ; le goût d'une perdrix rouge du Périgord n'est pas le même que celui d'une perdrix rouge de Sologne »[103]. Le terroir est alors bien considéré comme un indice de qualité et de différenciation. Dans ce manuel de gastronomie, il cite également les poulardes de Bresse, les pâtés de foie gras de Strasbourg et les truffes du Périgord. Tous ces produits ont alors une réputation bien établie et s'insèrent dans un marché de la gourmandise bien structurée, régie par les jugements des gastronomes et les goûts des élites[104].

Conclusions

La réputation des produits des terroirs du XVIIe à la première moitié du XIXe siècle est le fruit d'une construction complexe où se mêlent les nomenclatures commerciales, les consommations distinctives et l'imaginaire gourmand. Certains d'entre eux comme les truffes du Périgord, l'huile de Provence ou les fromages de Roquefort sont clairement identifiés et leur origine est considérée par les producteurs, les intermédiaires et les consommateurs comme un signe de qualité. Le déve-

---

[101] Ibid., 231.
[102] Jean-Anthelme Brillat-Savarin, *Physiologie du goût* (1826), dir. Jean-François Revel (Paris, 1982), 102.
[103] Ibid., 92.
[104] Le rôle central de ces « faiseurs de goût » à propos des produits des terroirs a été bien mis en exergue par Trubek, *Taste of Place*, 21.

loppement de la demande pour ces denrées au XVIIIe siècle entraine une valorisation de la localisation qui s'appuie principalement sur les villes-relais de ces produits. Comme il n'existe alors ni de certifications officielles ni de labels, la réputation fondée sur la durée et la localisation leur confère une plus-value distinctive qui les fait rentrer dans la définition donnée aujourd'hui des produits des terroirs, même si le terme n'est pas encore employé[105].

Le commerce joue un rôle de premier plan dans ce processus de hiérarchisation. Si l'action des producteurs reste difficile à mesurer, celle des marchands et des dictionnaires de commerce est plus manifeste. Afin de faciliter les échanges, ils mettent en place des classifications qui associent origine et qualité. Pour satisfaire à la demande d'une clientèle fortunée qui désire ces produits gourmands se met en place un marché spécialisé marqué par une forte dimension sociale et culturelle dans la seconde moitié du XVIIIe siècle. Loin de se réduire à un simple jeu d'équilibre entre l'offre et la demande, les effets de réputation induisent des mécanismes originaux illustrés par une sensibilité aux modes et la place tenue par les prescripteurs de goût (consommateurs prestigieux, voyageurs, écrivains gastronomes). Ce marché gourmand des produits des terroirs centrés sur Paris offre le cas intéressant d'une cohabitation au XVIIIe siècle entre, d'un côté des pratiques profondément ancrées dans l'Ancien Régime comme l'économie du don ou l'importance des réseaux personnels, et, de l'autre, des innovations comme le recours aux journaux d'annonces, l'attention à la préservation des produits ou l'appui sur des systèmes de dépôts-vente. La réputation de ces produits initiée par la culture de consommation des élites, notamment nobiliaires, engendre un désir de consommation, un élargissement de la clientèle et une structuration progressive de ce marché dont les magasins de comestibles parisiens à partir de la seconde moitié du XVIIIe siècle fournissent la vitrine. La multiplication des échanges dans les années 1770–80, grâce aux progrès des transports, et la croissance de la demande marquent assurément un tournant majeur dans le développement de ce marché gourmand. Durant la Révolution française, le recul des marchés extérieurs qui conduit à une valorisation des marchés intérieurs et le regard nouveau porté sur les provinces, bases de la richesse de la nation, ne représentent qu'une accélération

---

[105] Selon la définition donnée par les experts de l'INAO (Institut national des appellations d'origine), « un terroir est un espace géographique délimité, où une communauté humaine a construit au cours de l'histoire un savoir intellectuel collectif de production, fondé sur un système d'interactions entre un milieu physique et biologique, et un ensemble de facteurs humains, dans lequel les itinéraires sociotechniques mis en jeu révèlent une originalité, confèrent une typicité et engendrent une réputation pour un produit originaire de ce terroir » ; cité par Madeleine Ferrières, « Terroirs : Jalons pour l'histoire d'un mot », dans Ceccarelli, Grandi et Magagnoli, *Typicality in History*, 23–45.

d'un processus déjà largement initié que les écrits des gastronomes au début du XIXe siècle viennent simplement entériner[106].

L'étude de la réputation des produits des terroirs et de ce marché gourmand ne peut en effet être réduite à une simple approche économique. Les récits des voyageurs et les éloges des gastronomes sont autant de dispositifs de jugements qui font, défont et entretiennent les réputations. Ils contribuent aussi à l'élaboration d'un imaginaire gourmand de plus en plus partagé qui sert de toile de fond au commerce de ces denrées. Les origines géographiques deviennent au XIXe siècle des références pour ces produits. La constance de la mise en valeur de certaines spécialités par les cadeaux édilitaires du XVIIIe siècle, les dictionnaires de commerce et la littérature gastronomique confirme que leurs réputations sont déjà bien établies et qu'elles sont considérées comme des produits de qualité clairement identifiés géographiquement sur ce marché des produits gourmands. La notion de terroir y occupe une place grandissante qui témoigne de l'émergence d'une spécificité française dans cette valorisation des provinces et des campagnes à travers leur lien avec la qualité de l'alimentation ; l'Italie, avec la notion de typicité, offre de nombreux points communs qu'il conviendrait d'approfondir, mais la ville y est sans doute plus présente que la campagne. La reconnaissance des produits italiens s'opère beaucoup plus sur les marchés étrangers et l'absence d'une capitale unique comme Paris n'offre pas un pôle centralisateur à la valorisation des terroirs dans un cadre national[107]. Cette étude n'offre ici que les premiers éléments pour comprendre le fonctionnement de ce marché et l'effet des réputations. De manière plus systématique, par la multiplication des exemples et des comparaisons, il conviendrait de voir comment sont élaborés ces produits renommés, quels contrôles exercent les professionnels sur leur qualité, de quelle manière ils tentent de lutter contre les contrefaçons et comment fonctionnent précisément les réseaux commerciaux dans ce secteur singulier du marché de l'alimentation en France. Ces réputations ne sont en outre pas immuables ; elles se construisent au fil du temps. Soumises aux effets de mode et aux transformations des goûts des consommateurs, leurs évolutions, voire dans certains cas leur déclin, offrent un terrain propice à la réflexion sur le rôle de la demande et de la consommation dans l'Europe préindustri-

106 La construction de ce marché des produits des terroirs avant la Révolution s'opère en parallèle avec la valorisation des cuisines régionales ; voir Philippe Meyzie, *La table du Sud-Ouest et l'émergence des cuisines régionales (1700–1850)* (Rennes, 2007).

107 John Dickie, *Delizia ! The Epic History of the Italians and Their Food* (Londres, 2007) ; Massimo Montanari, « Une gastronomie urbaine : Cuisine(s) et culture(s) d'Italie entre le Moyen Age et l'époque contemporaine », dans *Manger en Europe : Patrimoines, échanges, identités*, dir. Antonella Campanini, Peter Scholliers et Jean-Pierre Williot (Bern, 2011), 209–20 ; Alberto Capatti et Massimo Montanari, *La cuisine italienne : Histoire d'une culture* (Paris, 2002), 18–19.

elle[108]. L'histoire de la réputation de ces denrées en replaçant l'analyse des produits des terroirs dans le temps long apporte des indications sur leur ancrage historique et spatial, mais aussi sur la question, si souvent mobilisée par le marché actuel, de leur authenticité qui apparaît bien comme une construction économique, sociale et culturelle[109].

---

[108] John Brewer, Neil McKendrick et John Harold Plumb, *The Birth of a Consumer Society : The Commercialisation of Eighteenth Century England* (Londres, 1982) ; John Brewer et Roy Porter, dirs., *Consumption and the World of Goods* (Londres, 1997) ; Grenier, « Travailler plus pour consommer plus ».

[109] Jean-Pierre Poulain, dir., *Dictionnaire des cultures alimentaires* (Paris, 2012), 144. « L'authentique est toujours un qualificatif qui contribue à la valorisation sociale, symbolique, économique, politique, d'originalité d'un aliment ou d'un produit alimentaire » ; Bonnain-Dulong et Brochot, « De l'authenticité des produits alimentaires ».

Workers' Lunch Away from Home in the Paris of the Belle Epoque: The French Model of Meals as Norm and Practice

Martin Bruegel

Abstract   *This article expands the anthropological notion of the "proper meal" to account for the quantitative aspects of workers' lunch away from home in Paris around 1900. It reconstructs the meals' caloric content and shows that male workers had easier access than their female colleagues to what they considered a full repast. Yet not everybody behaved according to the French model of the structured meal, namely, appetizer, entrée, and dessert. A full-fledged takeout food sector offered alternatives to the French model and allowed consumers to distance themselves from norms. Many French scholars have accepted the canonical dietary model as self-evident, which has led to neglect of this more informal food space where cultural rules exerted a weaker hold on eating behavior. Attention to the cultural importance and the material content of the commercial midday meal around 1900 offers a starting point to examine the developments of food practices and body weights in the twentieth century.*

Keywords   *consumption, working class, gender, social norms, belle epoque*

Historical research has shed light on the genesis of the so-called French dietary model, namely, a structured lunch and dinner of appetizer, entrée, and a dessert. Jean-Paul Aron showed the passage to the three-course menu over the course of the early nineteenth century,[1] and Claude Grignon delineated the compromises between a bourgeois way of life and a multitude of popular (food) cultures that resulted in the pattern of three daily meals (breakfast, lunch, dinner) by 1900.[2] Both developments normalized social rhythms. For one, the timetable of eating helped industrializing society link the replenishment of its members to its economic tempos and imperatives; the pressure to syn-

Martin Bruegel is a historian in the research unit Alimentation, Sciences Sociales of the Institut National de la Recherche Agronomique.

Parts of this article have been presented at the Centre Georges Chevrier at the Université de Bourgogne, at a workshop at the Université Libre de Bruxelles, at the Sorbonne seminar on the history of Paris, and in an in-house seminar at the Institut National de la Recherche Agronomique; the author's gratitude goes to the participants, among whom Aurélie Maurice, Anne Lhuissier, Marie Plessz, Stéphane Gacon, and Peter Scholliers deserve special mention. He also thanks the readers and editors of *French Historical Studies*, whose judicious comments and tireless work have made this a much better article.

1 Jean-Paul Aron, *Essai sur la sensibilité alimentaire à Paris au 19e siècle* (Paris, 1967), 48–55.

2 Claude Grignon, "La règle, la mode et le travail: La genèse sociale du modèle des repas français contemporains," in *Le temps de manger: Alimentation, emploi du temps et rythmes sociaux*, ed. Maurice Aymard, Claude Grignon, and Françoise Sabban (Paris, 1994), 275–309.

French Historical Studies, Vol. 38, No. 2 (April 2015)   DOI 10.1215/00161071-2842566

chronize biology and work led to the widely respected regular meal schedule. Then, too, the change from the simultaneous "French" to the sequential "Russian" food service streamlined workflow in the kitchen and at the table; it proved particularly tailored to consumption in restaurants, where seated clients expected individual menus and warm dishes. These conventions determined the forms (on menus) and the timing of meals in urban settings (but not in the countryside, where the seasons still determined both)[3] at the end of the nineteenth century. They do not, however, reveal how actual eaters dealt with these norms or the content of their meals. In other words, the extent to which consumers ate by the "French model" and what this meant in quantitative terms remain unknown. The lack of knowledge especially concerns artisans and workers, the group whose social rhythms and eating practices were most likely to endure the pressure of the arising urban organization. This is the gap that research into workers' lunch away from home is seeking to fill.

This article expands the anthropological notion of the "proper meal," to wit, the grammar behind a repast's composition and sequencing, to account for the quantitative aspects of workers' lunch away from home in Paris around 1900. It reconstructs the caloric content of what Parisians described as a normal meal and shows that male workers had easier access than their female colleagues to what many in French society considered a full repast. Crucially, a full-fledged takeout food sector offered alternatives to the French model of a structured meal. The history of these street and carry-away foods has fallen into oblivion, enabling contemporary fast foods to be interpreted as foreign and labeled as junk food.

Eating out during the workday was "an ineluctable necessity for many workers"[4] in Paris, "a hardworking" city of 2.7 million inhabitants "and many thousand workshops and factories"[5] at the turn of the twentieth century. Its importance notwithstanding, the midday meal taken away from home has received only scant historical attention. John Burnett details the burden such lunches taken by men put on family budgets in England,[6] and Kathleen Leonard Turner illustrates families' strategies of food provisioning in North American cities.[7] The supply

3 Rolande Bonnain, "Les campagnes françaises à table," in Tables d'hier, tables d'ailleurs, ed. Jean-Louis Flandrin and Jane Cobbi (Paris, 1999), 277–79.

4 Henri Labbé, "Le budget alimentaire des ouvriers et employés parisiens," Bulletin de la Société scientifique d'hygiène alimentaire 1, nos. 1–2 (1911): 330; Fernand Pelloutier and Maurice Pelloutier, La vie ouvrière en France (Paris, 1900), 212.

5 "City of Many Thousand Workshops and Factories," Omaha Daily Bee, Oct. 19, 1902, 6.

6 John Burnett, England Eats Out, 1830–Present (Harlow, 2004), 107–12.

7 Kathleen Leonard Turner, How the Other Half Ate: A History of Working-Class Meals at the Turn of the Century (Berkeley, CA, 2014), 51–90.

side is the focus of Jakob Tanner, Anne Lhuissier, and Abigail Carroll, who tie the emergence of industrial canteens—where Swiss, French, and American workers could find sustenance away from home—to economic pressure and sometimes to a philanthropic outlook, but mostly to bosses' growing comprehension of the relation between workers' rest and their productivity in the second half of the nineteenth and into the twentieth century.[8] While the importance of public drinking to workers' sociability and their political activism is the theme of W. Scott Haine's study of the Parisian café in the nineteenth century,[9] eating out turns up as an element of the bourgeois drive for social distinction in Rebecca L. Spang's and Rachel Rich's narratives about the invention of the restaurant and its social uses as places to stage power and influence.[10]

These histories point to areas that need further research. For one, the physiological aspects of workers' meals away from home require investigation, and insights into the meaning of eating one's fill during the workday expand our knowledge of workers' standard and quality of living. In other words, we learn about the social definition of metabolic "needs." Then, too, we do well to remember that the difference between middle-class and working-class households hinged on women's gainful employment, and in that respect married French women outpaced their counterparts in Germany, the United Kingdom, and the United States by a ratio of four to one at the beginning of the twentieth century (the fact did not escape contemporary observers).[11] Both income and work created specific problems for working women. Helen Harden Chenut has depicted their struggle to keep family and work in sync as "an exhausting routine,"[12] and Eliza Earle Ferguson has sketched out the tensions that existed between spouses over the distribution of household resources.[13] Yet most of the history of women's consumption

---

[8] Jakob Tanner, *Fabrikmahlzeit: Ernährungswissenschaft, Industriearbeit und Volksernährung in der Schweiz, 1890–1950* (Zürich, 1999), 209–53; Anne Lhuissier, "Un dispositif pratique de gestion de la main d'oeuvre: Les cantines industrielles dans le second XIXe siècle," *Consommations et sociétés* 2, no. 2 (2001): 53–65; Abigail Carroll, *Three Squares: The Invention of the American Meal* (New York, 2013), 120–26.

[9] W. Scott Haine, *The World of the Paris Café: Sociability among the French Working Class, 1789–1914* (Baltimore, MD, 1996).

[10] Rebecca L. Spang, *The Invention of the Restaurant: Paris and Modern Gastronomic Culture* (Boston, 2000); Rachel Rich, *Bourgeois Consumption: Food, Space, and Identity in London and Paris, 1850–1914* (Manchester, 2011), 142–61.

[11] Jean Frollo, "Le travail des femmes," *Le petit Parisien*, July 18, 1900, 1; Alain Cottereau, "The Distinctiveness of Working-Class Cultures in France, 1848–1900," in *Working-Class Formation: Nineteenth-Century Patterns in Western Europe and the United States*, ed. Ira Katznelson and Aristide R. Zolberg (Princeton, NJ, 1986), 137–42.

[12] Helen Harden Chenut, *The Fabric of Gender: Working-Class Culture in Third Republic France* (University Park, PA, 2005), 195–99.

[13] Eliza Earle Ferguson, *Gender and Justice: Violence, Intimacy, and Community in Fin-de-Siècle Paris* (Baltimore, MD, 2010), 57–60, 74–77.

concerns the private, middle-class household,[14] rather than working-class families. The significant involvement of women in the French labor market meant that many among them lunched away from home, and gender offers a prism through which to analyze the experience of the midday meal among the working class.

At the end of the nineteenth century, the question of "whether people lunching out of the home—and we know that they are plenty—get their money's worth with respect to their physical needs" had become a public preoccupation.[15] By that time, organic chemistry had succeeded in measuring a foodstuff's energy content, an achievement that made it possible to think of food as fuel.[16] In the 1870s French agronomists put a price on the calories of fodder and, by substituting oats, corn, and legumes according to their cost per energy unit, reduced the expenses of feeding the enormous number of horses drawing carts and coaches in Paris by more than 30 percent.[17] The publication of Wilbur O. Atwater's "Pecuniary Economy of Food" in 1888 prompted the application of the same quantitative method to human consumption, and it put the calculation of "the relation of the nutritive value of food to its cost" on the public agenda on both sides of the Atlantic.[18]

The idea found fertile ground in reform-minded France. Philanthropists and members of the academic establishment integrated it into the program of the Société Scientifique d'Hygiène Alimentaire et d'Alimentation Rationnelle (SSHA), founded in 1904 with financial support from the French state. The dean of the medical faculty, Louis Landouzy (1845–1917), a tuberculosis specialist, tireless promoter of improvements in public health, and frequent guest speaker at the SSHA, summed up the scientific rationale for making inquiries into popular food practices. "Human food," he wrote in 1908, "is a simple question of *must* and *have*. The *must* is the responsibility of the physiologist; the *have*, of the economist."[19] The aim of these investigations

---

[14] See, e.g., Victoria de Grazia, "Introduction," and Leora Auslander, "The Gendering of Consumer Practices in Nineteenth-Century France," in *The Sex of Things: Gender and Consumption in Historical Perspective*, ed. Victoria de Grazia with Ellen Furlough (Berkeley, CA, 1996), 15–16, 80–85.

[15] Dr. Dauzères, "A travers la science," *Le petit Parisien*, Aug. 7, 1905, 5.

[16] Kenneth J. Carpenter, "A Short History of Nutritional Science," *Journal of Nutrition* 133, nos. 3, 4, 10, 11 (2003): 638–45, 975–84, 2023–32, 3331–42; Anson Rabinbach, *The Human Motor: Energy, Fatigue, and the Origins of Modernity* (Berkeley, CA, 1992).

[17] Louis Grandeau et al., *Etudes expérimentales sur l'alimentation du cheval de trait* (Paris, 1882).

[18] Wilbur O. Atwater, "The Pecuniary Economy of Food," *Century* 35, no. 3 (1888): 437–46; for a brief description of the transatlantic discussion among physiologists, see Martin Bruegel, "Locating Foodways in the Nineteenth Century," in *A Cultural History of Food in the Age of Empire*, ed. Martin Bruegel (London, 2012), 11–17.

[19] Louis Landouzy, "L'alimentation rationnelle envisagée du point de vue physiologique et économique," *Revue scientifique*, Sept. 5, 1908, 289.

was to assess popular diets in order to reform them. The newly gained nutritional knowledge specified the guidelines for turning putatively profligate workers into efficient and healthy consumers.[20] Despite the moralizing impulse, it is precisely because investigators proceeded meticulously and aspired to produce incontrovertible data that the results of their studies provide many of the sources for the retrieval of workers' lunch practices.

There is more to the recovery of past popular consumer behavior than the retrospective assessment of agency, degrees of liberty with respect to norms, and indigenous (as opposed to scientific) conceptions of proper meals. The historical study of lunchtime away from home, as a constrained practice and a source of physical energy, has contemporary relevance. France's relative resistance to eating disorders has even been tied to the French model of meals.[21] While there is a vast literature on the increase in the size of portions and meals consumed in commercial environments and their contribution to the incidence of obesity in the United States, England, and, to a lesser extent, continental Europe,[22] smaller servings in restaurants seem to contribute to the lower rate of overweight in France.[23] Evidence from 1900, when empirical analyses and quantification were being institutionalized, expands the temporal horizon of current research and offers figures for comparison across time as well as space.

This article begins with a description of the demand for lunch away from home and the supply it met. The inquiry then examines whether the anthropological notion of the "proper meal" is an appropriate tool to portray French working-class practices circa 1900. This is followed by recovering the conventional portion size to reconstruct the canonical meal's calorie content and by comparing it to real consumption in Parisian working-class restaurants. Finally, I will argue that the infatuation with the so-called French model of meals creates a blind spot among present-day commentators on the street-food and carry-away sector, whose existence has allowed consumers to distance themselves from social norms, yesterday and today.

20 Martin Bruegel, "Un distant miroir: La campagne pour 'l'alimentation rationnelle' et la fabrication du consommateur au tournant du XXe siècle," *Actes de la recherche en sciences sociales*, no. 199 (2013): 28–45.

21 Faustine Régnier, Anne Lhuissier, and Séverine Gojard, *Sociologie de l'alimentation* (Paris, 2006), 3–4, 38–40.

22 Jenny H. Lediwike, Julia A. Ello-Martin, and Barbara J. Rolls, "Portion Sizes and the Obesity Epidemic," *Journal of Nutrition* 135, no. 4 (2005): 905–9; David M. Cutler, Edward L. Glaeser, and Jesse M. Shapiro, "Why Have Americans Become More Obese?," *Journal of Economic Perspectives* 17, no. 3 (2003): 93–118; "Fast Food Britain: More Than Half Our Meals Out Are Burgers or Kebabs," *MailOnLine*, Jan. 17, 2012.

23 Paul Rozin et al., "The Ecology of Eating: Smaller Portion Sizes in France Than in the United States Help Explain the French Paradox," *Psychological Science* 14, no. 5 (2003): 450–54.

The Working-Class Demand for
Lunch Away from Home

Three factors sustained the demand for lunch away from home: geography, women's employment, and industrial time. The difference in rental charges pushed working families to the periphery and into the suburbs of Paris, whereas shops remained in its center.[24] There was no way around the fact that "the great distance between work and home makes it impossible to have lunch with the family."[25] Portraits of artisans or lower-level employees—cabinetmakers, postmen, carpenters, ragmen, and dressmakers—mention the half-hour or hour walk to work (see fig. 1).[26] In 1900 the *Richmond (VA) Times* saw something picturesque in the crowds of dressmakers and milliners walking in the day's early hours from Montmartre, Batignolles, Clichy, and Belleville into the heart of the city,[27] while the reform-minded editor of *Demain* considered it an argument in favor of efficient and affordable public transportation, a long-running—and ongoing—political fight.[28]

Proximity was a relative term, Alain Faure has shown, and even the very specific and circumscribed recruitment patterns in Parisian industries (the abattoirs at La Villette; the gasworks, sugar refineries, and metal fabricators in the nineteenth arrondissement; and the *bijouteries* and the Imprimerie Nationale in the third arrondissement) often meant that workers walked a great deal.[29] The architects' professional association traced eating out as a self-evident routine among carpenters to budgets dating from the July monarchy,[30] and an 1851 parliamentary inquiry into the meat trade accorded so much importance to commercial meals that three restaurant owners were called to describe

---

24 Louis Duval-Arnoud, "L'influence du développement des moyens de transport sur le taux des loyers," *La réforme sociale*, 7th ser., no. 8 (1914): 362.

25 Armand Beauvy, "Le problème de l'alimentation," *La revue de Paris*, Nov.–Dec. 1906, 299.

26 Pierre Du Maroussem, "Charpentier indépendant de Paris," *Les ouvriers des deux mondes*, 2nd ser., vol. 3 (Paris, 1892), 334; Armand Imbert, "Une observation économique de vie ouvrière," *Revue de la Société scientifique d'hygiène alimentaire 3*, no. 2 (1906): 45 (henceforth *Revue SSHA*); Du Maroussem, "Ebeniste parisien de Haut-Luxe," *Les ouvriers des deux mondes*, 2nd ser., vol. 4 (Paris, 1895), 65; Ed. Demolins and B. Pocquet, "Précis d'une monographie ayant pour objet un chiffonnier instable," *Les ouvriers des deux mondes*, 1st ser., vol. 5 (1885): 193; Charles Benoist, *Les ouvrières de l'aiguille: Notes pour l'étude de la question sociale* (Paris, 1895), 193–94, 206, 211–13.

27 "The Paris Work Girl," *Richmond (VA) Times*, July 8, 1900, 14; the description is reminiscent of the opening scene in Emile Zola, *L'assommoir* (Paris, 1876), and Jules Adler's painting *Matin de Paris: Le faubourg* (ca. 1900).

28 Edouard Toulouse, "Pour préparer demain: Savoir est le moyen, créer est le but," *Demain—efforts de pensée et de vie meilleure 2*, no. 16 (1912): 295–97; "La ligue Paris-Banlieue: Les trains de nuit—les trains ouvriers," *Le rappel*, Aug. 17, 1896, 1–2.

29 Alain Faure, "'Nous travaillons 10 heures par jour, plus le chemin': Les déplacements de travail chez les ouvriers parisiens (1880–1914)," in *Villes ouvrières, 1900–1914*, ed. Susanna Magri and Christian Topalov (Paris, 1989), 93–107.

30 "Les variations des salaires dans l'industrie du bâtiment à Paris depuis 1830," *La réforme sociale*, 3rd ser., no. 2 (1891): 438–39, 442.

Figure 1 Somewhat idealized representation of breakfast taken on the way to work. Note that the vendor supplies the bowls. "Le déjeuner matinal en plein vent," *Le petit journal, supplément illustré*, Feb. 3, 1907

how their establishments served between 150 and 200 lunches per day to a working-class clientele. They probably represented the àverage eating place in central Paris, although they were overshadowed by "La Californie," located on the Chaussée du Maine, where three thousand people from "the poorest working class" took meals served nonstop from eight in the morning to eleven at night.[31] In the early 1880s phi-

---

[31] Archives Nationales (hereafter AN), C//1014, Commission d'Enquête Relative à la Production et à la Consommation de la Viande, Apr. 12 and 24, 1851.

lanthropists and humanitarian activists believed that "the worker who lunches with his family is a veritable exception in Paris; the distances are set against it, and often the wife works, too, so she lacks the time, the desire, and even the capacity to manage the household."[32] The city's demographic and industrial growth and the spread of its working population into the suburbs had made eating out one of its salient features.[33] This was a reason that, for example, unions argued in favor of cooperative restaurants for workers in central Paris.[34]

Women's gainful employment was the second determinant of eating away from home. It, too, had a long history, and it gained in significance as job opportunities were added. The number of seamstresses stood at about ninety thousand in the mid-1890s, and Charles Benoist, who cites this figure, also lists a selection of thirty-five industrial occupations from food production (sugar refining, canning, chocolate) to pharmaceuticals and leather goods (bags as well as harnesses) that hired women.[35] As one observer noted, there were "multiple industries where women [could] apply their skills."[36] This meant that ever more women were eating out. For families, this had a doubling effect: expenses for food increased more when both husband and wife ate out. "In most working households in Paris," the *Journal du dimanche* reported in 1893, "the husband works, and so does the wife; they leave home at dawn, each one in a different direction, to go to the shop, the factory or the building site; one goes to Batignolles, the other to Grenelle, Montrouge or Ménilmontant, and they see each other again only in the evening." At noon, both had lunch away from home.[37]

Finally, the need for the close coordination of production tasks even trumped proximity. Industrial time tends to speed up the rhythm of work and induces the need for the synchronization of diverse tasks. Meal breaks and working cadences conflict, and indeed the time allotted to the lunch break became an issue between owners and workers.[38] Strikes occurred to allow women to leave work early so as to prepare lunch for the family or to have owners install stoves to heat up food that workers had brought to the plant.[39] In some cases, industrial

---

32 Antonin Rondelet, "Le régime alimentaire de l'ouvrier à Paris," *La réforme sociale*, 2nd ser., no. 4 (1882): 396.

33 Haine arrives at the same conclusion (*World*, 93–95).

34 "Restaurant coopératif," *La voix du peuple*, July 28–Aug. 4, 1901, 3.

35 Benoist, *Les ouvrières*, 234, 229–30.

36 Nicolas Fanjung, "Précis d'une monographie du serrurier poseur de persiennes en fer de Paris," *Les ouvriers des deux mondes*, 2nd ser., vol. 5 (Paris, 1899), 363.

37 "Ce que mangent les pauvres gens," *Journal du dimanche*, Apr. 5, 1893, 2.

38 Michelle Perrot, *Les ouvriers en grève: France, 1871–1890*, vol. 1 (Paris, 1974), 291–92.

39 Martin Bruegel, "Le repas à l'usine: Industrialisation, nutrition et alimentation populaire," *Revue d'histoire moderne et contemporaine* 51, no. 3 (2004): 190–91.

working conditions led companies to offer meals on-site. The railway enterprise Compagnie d'Orléans sponsored a canteen for its workers where, already by the 1880s, eight hundred meals were served daily,[40] and the chocolate factory Menier in Noisiel opened a dining hall to allow "homemakers whose job keeps them at the factory and who lack the necessary time to prepare suitable food, to have nevertheless access to hot, hygienic and affordable dishes."[41] The restaurant reserved for the unmarried women in the female workforce at the Maison de la Bonne Presse served "an excellent lunch (that includes some bread for the afternoon snack)" to its 220 typographic composers and other personnel involved in the usually hurried newspaper production process.[42]

Distance to work, women's employment, and industrial time determined working people's demand for food away from home but did not determine the form that eating out really took. Monographs on blue-collar Parisians by the Le Play school of sociology and published in *Les ouvriers des deux mondes* (1857–1928) show that in eleven of seventeen households at least one member ate out during the workday. This is a small sample, to be sure, but one that shows the variety of arrangements for having lunch away from home: some did it daily, some once a week; some were regular customers of commercial establishments, and some carried their billycan or a basket to work where they may, or may not, have heated its contents (oftentimes the leftovers from the previous evening). Sometimes a family member brought a packed lunch to the eater. What emerges clearly, however, is the insignificance of wages as determinants of lunch away from home: just as today, revenues bear no relation to eating out (the coefficient of correlation is close to zero).[43]

Demand is thus hard to quantify. The newspaper *La croix* speculated in 1912 that seamstresses alone accounted for one hundred thousand midday restaurant meals per day.[44] There is some circumstantial evidence concerning the proportion of working families relying on commercial foods at lunch. Among 296 workers' households at the Vincennes cartridge factory (La Cartoucherie) investigated in June 1910, 189 (or 64 percent) returned home for lunch, 59 (about 20 percent) brought their *gamelle* to the refectory, and 43 (about 15 percent) relied

40 Joseph Barberet, *Le travail en France: Monographies professionnelles*, vol. 7 (Paris, 1890), 290; Marcel Labbé, "Les oeuvres d'alimentation," *Journal des débats*, July 26, 1908, 3.

41 Ch. Quillard, "Visite aux établissements Menier, à Noisiel, le jeudi 26 octobre 1906," *Revue SSHA* 3, no. 3 (1906): xlvi. Nine hundred of Menier's twenty-two hundred workers were women: "La cité ouvrière de Noisiel," *La revue philanthropique*, May–Oct. 1911, 83–87.

42 "Nos ouvriers," *La croix*, Sept. 26, 1899, 1.

43 Revenues, however, do secondarily influence the price of the menu: France Caillavet and Véronique Nichèle, "L'activité féminine détermine la consommation de repas hors domicile," *INRA—Sciences sociales* 1, no. 2 (2002): 2.

44 "Les restaurants féminins à Paris," *La croix*, Sept. 27, 1912, 1.

on commercial meals in restaurants or the canteen.[45] In 1901 a feather-making entrepreneur whose business employed 250 women affirmed that fewer than 50 (or 20 percent of his workforce) could afford to eat in restaurants, 150 (or 60 percent) brought their meals in baskets, and the remaining fifth lived in the neighborhood and thus could eat at home.[46] A secondary analysis of a 1906 survey into savings behavior among the poor in the eastern, working-class arrondissements carried out by the Ligue contre la Misère shows that 301 households out of 725 (or 42 percent) spent money on meals away from home.[47] A 1908 inquiry of New York working-class families arrived, coincidentally, at the same percentage of households incurring expenses for take-away or eat-out food.[48] For Paris, no such precision is possible. But these data mean that one-fifth and possibly two-fifths of workers' families had a member who regularly paid for lunch in a commercial or cooperative establishment. With almost a million workers in the city, this made for a lot of lunches.

The Supply of Working-Class Lunches Away from Home

Given the heavy demand, commercial restaurants were ubiquitous in Paris. "Restaurants abound in all popular neighborhoods, and even on the boulevards," the *Almanach illustré* noted in 1908.[49] By 1900 the city counted fifteen hundred restaurants, over two thousand cafés and *brasseries*, and at least nine thousand *marchands de vin*.[50] The literary journalist Emile Goudeau (1849–1906) captured the ambiance—and the possibility to get a bite to eat throughout the day—when he provided the rich nomenclature required to sketch the portrait of these "temples of consumption that we call restaurants, breweries, wine joints, cafés, dégustations, distilleries, greasy spoons, holes-in-the-wall, debits: everything for the service of the belly. There are streets in Paris where ninety out of a hundred businesses relate to food and drink."[51] The profusion of eating places made for a very competitive scene, and it

[45] Albert Dejouany, "L'alimentation du personnel civil de la Cartoucherie militaire de Vincennes," *Bulletin de la Société scientifique d'hygiène alimentaire* 4, no. 3 (1914): 115–16.

[46] AN, F/22/479, Travail et Sécurité Sociale, Comité Consultatif des Arts et Manufactures, Rapport de M. Roy, "Fabriques de plumes pour parures [entreprise Jules Vialle]," June 4, 1902.

[47] "Une nouvelle preuve de la nécessité de l'enseignement ménager," *Bulletin de l'union familiale*, no. 32 (1906): 3; Dr. Lemière, "L'enseignement ménager," *Quand même! Bulletin mensuel d'études sociales et d'action catholique*, Dec. 25, 1907, 376–77.

[48] Kathleen Leonard Turner, "Buying, Not Cooking: Ready-to-Eat Food in American Working-Class Neighborhoods, 1880–1930," *Food, Culture and Society* 9, no. 1 (2006): 33.

[49] "A quel prix voulez-vous déjeuner?," in *L'almanach illustré du petit Parisien* (Paris, 1908), 41.

[50] Pierre Andrieu, *Histoire du restaurant en France* (Paris, 1950), 103; for a longer-term view of the number of restaurants, see Rich, *Bourgeois Consumption*, 146.

[51] Emile Goudeau, *Paris qui consomme* (Paris, 1893), v.

was conventional wisdom that many—one official put the share at two-thirds—of the smaller eating places were up for sale because profits were small and survival precarious.[52]

The multiplicity of food and catering businesses should not hide the reality of a segmented market. Naturally, price limited access to restaurants, and a 1908 report distinguished between cheap dives and palaces whose clienteles never sat next to each other.[53] Such segregation was nothing new, of course. The Paris World Fairs of 1889 and 1900 confirmed and solidified a tripartite division. Concessions concerned "luxurious restaurants, comparable to the best establishments in Paris," middlebrow "fixed-price restaurants of a more modest character," and popular restaurants whose menus were affordable, respectable, but (during exhibitions at least) by no means cheap.[54] As a rule of thumb, this three-tiered economic breakdown helped navigate the large number of eating places in Paris. Tourist guides usually offered it as a mental map to the alimentary topography of a city where eating "is considered a fine art."[55] Yet a careful eye could distinguish how even working-class customers sorted themselves when eating away from home. Retail employees patronized the prix fixe restaurants, their less-esteemed colleagues from wholesale businesses would sit apart in a particular room set aside at the *marchand de vin-restaurateur,* while artisans and workers patronized the *gargotes* and other bistros, some of which served only beverages to accompany the meals brought in.[56]

In addition to purchasing power, gender influenced the restaurant business. Of course, women and men rubbed elbows in many places where the working class went for lunch. But contemporary observers tended to assign a rather male clientele to the so-called *mastroquets* (Parisian slang for *marchands de vins* who also served food).[57] In contrast, the newcomer among commercial eating places, the *crèmerie*—"a modern establishment . . . somewhere between the restaurant and the café" according to Pierre Larousse's *Grand Dictionnaire*—catered

---

52 About one-quarter of the 1,574 bankruptcies in 1896 concerned food and beverage retailers. See Archives de la Préfecture de Police, BA 505, Situation industrielle 1896–97.

53 "A quel prix voulez-vous déjeuner?," 39–44.

54 France, Ministère du commerce, de l'industrie et des colonies, *Exposition universelle internationale de 1889 à Paris: Rapport général,* vol. 3 (Paris, 1889), 282–83; France, Ministère du commerce, de l'industrie, des postes et télégraphes, *Exposition universelle internationale à Paris: Rapport général administratif et technique,* vol. 7 (Paris, 1903), 191, 196.

55 "I shall introduce my readers to three classes of restaurants," begins an article titled "Reminiscences of Paris by an Anglo-Frenchman: Restaurants and Cafés," *South Australian Register* (Adelaide), July 3, 1879, 5; "Paris Restaurants," *Evening Star* (Washington, DC), Jan. 20, 1900, 20; "Où prendre ses repas?," *1900: Paris Exposition, guide pratique du visiteur de Paris et de l'Exposition* (Paris, 1900), 14–21.

56 Georges Montorgueil, *Les minutes parisiennes: Midi; Le déjeuner des petites ouvrières* (Paris, 1899), 22–27.

57 "Ce que mangent les pauvres gens," 2; "Devant le Zinc," *La lanterne,* Dec. 3, 1907, 3.

mostly to women.[58] Its rise in the fierce world of eateries had profited, says Larousse, from the extension of its menu. It had started out with simple cups of coffee with cream (or milk), added scrambled and fried eggs, and from there expanded into grilled meat. Their menu boards did not carry strong liquor, and even wine did not appear in every one, a major distinction with respect to the *mastroquet*.[59]

The way gender shaped the perception of consumer habits appears in efforts to reform them. Temperance restaurants clearly targeted men.[60] Women posed a different problem. For most philanthropists, the wife as homemaker and the family meal were the norm, while working outside the home should have remained the exception. "The wife's absence from the home is a deplorable fact," noted *Le Figaro* in 1906.[61] However, the demand for women's labor was pressing in Paris, and so was the need for supplementary income in many families. To send women back into their homes would have been a lost cause to reformers, who consequently aimed at improving conditions surrounding work. Lunch and freedom from supervision (and hence the temptation to succumb to vice) went hand in hand, and this was a predicament that mostly Catholic activists—"pious ladies," noted the reporter of the Washington, DC, *Evening Star*[62]—meant to tackle. Their goal was to provide meals and morality. The first two *restaurants féminins* opened in 1893, and although they were not self-supporting at first, their example inspired the subsequent creation of at least three dozen similar establishments by 1912.[63] These few restaurants did not weigh heavily in the production of commercial meals in Paris, and yet, wrote the *Annales politiques et littéraires* in 1908, "it would be impossible to count the number of female teachers, state and bank employees, professors of music and languages; students of the Fine and Decorative Arts at the Sorbonne; saleswomen, cashiers, stenographers, typists and seamstresses who came [to the *restaurant féminin de la Rive gauche*] to have a healthy, comforting meal and get a little bit of encouragement."[64] Unable to

58 "Crèmerie," in *Grand Dictionnaire universel du XIXe siècle*, ed. Pierre Larousse, vol. 5 (Paris, 1869), 486; "Paris consommateur," *La gazette de Lausanne*, Feb. 17, 1868, 1–2; Henri Collière, "L'alimentation de la classe ouvrière," *La réforme alimentaire* 10, no. 9 (1906): 217; Dauzères, "A travers la science," 5.

59 "Crèmerie," 486.

60 "Un restaurant de tempérance," *Journal des débats*, Aug. 13, 1899, 1.

61 "L'aide sociale—le réchaud," *Le Figaro littéraire*, June 16, 1906, 4.

62 Sterling Heilig, "Worship of Food: The French Can Live on What Americans Waste," *Evening Star* (Washington, DC), Jan. 26, 1895, 16.

63 "Chronique," *La semaine des familles*, Jan. 14, 1893, 669–70; "Pour soixante-quinze centimes," *Le Gaulois*, Jan. 15, 1894, 1; "Restaurants de dames seules," *Le Figaro*, May 13, 1894, 2; "Courrier de la semaine," *Le petit Parisien*, supplément littéraire, Oct. 7, 1894, 322; "Restaurants—Homes pour dames et jeunes filles," *La femme* (1911–12). (This information appears on the second-to-last, unnumbered page of every installment of *La femme* at that time.)

64 Yvonne Sarcey, "Restaurant féminin," *Les annales politiques et littéraires*, no. 1311 (1908): 138.

transform the labor market and to reinstate the home as women's natural sphere of activity, the promoters of ladies' restaurants endeavored to alleviate the real cost of, and remove putative moral perils inherent in, commercial midday meals taken amid a mixed public.

The variety of eating places and the representation of their clientele notwithstanding, menus espoused, with the one exception of the *crèmeries*, the same form. The sequence of propositions was couched in the categories of appetizer, meat dish with vegetables, and dessert. Bread and wine were almost incontrovertible accompaniments to the meal.[65] This standard structure had come into its own only recently, at least in eating places patronized by the working class.

As late as the 1860s, artisans in the building trades lunched around eleven a.m. on "the ordinaire," a piece of beef in a somewhat vegetable-augmented bouillon, part of which they ate cold as a sandwich at two p.m. ("le coup de deux heures").[66] The down-and-out heroine of *La porteuse de pain*, an enormous melodramatic success in print and onstage in the 1880s (and in film and even on television later), spent her piteous small change on a last lunch consisting of an "ordinaire" (from then on, things looked up for her).[67] Gastronomer Eugène-Victor Briffaut thought it still the defining aspect of a Parisian lunch in the July monarchy, and, according to the *Petit Journal* of 1869, it constituted "the most indispensable element of public [i.e., popular restaurant] food."[68] It was only in the second half of the nineteenth century that separately prepared vegetables garnished the meat of the "ordinaire" and helped reduce the role of the bouillon.[69] The American traveler Lee Meriwether, unaccustomed to French ways in the mid-1880s, came to know this new configuration of lunch with the help of the working-class clients in a popular *bouillon*. His meal duly consisted of three parts: soup, a dish of meat accompanied by potatoes, and plums for dessert.[70] Meriwether had gone native, so to speak, and by doing so he discovered what it meant to have a "proper meal" in Paris around 1900.

65 "Ce que mangent les pauvres gens," 2; "A quel prix voulez-vous déjeuner?," 41–43.

66 "Les variations des salaires," 442.

67 The pivotal scene is highlighted in "Premières représentations," *Le Figaro*, Jan. 12, 1889, 2; for a later edition of the novel first serialized in *Le petit journal*, see Xavier de Montépin, *La porteuse de pain* (Paris, 1903–5), 374–75.

68 Eugène-Victor Briffaut, *Paris à table* (Paris, 1846), 63; "De l'alimentation," *Le petit journal*, May 29, 1869, 3.

69 See the account by a working-class representative in Paris: Conseil Municipal, *Bulletin officiel*, Dec. 9, 1885, 694.

70 Lee Meriwether, *A Tramp Trip; or, How to See Europe on Fifty Cents a Day* (New York, 1887), 252.

Quantitative Criteria: The "Strictly Necessary" and the "Proper Meal"

Anthropologists use the notion of the "proper meal" to pinpoint the rules that determine the association of dishes, their sequencing, and so on.[71] This definition derives from private, sit-down meals in families and highlights the sexual division of labor. Meriwether's encounter with French food culture suggests its parallel (and maybe prior) public existence. But the structural makeup of a meal does not exhaust its meaning, and the commercial context may yet accentuate a quantitative expectation. After all, a meal taken during the workday ought to satiate a customer's hunger. Historians have paid attention to provisioning in collective households (hospitals, prisons, armies, and navies) to gauge empirical definitions of what amount of food it takes to survive, work, and fight.[72] Budgets have helped re-create private consumption patterns in single households. Meals away from home and their contribution to an individual's metabolism have, however, so far eluded historical analysis.[73] French sources allow them to receive a closer look, especially as there was a consensus on the meaning of the complete lunch. When the professor of medicine Louis Landouzy and his collaborators inquired into popular food habits in 1905, they noted that "they looked, of course, at the usual food that conforms to the taste of the greatest number, such as that found at the *marchand de vins-restaurateur* where most of the workers usually take at least one of their daily meals."[74] The physiologist Jean Laumonier declared that the success of popular restaurants depended on portions "calculated to respond to the expectations of adult workers."[75] It is to the retrieval of their quantitative aspect that we turn now.

A condition for the assessment of meals' caloric content around 1900 is the retrieval of portion size. The rise of nutritional science

---

[71] Mary Douglas, "Deciphering a Meal," *Daedalus* 101, no. 1 (1972): 61–81.

[72] For a recent example that compares official ration scales and actual incapacity to live up to them, see Rachel Duffett, *The Stomach for Fighting: Food and the Soldiers of the Great War* (Manchester, 2012); and Robert Mandrou, "Le ravitaillement d'une ville dans la Ville: La ration alimentaire de restauration à l'Assistance publique de Paris (1820–1870)," *Jahrbücher für Nationalökonomie und Statistik* 179, no. 3 (1966): 189–99.

[73] Ulrike Thoms, who lists the sizes of portions served in the canteen at the Krupp Iron Works in Essen, Germany, between 1901 and 1910 is silent on the method of calculation but gives the impression that she simply divided provisioned quantities by the number of meals, without paying attention to the frequency with which dishes were served. See Thoms, "Industrial Canteens in Germany, 1850–1950," in *Eating Out in Europe*, ed. Marc Jacobs and Peter Scholliers (Oxford, 2003), 362.

[74] Louis Landouzy, Henri Labbé, and Marcel Labbé, *Enquête sur l'alimentation d'une centaine d'ouvriers et d'employés parisiens. Ce qu'elle est: irraisonnée, insuffisante, insalubre, dispendieuse; ce qu'elle pourrait être: rationnelle, suffisante, salubre, économique* (Paris, 1905), 16.

[75] Jean Laumonier, "Bouillons ouvriers et restaurants populaires," *Bulletin général de thérapeutique*, no. 141 (1901): 287, 291.

in the nineteenth century promoted the identification of foodstuffs by calorie. The diligent agricultural engineer J. Tribot, a member of the Brussels-based Institut Solvay who worked at the Laboratoire de Physiologie des Sensations at the Sorbonne, compiled a list of portion weights and their corresponding energy content between 1905 and 1907 when he carried out an analysis of more than 130 meals in Parisian working-class restaurants. The enumeration comprised nine appetizers, twenty-four entrées (meat and eggs, but no fish), thirteen side dishes (legumes, pasta, vegetables), and ten desserts (six kinds of cheese, a cake, three kinds of fruit).[76] These empirical numbers correspond quite closely to the estimated helpings served in Duval's restaurants during the World Fair in 1889, when it supplied more than 2.4 million meals (or around forty-three thousand per day).[77] A comparison with the recommendations provided by a pre–World War I self-help manual to "compose salutary meals"[78] concurs with Tribot's figures. Menus suggested by one of the first domestic science handbooks to evaluate servings in calories, whose aim was to provide information on adequate meals at the least expense, no doubt diverged from the firsthand evidence, which merely shows that campaigns to educate consumers had a long way to go against habit.[79] Overall, however, these data suggest the pervasiveness of a cultural definition of portion size. Laumonier brought the point home when summing up his practical research into menus at Parisian working-class restaurants: "In the *bouillons* of Paris . . . the portion of meat weighs, according to its nature, between 100 and 150 grams, vegetables [and legumes] between 250 and 300 grams. But note that the French worker, and surely the Parisian worker, is not satisfied with a single plate; he often adds either a bowl of soup, a piece of cheese or some other dessert." Once Laumonier factored in 250 to 300 grams of bread, the weight of the standard lunch—soup, meat and vegetables, cheese, bread, and dessert—climbed to at least 800 and often 900 grams.[80] It is this quantitative convention that authorizes the use of menu compositions to calculate a meal's energy value.

The historical reconstruction of the "proper meal" in 1900 can now proceed with indications drawn from restaurant menus. Yet public

[76] J. Tribot, "La composition chimique et la valeur énergétique des aliments servis dans les bouillons populaires à Paris," *Revue SSHA* 2, no. 4 (1905): 462–65; Tribot, "Sur la valeur énergétique des repas servis dans les crémeries, les bouillons populaires et les restaurants à prix fixe," *Revue SSHA* 3, no. 2 (1906): 66–68.

[77] "Courrier de l'Exposition," *L'univers illustré*, Nov. 30, 1889, 762; supplies divided by number of served meals.

[78] *Voulez-vous réussir? Santé + succès = bonheur* (Paris, n.d.), 2–3.

[79] René Leblanc, *Notions scientifiques d'enseignement ménager* (Paris, 1913), 162–67.

[80] Laumonier, "Bouillons ouvriers," 294.

discussion in France on the standard of living (especially when applied to the weak, the elderly, and working families) centered on the notion of the *strict nécessaire*, that is, the biological and social minimum it took to survive. In an 1897 article titled "L'argent des pauvres," *Le matin* wondered whether "any Parisian lacked the bare necessities."[81] The question inevitably involved food consumption, which took up 60 percent of the typical working-class family's budget and was by far the most important item.[82] The debate revolved around managing the resources of modest households, "to join the two ends, to keep out of difficulties [*se tirer d'affaires*] as the saying goes, without cutting into the strictly necessary, especially with respect to food."[83] A social investigator on the conditions of female workers in Paris considered that many among them had "reduced their needs to the *strict nécessaire*."[84]

Attention to collective representations can supplement the anthropological approach to commensality with its single reference point of the proper cultural standard. French society appreciated the full-blown incarnation of the meal but also envisioned a lower bound defined by the benchmark of provisioning at the "strictly necessary" level. While physiologists, too, searched for the discrete quantities of energy provisioning to maintain the basal metabolism or to fuel hard work, the "strictly necessary" and the "proper meal" constituted meaningful—and practical—categories of everyday life and, as such, helped organize such an ordinary habit as eating lunch.

Prolonged hardship and dire straits uncover the value of the strictly necessary amount of calories at lunch to get through the day. In 1899 a philanthropic refectory in the wealthy sixteenth arrondissement provided workers with half a pound of bread, a ragout, and a quarter liter of wine, which amounted to somewhere between 900 and 950 kcal.[85] When *Le matin* asked "at what price it was possible to eat" in Paris, the least expensive (*la façon la plus économique*) provided 900 kcal.[86] Landouzy's menu plan for retired working men delivered between 900 and 950 kcal at the day's most important meal.[87] But the medical opinion of Albert Dejouany considered a midday meal of less than 1,000 kcal

81 "L'argent des pauvres," *Le matin*, Sept. 10, 1897, 1. See also "Les invalides," *La croix*, May 3, 1888, 3; "Mouvement social: Les gardes-cantonnier des stations de voitures," *Le rappel*, Feb. 27, 1893, 2; "Assistance familiale: Les vieillards," *Le rappel*, Apr. 26, 1903, 1; "Les demi-infirmes," *Le matin*, Oct. 9, 1905, 1.

82 Lenard Berlanstein, *The Working People of Paris, 1871–1914* (Baltimore, MD, 1984), 46–48.

83 "Budgets de famille," *Le petit Parisien*, June 17, 1905, 1; "Budgets ouvriers," *Le Figaro*, supplément littéraire, Jan. 26, 1907, 3–4.

84 Mme. Froment, *Ouvrières parisiennes* (Lille, 1903), 3.

85 "L'assistance par le travail," *Le petit Parisien*, June 12, 1899, 1.

86 "Pour quel prix peut-on se nourrir?," *Le matin*, Feb. 12, 1906, 2.

87 Louis Landouzy, *La loi de 1905 sur l'assistance obligatoire aux septuagénaires et l'alimentation rationnelle du vieillard assisté* (Paris, 1907), 10–11; see also "Un menu d'ouvrier," *L'humanité*, Jan. 3, 1907, 2; "Cantines populaires," *Journal des débats politiques et littéraires*, Jan. 5, 1902, 3.

"quantitatively and qualitatively insufficient for a worker of average weight and constitution."[88] For women, the smallest complete lunch contained bread, cheese, and vegetables, whose energy value was 740 kcal,[89] and when Augusta Moll-Weiss assessed available repasts for women workers, she considered the soup kitchen's portion of split peas and lard with bread at 753 kcal a decent, if minimal, meal.[90]

Evidence culled from eyewitness accounts provides a first step toward determining the "proper meal." In the 1880s and 1890s the seamstress and future union organizer Jeanne Bouvier (1865–1964) typically lunched on the "ordinaire," plus bread, cheese, and wine. This meal, whose price remained below the expense incurred "by the best paid working women" (who probably added an hors d'oeuvre), contained 1,200 kcal. Bouvier's choice was driven by pride, as she did not want to lose face in front of her colleagues. And self-respect was costly at 1.20 francs per lunch (a seamstress's daily wages amounted to about 2.50 francs). The outlay left practically no room for indulgence at breakfast and dinner. Bouvier notes that she saved part of the beef from lunch for the evening, when she ate it with half a pound of bread bought at ten centimes.[91] Her "proper" lunch amounted thus to about 1,000 kcal.

Men's proper lunch included soup, bread, a meat dish, vegetables, and wine.[92] Its caloric value rose to 1,300 kcal. The chronicle by the journalist Henry Leyret (1864–1944), who led an early experiment in participant observation by running a "troquet" in Belleville, breathes life into the anthropological abstraction: "The faubourien, in a pronounced natural concern for his health, takes care of himself, seeks a good cuisine, eating if he can meat at each meal; the common menu goes something like this: at eleven o'clock or noon, a soup, beef or the meat dish of the day, a vegetable, a piece of cheese, a pint of wine, and a small coffee—all for thirty sous [1 franc 50]; in the evening, half of this has to suffice."[93] While Leyret's computation of the meal's price seems high (average daily wages for artisans amounted to five or six francs), its composition corresponded to the widely shared convention. When discussing why he had authorized the workers' canteen on the building site of the Exposition in 1900, Henry Boucher, minister of commerce, industry, post, and telegraphs, declared that "a normal meal, composed of an ordinaire, a portion of vegetables, a piece of cheese,

88 Dejouany, "L'alimentation," 118.

89 Suzanne Bidgrain, "Le travail à domicile et le 'sweating system,'" *Le christianisme social* 23, no. 5 (1910): 274–75.

90 Augusta Moll-Weiss, "Les restaurants populaires," *La revue*, Feb. 1, 1908, 286.

91 Jeanne Bouvier, *Mes mémoires ou 59 ans d'activité industrielle, sociale et intellectuelle d'une ouvrière, 1876–1935*, 2nd ed. (Paris, 1983), 82.

92 "Pour quel prix peut-on se nourrir?," 2.

93 Henry Leyret, *En plein faubourg (moeurs ouvrières)* (Paris, 1895), 82–83.

and the traditional cup of coffee, with half a liter of wine" at 1 franc 60 or 1 franc 70 was beyond the reach of construction workers. An assemblyman zeroed in on 0.85 to 1.05 francs that workers could and would pay for lunch,[94] and that was congruent with the sum of 0.80 to 1.00 franc the Cooks' Union of Paris provided for its unemployed members as a restaurant ticket for lunch in 1912.[95]

The fact of the collective representation of a "proper meal" is not in doubt. The depictions of what modest Parisians could obtain as lunch in public eateries conveyed a common understanding of its qualitative profile and quantitative makeup, which differed for men and women. Women's menus offered 850–1,050 kcal and ranged from sixty to ninety-five centimes. Men's menus offered 1,250 to 1,600 kcal and ranged from sixty centimes to a franc and a half. For both men and women, the cost of a meal did not correlate directly to the amount of food it contained.[96] So much for the possibilities, but what about the plates of real consumers?

A Full Plate?

Eating out was an item on the agenda of the SSHA. Its journal published the results of Tribot's quantitative investigations into workers' lunch at three kinds of establishments: *crèmeries, restaurants à prix fixe,* and *bouillons.* At the *crèmeries* in the center of Paris, he analyzed ninety meals, assuring his readers that "all the figures correspond to the real value of meals consumed by a very great number of people, in general small employees and above all the small hands in the fashion and clothing business whose salary barely amounts to twenty francs per week and who it is absolutely necessary to instruct on the physiological value of their diet."[97] He examined forty meals taken by artisans at the *restaurants à prix fixe,* at which the client chooses a dish among a small list of possibilities for each course, as the overall price is set in advance. Tribot picked lunches that cost either 1.15 or 1.25 francs.[98] Finally, he

94 *Journal officiel de la République française: Débats parlementaires; Chambre des députés,* séance du 5 févr. 1898, 435–36.

95 Archives Départementales de Seine-Saint-Denis, 46 J 16, Chambre Syndicale Ouvrière des Cuisiniers de Paris, Conseil Syndical, Dec. 5, 1912.

96 Information culled from *La semaine des familles,* Jan. 14. 1893; *Le Gaulois,* Jan. 15, 1894; *Le journal du dimanche,* Apr. 5, 1893; *Le petit Parisien,* Apr. 2, 1894; *Le Figaro,* May 13, 1894; Laumonier, "Bouillons ouvriers," 294; *Gil Blas,* Mar. 9, 1904, and Jan. 5, 1908; Landouzy, Labbé, and Labbé, *Enquête,* 11; *Le Figaro,* supplément littéraire, June 16, 1906; *La lanterne,* July 25, 1908; *Le petit journal,* Oct. 27, 1906; Dejouany, "L'alimentation," 117–18; Joseph Durieu, "L'éducation de la prévoyance par le métier," *Bulletin de la Société internationale de science sociale,* June 1911, 105; *La bataille syndicaliste,* Oct. 23, 1912; Jacques Valdour, *Ouvriers parisiens d'après-guerre: Observations vécues* (Paris, 1921), 12.

97 Tribot, "Sur la valeur énergétique," 57.

98 J. Tribot, "Les repas dans les restaurants à 1 fr 15 et 1 fr 25," *Revue SSHA* 2, no. 2 (1905): 170.

weighed the dishes at the popular *bouillons*, the model of which were the Bouillons Duval, "a Parisian institution," according to the *San Francisco Call*, "and a striking feature of metropolitan life," with over forty restaurants feeding forty thousand people daily in 1896. Duval's trademark was the card on which uniformed waitresses inscribed consumed items, which thus enabled the client to adjust appetite and pocketbook.[99] Tribot targeted lunches between 1.00 and 1.25 francs.

Tribot's studies were well received. Empirical, their originality trumped laboratory experiments that often appeared theoretical and were too remote from the everyday experience of real eaters.[100] Nutritional science had almost come into its own by 1900, but certain tools were still being refined. Atwater coefficients—the calorie content of macronutrients (1 g carbs = 4 kcals, etc.)—required stabilization. Tribot's computations of energy value sometimes overlooked the difference between raw and cooked food, and they may, in general, slightly overestimate the caloric contribution of other foods. It is therefore necessary to verify Tribot's calculations. From a synchronic point of view, they are set against the nutritional nomenclatures elaborated by chemist Jules Alquier at the beginning of the twentieth century.[101] Today's *Répertoire général des aliments* provides a diachronic checkpoint, although it is necessary to keep in mind that both foods and tastes for foods have changed (e.g., the appreciation of fatty meat has declined).[102] Tribot's weighings remain the basis of the estimation of the meals' calories, but recalculation shows that he overestimated their energy content— especially when the servings included pasta and legumes. (Table 1 provides Tribot's figures, as well as estimations based on current conversion coefficients.)

If the question was "to speak about money to the consumer," as Alquier stressed,[103] it was clear that Parisians of modest means received the best value at the *restaurants à prix fixe*, as long as they did not have access to canteens—or did not want to patronize them because, as it was said about the employees of the *grands magasins*, they preferred the "free air of the street" to the confining atmosphere in the refectory.[104] If, at the high caloric end, customers may have carried away part of the

99 Tribot, "Sur la valeur énergétique," 56–69; J. Tribot, "Enquête sur l'alimentation ouvrière (suite)," *Revue SSHA* 4, no. 1 (1907): 17–24; "A Parisian Institution: A Concern That Owns and Controls Fifty Huge Restaurants," *San Francisco Call*, May 17, 1896, 10.

100 Jules Alquier, "Les aliments de l'homme," *Revue générale des sciences pures et appliquées* 18 (1907): 417; "Le Congrès de l'hygiène alimentaire," *Le petit Parisien*, Oct. 25, 1906, 2.

101 Alquier, "Les aliments de l'homme," 356–65, 406–18; see also Marcel Labbé, *Régimes alimentaires* (Paris, 1910), 132–40.

102 See Jean-Claude Favier et al., *Répertoire général des aliments: Table de composition*, 2nd ed. (Paris, 1995), xxi–xxviii, for the development of analytic methods.

103 Alquier, "Les aliments de l'homme," 417.

104 Montorgueil, *Minutes parisiennes*, 31–32.

Table 1 Energy value of commercial lunch in Paris ca. 1900

Place	Tribot (kcal)	Estimate (kcal)[a]					Price (frs)	Price/1,000 kcal (frs)
		Total	Carbs	Proteins	Fats	Wine		
Cantine Menier[b]	2,096	1,764	872	339	445	108	0.65	0.37
Prix fixe 1	2,845	2,318	1,328	330	463	197	1.15–1.25	0.52
Prix fixe 2	2,083	1,865	1,171	296	233	165	1.15–1.25	0.64
27 individual meals[c]	1,685	1,516	623	227	531	135	1.13	0.75
Bouillon 2	1,914	1,343	657	222	329	135	1.05	0.78
Bouillon 1	1,316	1,320	626	197	227	270	1.25	0.95
Crèmerie 2	771	746	244	160	342	no	1.00	1.34
Crèmerie 1	698	669	204	204	261	no	1.00	1.49
Crèmerie 3	557	538	252	160	126	no	1.00	1.86

Sources: "Le restaurant et les réfectoires ouvriers de Noisiel," *Revue SSHA* 1, no. 3 (1904): 207–15; Tribot, "Les repas dans les restaurants," 168–75 (see n. 98); J. Tribot, "Sur la valeur physiologique des aliments des bouillons de Paris," *Revue SSHA* 2, no. 2 (1905): 176–79; Tribot, "La composition chimique" (see n. 76); Tribot, "Sur la valeur énergétique," 56–69 (see n. 76); Tribot, "Enquête sur l'alimentation ouvrière (suite)" (see n. 99); Jules Alquier, "Les aliments de l'homme," *Revue SSHA* 3, no. 1 (1906): 1–15 with tables on unnumbered pages; Favier et al., *Répertoire général des aliments* (see n. 102).

[a]My computation with current Atwater coefficients and correcting for Tribot's oversights.

[b]Value provided in "Le restaurant."

[c]This is Tribot's composite control group; researched in 1906, the results were published in 1907, basic data augmented by 200 grams of bread and 0.25 liter of wine (9 percent alcohol), as suggested by observations reported in Labbé, "Le budget alimentaire," 316 (see n. 4).

complimentary pound of bread (or 1,200 kcal) to constitute the basis of the afternoon snack, Tribot's findings based on a sizable data set were not out of line with the conclusion reached by René Martial; his monograph of a hatter's consumption pattern described a common, if more expensive, lunch providing between 1,500 and 1,600 kcal.[105] The second point concerns the rift between the *crèmeries* and the rest of the commercial eating places. Not only were meals in *crèmeries* below the standard of the "strictly necessary" for men and (in two cases) for women, but the cost per calorie was much higher than elsewhere.

This brings us back to the clientele. The purpose of the *crèmeries* was to serve a majority of women, yet their menus were not particularly close to what workers understood as "bien manger." If economic considerations exerted no influence on this choice, what advantages did the female customers find at the *crèmerie*: camaraderie, informality, swift service, a short escape from the atelier? It was a choice that preoccupied ironic commentators such as Georges Montorgueil ("the meals of female workers are often only simulacra"),[106] raised concerns among distant observers (an early description mentioned women's willingness to cheat their stomachs),[107] and infuriated reformers like Augusta Moll-Weiss who considered the insufficient food consumption among working women a moral outrage.[108]

Time may well be an explanatory factor, since it was a scarce resource among the Parisian working class.[109] The myth notwithstanding,[110] all Paris did not take an hour for lunch. Women tended to eat more quickly than men—barely a quarter of an hour in the feather-making business, where the workforce was almost exclusively female,[111] and one and a half hours in the case of cabinetmakers, an exclusively male occupation.[112] This phenomenon was not purely Parisian. An investigation of the Bordeaux working class came to the same conclusion: "Whereas men take all the time to lunch [between 25 and 90 minutes], working women, for diverse reasons, spend hardly a quarter of an hour and at most twenty minutes on their midday meal."[113] *Crèmeries* most obviously

---

[105] René Martial, "L'alimentation des travailleurs," *Revue d'hygiène publique et de police sanitaire* 29 (1907): 518.

[106] Montorgueil, *Minutes parisiennes*, 75–76.

[107] "Paris consommateur," 1.

[108] Augusta Moll-Weiss, "La ligue des acheteurs," *La revue*, Jan. 15, 1907, 217.

[109] "Hygiène," *La revue*, June 1, 1907, 402.

[110] "Paris, a Matrimonial Market for Artists," *Los Angeles Herald Sunday Supplement*, Jan. 21, 1906, 27.

[111] AN, F/22/479, Travail et Sécurité Sociale, Comité Consultatif des Arts et Manufactures, Rapport de G. Roy, "Industrie du montage de plumes pour parures [entreprise Pellissier]," June 4, 1902.

[112] Du Maroussem, "Ebeniste," 65; see also Landouzy, Labbé, and Labbé, *Enquête*, 13.

[113] Meyer Adda, *Alimentation et tuberculose* (Bordeaux, 1908), 35–37.

allowed their clientele to move outside of the French meal canon and to grab a quick bite to eat. They offered an alternative to the French model and so formed a bridge to other modes of eating out during the workday.

Alternatives to the French Model

Alternatives to restaurant eating surely combined economic and social considerations. There are examples of fathers bringing meat to the restaurant to reduce the expense for lunch.[114] The savings were greatest when workers carried all their food in a basket or in a container so as to reheat it in the shop, a customary practice among female garment workers in Paris.[115] At the Crédit Foncier employees used a refectory with a gas stove to warm up their repast.[116] Wives brought lunch pails to the building site or the atelier.[117] Others profited from the supply of carry-away portions. In fact, many a publicity flier for restaurants catering to a working-class clientele—the Restaurant Populaire near the city hall in the first arrondissement, as well as the Grande Pension Ouvrière on the Rue de Flandre near La Villette (fig. 2) and the Grand Restaurant Ouvrier on Rue d'Alésia in the fourteenth arrondissement—carried the line "Cuisine à emporter" or "Vente à emporter."[118]

Age influenced the form these diverse practices took. Younger workers appeared to rely on takeout foods. Some among them simply ate cold cuts and reserved warm food for dinner. Sandwiches composed of a hundred and forty grams of bread and forty grams of charcuterie provided an overall energy value of less than 500 kcal.[119] Combinations varied. Unmarried seamstresses brought cold meats or cheese from home, fetched fried potatoes in the street or bread at the nearest bakery, and finished their lunch hour with a "petit noir [small cup of coffee]."[120] They took advantage of "the public benches in our parks at

114 Du Maroussem, "Ebeniste," 65, 79.
115 AN, F/22/474, folder 4, Dossier d'un projet de modification des art. 5, 6, 8 et 9 du décret du 10 mars 1894, Ouvrières de la Maison Vve A. Ettlinger et fils à Monsieur le Ministre du Commerce et de l'Industrie, Nov. 7, 1901; AN, F/22/474, folder 4, Un groupe d'ouvrières plumassières à Monsieur le Ministre du Commerce et de l'Industrie, Feb. 10, 1902; see also Dejouany, "L'alimentation," 116; "Le déjeuner de l'ouvrière," Le temps, Sept. 29, 1892, 1; "La sécurité et l'hygiène dans les ateliers," L'alimentation ouvrière, May 1, 1904, 2.
116 "Les coulisses d'un emprunt," Le Figaro, Oct. 6, 1879, 1.
117 "Paris qui peine: Ouvriers du bâtiment—les terrassiers," Le Figaro, supplément littéraire, Sept. 5, 1891, 142; A.-F. Badier, "Compositeur-typographe de Paris," Les ouvriers des deux mondes, 1st ser., vol. 4 (1862): 250.
118 Bibliothèque Historique de la Ville de Paris, Collection des Ephémères, Cartes et menus de restaurants.
119 Jean Lahor and Lucien Graux, L'alimentation à bon marché saine et rationnelle (Paris, 1908), 31.
120 "Lunch Hour Is a Riot of Hugs and Kisses for the Pretty Paris Working Girls," Day Book (Chicago), July 10, 1913, 22. Beauvy asserts that coffee was a necessary stimulant for working women ("Le problème," 294).

PLUS DE CUISINE CHEZ SOI!

ALLONS A LA

GRANDE PENSION OUVRIÈRE

28, Rue de Flandre, 28 (La Villette)

« *Qui bien se nourrit, bien se porte.* »
D' DOSMONDUS.

30 Plats de viande garnis et Poisson	0 20
Tous les Rôtis	0 30
Veau Marengo	0 30
Entrecôtes, Filet aux champignons, Blanquette de veau, Lapin sauté.	0 30
Côtelette2, Beefsteaks garnis	0 30
Soupe, Bouillon, Vermicelle.	0 10
Tous les Légumes	0 10
Desserts.	0 10
Primeurs.	0 15
Vin garanti nature sans addition d'eau . . .	0 60
Café svec petit verre.	0 15
Apéritifs 1er choix.	0 15

VENTE A EMPORTER AUX MÊMES PRIX

PAIN 1re qualité au prix du Boulanger

MÊMES MAISONS :
40, Rue Notre-Dame-de-Nazareth, 40
47, Rue des Francs-Bourgeois, 47
122, Rue de Flandre, 122 (Villette)

c.5994. — Imp. DOSMOND, 147, rue du Temple.

Figure 2 Eat in or carry away: menu from a working-class restaurant near La Villette, ca. 1900. Bibliothèque Historique de la Ville de Paris, Collections des Ephémères

noon."[121] in the Tuileries (to the great annoyance of the park adminis-tration, which needed to employ three caretakers to collect the greasy papers in which food had been wrapped)[122] or were "lunching on a small bag of fries leaning against the wall of the post office where the sun shines."[123] The Catholic-leaning social critic Lucien de Vissec described the "hubbub [tohu-bohu]" on the streets, the lines in front of the crèmeries, the bakeries, the charcutiers, and the stalls sporting signs such as "cui-sine à emporter—portions à 30, 40 et 50 centimes," and the bars where working-class girls "gulp down" their pittance with a glass of white wine and a coffee. De Vissec expressed concern for these "poor stomachs."[124]

To American observers, there was a romantic element to the splendid misery of French working girls.[125] But at the opposing Catho-lic and socialist ends of the political spectrum, eating in the open air had less to do with choice and romanticism than with inadequate reve-nues that induced the obligation to consume food "on a bench, in the street, in the Tuileries or the Champs Elysées, or if permitted, in a cor-ner of the shop."[126] If workers ate "unhealthy food in an unhealthy environment,"[127] that called for reform. The Paris municipality sup-ported efforts to provide refectories to women who worked in the arti-sanal district between the Place Vendôme and the Arts et Métiers.[128]

Fast food was a normal feature of Parisian life around 1900 because, as left-leaning reporters Léon Bonneff and Maurice Bonneff put it, lunch was a luxury affordable only to those who could pay ninety centimes or a franc.[129] A whole street-food sector existed—from oyster stalls to fried tripe merchants. One very common dish was soup (the vendor provided the bowl), and the fried potato was a working-class indulgence ("main course and treat," Montorgueil noted).[130] Some hygienists may have frowned upon such foods, but others commended butchers and caterers who supplied soup and meat that workers could carry away during "the short time allotted to lunch."[131] The presence

121 Beauvy, "Le problème," 298; Georges Montorgueil and Auguste Lepère, Paris au hasard (Paris, 1895), 178–79.

122 "Les vandales du Louvre," La presse, Sept. 18, 1903, 3.

123 "Le meeting de la place de la Bourse," Le petit Parisien, Dec. 9, 1883, 2.

124 André Vernières [Lucien de Vissec], Camille Frison: Ouvrière de la couture (Paris, 1908), 38–39.

125 "Lunch Hour," 22–23. "Many of these girls eat their lunch box in the Tuileries Gardens," noted an article on the quixotic and romantic superstitions among the midinettes: see "Signs and Omens of the Paris Midinettes," Sun (New York), Sept. 28, 1913, 10.

126 "Les restaurants féminins," 1.

127 "Pour les midinettes," L'humanité, May 29, 1905, 2.

128 "Les midinettes auront des réfectoires," Journal du dimanche, June 11, 1911, 371.

129 Léon Bonneff and Maurice Bonneff, La classe ouvrière (Paris, 1911), 97.

130 Montorgueil, Minutes parisiennes, 55.

131 Félix Putzeys, Emile Putzeys, and Maurice L. M. Piettre, Approvisionnement communal, vol. 14 of Traité d'hygiène, ed. A. Chantemesse and E. Mosny (Paris, 1908), 345.

of street sellers of prepared foods increasingly posed problems to the police, but an 1894 assessment of the situation noted "the growing fondness of the consumers for sales in the open air."[132] The *Journal du dimanche* described these "friandises parisiennes à bon marché": "In our era of so many hurried, busy and rushed people, it is possible to eat a lunch worthy of Lucullus, while walking, without losing time and cheaply, to boot."[133] This was an opinion that the correspondent of the Washington, DC, *Evening Star* shared: "The black pudding [*boudins*], sausages and fried potatoes are peculiar specialties of the Parisian street. In alleyways and doorways the concern is set up regularly by a motherly old woman glad to make a moderate day's wage for her profit, and 'two sous of fried potatoes' make the most famous of all hunger stoppers."[134]

An economy of food expedience offered provisions to workers and their families who avoided—or could not spare the money or time to patronize—restaurants with menus structured according to the French model. Note that an observer of the cooperative restaurant for female postal employees considered lunch at seventy-five and eighty centimes "maybe a bit high, though the meal is excellent,"[135] whereas the five female workers at a small lace-paper firm argued in favor of bringing in their food baskets because they "could not spend twenty sous [or one franc] for lunch."[136] L'abbé Georges Mény offered the reformers' point of view. He held in 1910 that it was not possible "to pass in front of these cooked-food merchants [*marchands de mets cuits*], often installed in the narrow corridor of a more or less unwelcoming building, without getting sick. It's there that working-class women [who work at home] go to grab their victuals at ninety cents per day."[137] While Mény meant to show the need to improve and possibly outlaw such practices, he also made clear that every aspect seemed measured when it came to carry-away dishes: time, money, quality, and, one supposes, quantity.

Takeout, carry-away, *crèmeries*: all these forms of getting lunch during the workday were very different from the canonical French meal. But the single dish, perhaps a carryover from earlier times when the *ragoût* dominated working-class lunch, was served even in places where

132 Archives de la Préfecture de Police de Paris, DB/257, Embarras de la Voie Publique, "Rapport sur les étalages devant les boutiques," Jan. 31, 1894.

133 "Les friandises parisiennes à bon marché," *Journal du dimanche*, Feb. 9, 1913, 89. Many scattered references document this activity: "La pomme frite se meurt," *Femina*, Dec. 15, 1912, xxviii; "Les restaurants féminins," 1.

134 "The Midinettes of Paris: Smart Little Sewing Girls in Swell Shops Lead a Hard Life," *Evening Star* (Washington, DC), Nov. 28, 1903, pt. 3, 2; see also Elie Frébault, *La vie de Paris: Guide pittoresque et pratique du visiteur* (Paris, 1878), 114–15.

135 "Pour les petites ouvrières," *Le XIXe siècle*, Sept. 11, 1902, 1.

136 AN, F/22/474, folder 4, Dossier d'un projet de modification des art. 5, 6, 8 et 9 du décret du 10 mars 1894, Ouvrières de la Maison Blouin à Monsieur le Ministre, Oct. 4, 1901.

137 Georges Mény, *Le travail à domicile: Ses misères—les remèdes* (Paris, 1910), 94.

the standard menu card was presented. The "restaurant féminin de la rive gauche" had a by then typical *carte* with a tripartite arrangement (hors d'oeuvres, meat and vegetables, dessert), but, so a commentary went, "many clients do not allow themselves to indulge in such follies. They keep to their single dish, accompanied by a *sous* de pain, and spend all in all thirteen sous [sixty-five centimes]."[138] The *Union chrétienne des ateliers de femmes* divided its clientele into three categories: the very poor, who spent fifteen centimes per meal on a portion of bread and cheese; the poor, who spent sixty centimes for a lunch consisting of two vegetable or legume dishes accompanied by bread and wine; and the rich, whose eighty-centime meals included all three courses (i.e., meat too).[139] The customer at the *bouillon populaire*, "recruiting their clientele among workers,"[140] could compose meals to suit their taste and pocketbook. The keystone was *l'addition*, the note on which each consumed dish and its price were added upon its serving, the sum of which was collected at the cash register when exiting the establishment (just as in the American diner). The fact that "you may retire after partaking of only a plate of soup as unnoticed as if you had patronized half the menu" was—according to an American reporter—a distinct advantage of the *bouillons*,[141] one that *Le temps* deemed a convenient means to apportion expenses according to the content of one's purse.[142] The French model functioned as a reference, but it constrained neither the composition of the meal nor its order.

Conclusion: What Is the Reach of a Model?

The nature of the trade, the distance to work, and timing were the three elements that determined the decision of workers to eat a commercial lunch away from home around 1900. Income did not prompt the routine. The phenomenon touched about one-third of the Parisian working class and reveals a rift between the consumption patterns of women and men. While male workers and employees found a supply that answered the cultural definition of the proper meal in its qualitative as well as in the hitherto unexplored quantitative aspects, their female colleagues confronted a situation at odds with the French

138 Sarcey, "Restaurant féminin," 138.

139 Georges Risler, "Restaurants, hôtels et pensions de famille," *La réforme sociale*, 7th ser., no. 3 (1912): 257.

140 "Les restaurants à bon marché," *Le petit Parisien*, Aug. 7, 1905, 5.

141 "'Restaurant Duval': The Great Eating Houses of Paris—How They Are Conducted and Supplied," *Evening Star* (Washington, DC), Aug. 2, 1884, 3.

142 "Fagots," *Le temps*, Apr. 14, 1899, 2; see also *Huit jours à Paris: Septembre 1875* (Orléans, 1875), 108.

model. Incidentally, Giacomo Puccini transformed the young working women's dire condition[143] into *La Bohème*, which premièred in 1896; its protagonist, Mimi—Mimi Pinson being the popular representation of a young, unmarried female wage earner, also known as *midinette* because she hurries through lunch on a summary repast—dies of poverty-induced tuberculosis; the second act stages facets of the street-food business in Paris (set, it must be said, about 1840). There lies a point to ponder: next to the orderly restaurant business that thrived on lunch and dinner and three courses per meal, a more informal ready-to-go food sector made it possible for a great many consumers to circumvent a norm of quite recent origin. Their point of reference may well have been the "strict nécessaire." Jean-Paul Aron sketched the existence of a secondary food market in which leftovers from the legitimate restaurant industry supplied street vendors,[144] yet historians of the nineteenth century have preferred to describe the most exalted features of French cuisine rather than explore its less lofty aspects. In any case, the French model was not the norm, especially for the working class.

Attention to the cultural importance and the material content of the commercial midday meal around 1900 thus has implications for today. The results offer a starting point to examine the developments of food practices and body weights in the twentieth century. A transatlantic comparison raises questions. In the late 1870s Mark Twain famously observed middle-class American tourists who found that meals in Paris would have been improved by the addition of a large, American-style roast of beef or mutton.[145] Even so, American travelers spending 1.50 francs usually got "what the Americans would call a square meal of the ordinary kind."[146] In 1901 a *Washington (DC) Times* correspondent recommended a *restaurant à prix fixe* on Rue Turbigo where the *déjeuner* "is 1.25 francs, about 25 cents, and while the variety is not great, the cooking is good and the portions quite generous."[147] Such a proper meal, we now know, provided somewhere around 1,500 kcal. The Parisian data shine light on the reason that the members of the so-called diet squad, New York police rookies participating in an experiment of eating a number of calories scientifically determined to make for complete nourishment in January 1917, complained about their 1,000-kcal

143 As portrayed in Henry Murger, *Scènes de la vie bohème* (Paris, 1851).

144 Jean-Paul Aron, "Sur les consommations avariées à Paris dans la deuxième moitié du 19e siècle," *Annales: Economie, société, civilisation* 30, nos. 2–3 (1975): 553–62.

145 Mark Twain, *A Tramp Abroad* (New York, 1905), cited in Harvey Levenstein, *Seductive Journey: American Tourists in France from Jefferson to the Jazz Age* (Chicago, 2000), 169–73.

146 "A Model Restaurant," *Colac Herald* (Victoria, Australia), July 16, 1886, 1.

147 "Paris Restaurant Life," *Washington (DC) Times*, Sept. 8, 1901, 3.

lunches (dinners were on average somewhat larger).[148] The scientific diet obviously fell short of the square meal.

There is a need for further research here, too, but it is possible to broach the hypothesis that the American and French ideas of a full commercial midday meal may not have differed that much at the turn of the century (breakfast was altogether different, as its continental and American forms did not share much beyond the label). The similarity matters because energy values of commercial midday meals had diverged significantly in the long run. By the 1980s French women consumed 737 kcal at lunch away from home during work days, men 1,069,[149] a value that further declined to 583 kcal for women and 846 for men in 2006.[150] In the United States research into popular full-service restaurant meals in Boston puts the current average at 1,327 kcal.[151] Social scientists thus confront a puzzle. They need to explain the practices of food away from home in France and the United States, where developments in the twentieth century almost look like mirror images. On the one hand, there is the persistence of the average lunch's energy content in the United States during the growth of fast-food chains. On the other, there is the reduction of calories per average lunch in France, where the canonical model of the three-course meal asserted its hold to the point of removing the street-food and carry-away trade from the purview of academic research. Yet these calories weigh in on the scales of the people who consume them.

---

[148] "Second Helpings, Bane on Diet Test, Meals May Be Cut," *Evening World* (New York), Jan. 11, 1917, 3.

[149] Catherine Rouaud, L. Château, Anne-Marie Berthier, and Henri Dupin, "Apports nutritionnels des déjeuners hors domicile de 204 personnes," in *Essais d'évaluation des apports nutritionnels en France*, ed. Jean-Louis Lambert (Nantes, 1987), 93–94.

[150] *Etude individuelle nationale des consommations alimentaires (INCA2), 2006–2007* (Paris, 2009), www.anses.fr/Documents/PASER-Ra-INCA2.pdf.

[151] Lorien E. Urban et al., "The Energy Content of Restaurant Foods without Stated Calorie Information," *Journal of the American Medical Association—Internal Medicine*, 173, no. 14 (2013): 1292–99, archinte.jamanetwork.com/article.aspx?articleid=1687518. See also Jane E. Brody, "Dietary Report Card Disappoints," *New York Times*, Sept. 23, 2013.

"Sa Coquetterie Tue la Faim": Garment Workers, Lunch Reform, and the Parisian *Midinette*, 1896–1933

Patricia Tilburg

Abstract   *This article understands the* midinette *as a key figure in the early twentieth-century Parisian pic-turesque. Specifically, the article examines popular depictions of the noon lunch break that romanticized the* midinettes *and warned of (and celebrated) the amorous seductions and picturesque allure of these women. A defining part of that allure was undereating. The Parisian garment worker was understood to be a delightfully frivolous undereater who happily sacrificed food for fashion and pleasure. Pulp fiction, songs, vaudeville shows, and even reform campaigns in this period proffered a novel representation of undereating and noneating in depictions of the* midinette. *The undereating* midinettes *of the early twentieth-century Parisian imaginary did so as a means of engaging more fully in the capitalist marketplace, making their bodies more appealing advertise-ments for and objects of urban consumption.*

Keywords   *Paris, restaurants, workingwomen, labor history*

In a lavishly illustrated 1899 study of the Parisian lunch hour, Georges Montorgueil, a journalist and practiced connoisseur of *les moeurs parisi-ennes*, noted wistfully: "[La Parisienne] only has an appetite to be pretty. To be appealing is the yoke under which all other needs of her nature are bent. Her vanity dominates her stomach; her interest in her appearance kills her hunger [*sa coquetterie tue sa faim*], or at least staves it off and allays it. . . . Her gourmandise recedes before the desire to be noticed."[1] A reader familiar with turn-of-the-century French femi-ninity might well presume that Montorgueil here alluded to the efforts by chic bourgeois ladies to maintain a fashionably slender form. But in fact this quotation is taken from a volume entirely devoted to the work-ingwoman's lunch, and the sacrifice of food described above is made in

Patricia Tilburg is associate professor of history and chair of the Gender and Sexuality Studies program at Davidson College. She is author of *Colette's Republic: Work, Gender, and Popular Culture in France, 1870–1914* (2009) and is completing a book that interrogates representations of Parisian garment workers in popular culture, social reform, and labor activism from the 1880s through the interwar.

The author wishes to thank members of the Charlotte Area French Studies Workshop and the Nineteenth-Century French Studies Association for comments on earlier versions of this article, as well as Scott MacKenzie, Melissa González, and Jane Mangan. All translations are those of the author unless otherwise noted.

1 Georges Montorgueil, *Midi: Le déjeuner des petites ouvrières* (Paris, 1899), 39. Georges Mon-torgueil (1857–1933) was the pseudonym of the journalist, *homme des lettres*, and native Parisian Octave Lebesgue.

the service of consumer purchases, not dieting; the laboring Parisienne "has cut back on roast beef for ribbons."[2] Montorgueil's lyrical reimagining of sweated garment workers' privation as girlish vanity, far from idiosyncratic, was a common assessment of Parisian workingwomen in the first decades of the twentieth century.

The *midinette*—the ideal Parisian garment worker who took her very name from the noon lunch hour—loomed large in the social imaginary of early twentieth-century Paris. A capacious and imprecise term, *midinette* could refer to any (typically young) woman in the Parisian garment trades: milliners, dressmakers, flower makers, feather and fur workers, shopgirls, laundresses, poorly paid pieceworkers, or relatively well-paid seamstresses in the haute couture shops.[3] This attractive young garment worker with inimitable Parisian taste and a ready smile was featured in countless guide books, novels, films, songs, social commentary, and even reform campaigns from the era as an inescapable urban type. The great-granddaughter of the 1830s grisette,[4] the *midinette* also has played a supporting role in scholarly studies of the belle epoque but has only recently begun to be considered as a historical phenomenon in her own right.[5] In line with recent ethnographic and

---

[2] Ibid.

[3] Anaïs Albert suggests that only seamstresses and workers in haute couture could be deemed *midinettes*. However, press and popular culture references in this period often blurred this distinction. Thus, for example, press coverage of strikes in the confection industry in 1910 commonly used the term *midinette* to refer to the strikers. This blurring is significant, since, as Albert points out, seamstresses and milliners in haute couture were much better paid than other workingwomen ("Les midinettes parisiennes à la Belle Epoque: Bon goût ou mauvais genre?," *Histoire, économie, et société* 32, no. 3 [2013]: 61–74).

[4] The *midinette* was the turn-of-the-century and early twentieth-century version of the grisette, who had had her own moment as a literary and pop-cultural darling in the 1840s and 1850s. See Victoria E. Thompson, "*Splendeurs et Misères des Journalistes*: Female Imagery and the Commercialization of Journalism in July-Monarchy France," *Proceedings of the Western Society for French History* 23 (1996): 363–64. For the grisette and other eighteenth- and nineteenth-century antecedents to the *midinette*—that is, other cultural types of working-class femininity—see Thompson, *The Virtuous Marketplace: Women and Men, Money and Politics in Paris, 1830–1870* (Baltimore, MD, 2000); and Jennifer Jones, *Sexing La Mode: Gender, Fashion, and Commercial Culture in Old Regime France* (New York, 2004).

[5] See the work of the ethnographers Anne Monjaret and Michela Niccolai, "La midinette en chansons: Représentations masculines d'un idéal féminin populaire (1830–1939)," in *Représentations*, vol. 3 of *Le genre à l'oeuvre*, ed. Mélody Jan-Ré (Paris, 2012), 101–16; and Anne Monjaret et al., *Le Paris des "Midinettes": Processus de mise en culture et/ou en patrimoine de figures féminines, XIX–XXI siècles; Ethnologie des traces et mémoires d'ouvrières parisiennes* (Paris, 2008); as well as the sociologist Claude Didry, "Les midinettes, avant-garde oubliée du prolétariat," *L'homme et la société*, nos. 189–90 (2013): 63–86. Judith Coffin refers to the way that the attractive image of the *midinette* increased public sympathy for *midinettes* in strikes of 1901, 1910, and 1911: the anti-Semitic press portrayed this as a battle of exceptionally French *midinettes* against "foreign" Jewish manufacturers (*The Politics of Women's Work: The Paris Garment Trades, 1750–1915* [Princeton, NJ, 1996], 179). Charles Rearick's study of the Parisian picturesque includes some discussion of the "pretty midinette" (*Paris Dreams, Paris Memories: The City and Its Mystique* [Stanford, CA, 2011]). On labor activism and *midinettes* during the era of World War I, see Patricia Tilburg, "Mimi Pinson Goes to War: Taste, Class and Gender in France, 1900–18," *Gender and History* 23, no. 1 (2011): 92–110; and

sociological studies by Anne Monjaret, Michela Niccolai, and Claude Didry, I propose the *midinette* as a key figure in the early twentieth-century Parisian "imaginary" and interrogate the "symbolic work" performed by this type in French pop culture in the decades straddling World War I.[6] This article considers one defining moment of the working Parisienne's day to which early twentieth-century French observers returned again and again: *midi*.

The noon lunch break was envisaged as affording Parisian artists, writers, and tourists alike a daily glimpse of the "fairies" (as they were repeatedly called) of the city's luxury garment workshops as they took to the boulevards and parks for an hour in the sun: an hour of flirtation, window-shopping, laughter, and, I will establish, conspicuous undereating. Indeed, crucial to the picturesque allure of the lunchtime seductions that filled popular *midinette* literature was the notion of the female garment worker as a frivolous undereater who cheerfully forfeited food for fashion and pleasure. No longer the tragically starving workingwoman of nineteenth-century fiction and art, nor her virtuous, anorectic middle-class sister, whose physical wasting increased their moral fortitude,[7] the undereating *midinette* of the early twentieth century was imagined to do so as a means of engaging more fully in the capitalist marketplace—making her body a more appealing advertisement for and object of urban consumption.[8] This cultural fantasy of the *midinette*'s lunch hour, which fetishized the supposed moral precariousness of her lifestyle, as well as the sparseness of her diet, was echoed by bourgeois reformers who, in this same period, sought to carve out spaces for workingwomen's lunches that kept them from the cafés and parks where they were believed to flirt much and eat little.

Paris has long been a prime site for scholars drawn to urban typology as a way of understanding social and economic change, with popular Parisian myths cementing, in the words of Adrian Rifkin, "the

---

Maude Bass-Krueger, "From the '*Union Parfaite*' to the '*Union Brisée*': The French Couture Industry and the *Midinettes* during the Great War," *Costume* 47, no. 1 (2013): 28–44.

6 Here I find tremendously useful Rearick's elucidation of the "Parisian imaginary" as a concept that scholars use to reference centuries of "awestruck description of Paris" and that becomes "crystallized as collective memories" that "[structure] how Paris has been viewed, described, and admired" (*Paris Dreams, Paris Memories*, 3). I use the term *symbolic work* in the sense employed by Mary Louise Roberts, *Civilization without Sexes: Reconstructing Gender in Postwar France, 1917–1927* (Chicago, 1994).

7 See Patricia McEachern, *Deprivation and Power: The Emergence of Anorexia Nervosa in Nineteenth-Century French Literature* (Westport, CT, 1998); Bram Dijkstra, *Idols of Perversity: Fantasies of Feminine Evil in Fin-de-Siècle Culture* (New York, 1986); and Helena Michie, *Flesh Made Word: Female Figures and Women's Bodies* (New York, 1990).

8 Monjaret and Niccolai argue that the *midinette* archetype occupied "la marge entre monde ouvrier et monde bourgeois" (the margin between the working and bourgeois worlds) and was thus a "personnage hybride" (hybrid figure), but they do not link this hybrid status specifically to consumption practices ("La midinette en chansons," 101).

representation of change as a succession of mere appearances and nostalgias."[9] I maintain that the *midinette* was just such a useful urban type, a modern yet nostalgic figure deployed to make palatable a novel system of economic and social relations. The novel system in question was what Lenard Berlanstein has called the "reorientation from manufacturing to services" in the French economy that began in the nineteenth century.[10] During that shift, the dominance of a highly skilled artisan class ceded before the less skilled, specialized industrial worker who made up the majority of the Parisian workforce by the turn of the century.[11] This shift appeared starkly in Paris, where ready-to-wear manufacture (*confection*) in the neighborhood of the Sentier existed alongside more traditional couture workshops run by the *grands magasins* and Parisian fashion houses.[12] At the same time, unprecedented strike activity and labor activism burst across France (as well as Germany, England, and the United States); strikes in the heavily feminine Parisian garment trades in 1901, 1910, 1911, and 1917–18 were part of this newly combative French labor movement from the 1890s through the Great War.[13] Indeed, this period witnessed, according to Gérard Noiriel, "more intense working-class militancy than any other period in recent French history," including in the garment trades.[14] These first decades of the twentieth century also witnessed, not coincidentally I argue, a swell of romantic pop-cultural reimaginings of Paris's workingwomen.

Women in the needle trades were some of the first to feel the pinch of these broader transformations and were on the front line of France's struggle with increasingly competitive international markets for luxury fashion goods.[15] In addition, female garment workers made up the

---

9 Adrian Rifkin, *Street Noises: Parisian Pleasure, 1900–1940* (New York, 1993), 7. See also Walter Benjamin, "Paris, the Capital of the Nineteenth Century," in *The Arcades Project*, trans. Howard Eiland and Kevin McLaughlin (Cambridge, 1999), 3–26.

10 Lenard Berlanstein, *The Working People of Paris, 1871–1914* (Baltimore, MD, 1984), 6–7.

11 Ibid., 15. See also Roger Magraw, *Workers and the Bourgeois Republic*, vol. 2 of *A History of the French Working Class* (Oxford, 1992).

12 Nancy Green, *Ready-to-Wear, Ready-to-Work: A Century of Industry and Immigrants in Paris and New York* (Durham, NC, 1997), 78–80.

13 See Judith F. Stone, *The Search for Social Peace: Reform Legislation in France, 1890–1914* (Albany, NY, 1985), 2. Though beyond the purview of this project, labor militancy outside Paris also involved workingwomen in a spectacular fashion. See, e.g., John M. Merriman, *The Red City: Limoges and the French Nineteenth Century* (New York, 1985).

14 Gérard Noiriel, *Workers in French Society in the Nineteenth and Twentieth Centuries*, trans. Helen McPhail (New York, 1990), 73. Noiriel refers here specifically to the period 1890–1910.

15 Berlanstein, *Working People of Paris*, 84–90. Berlanstein adds that "in the forty years before the Great War this capital of conspicuous consumption, audacious ideas, and sensual pleasures [Paris] did not simply preside over a Europe in rapid transition from a preindustrial to a mature industrial society. It participated quite fully in the transition" (202). As Noiriel points out, this was also "the first distinct phase of popular consumption's importance," as working-class purchasing power increased markedly at the turn of the century (*Workers in French Society*, 85).

majority of French workingwomen in manufacturing (three-fifths in 1896) and were often paid the lowest wages.[16] As a result, contemporary discourse on changing structures of labor after 1900—everything from pulp novels to ministerial correspondence—tended to fix attention on the female Parisian garment worker. The lunching *midinette*, whose eager consumption of the city's noncomestible pleasures complemented her meager food consumption, was a compelling capitalist invention in which labor was offered up as an attractive affirmation of the social hierarchy.

The *midinette*, I suggest, was also a compelling and politically useful antidote to the *femme nouvelle* of the early twentieth century. Mary Louise Roberts traces the potent discourse surrounding "bad" women in the period 1917–27: *femmes modernes* whose egotism and androgyny offered a convenient means for French men and women to make sense of the disruption of these years. Roberts demonstrates that the *femme seule* operated as a particularly effective symbolic reconciliation of traditional femininity and agitated socioeconomic relations in this period.[17] Following Roberts, I assess the discursive utility of the *midinette* as a feminine type that allowed one to reimagine both the working classes and the New Woman as pliant, (sexually) submissive, and content— just the qualities these groups were feared to lack. A proliferation of lunchtime narratives that established the *midinette*'s delicate appetite, coquettishness, and erotic appeal speak to, I contend, tremendous anxiety surrounding issues of production, consumption, and gender in the decades straddling World War I.

Midi and the Parisian *Pittoresque*

Lunch breaks during which women laboring in Paris's luxury garment trades spread out across the city, particularly along the Rue de la Paix and in the Jardin des Tuileries, were the central setting for numerous films, novels, songs, and plays from the early twentieth century (most, though not all, written by men). As Anaïs Albert argues, the fact that the offices of the Parisian mass press abutted those of the couture workshops meant that lunching garment workers shared a daily space with many of the city's journalists and writers, who, according to Albert, devoted substantial space in their writing to the workingwomen of

16 Mary Lynn Stewart, *Women, Work, and the French State: Labour Protection and Social Patriarchy, 1879–1919* (Kingston, ON, 1989), 37–38. "While tailors earned four francs daily in the provinces and 7.5 francs daily in Paris," Stewart notes, "dressmakers earned two and four francs respectively. Broadly speaking, the higher the proportion of women, the lower the wages" (38). By the mid-1920s some four million Parisian workers toiled in some sector of the garment industry: Stewart, *Dressing Modern Frenchwomen: Marketing Haute Couture, 1919–1939* (Baltimore, MD, 2008), 92.

17 Roberts, *Civilization without Sexes*, 150.

haute couture; in this way, "the *midinette* enters into the pantheon of the fin-de-siècle erotic imaginary."[18] The narrative possibilities opened up by this setting were evident, removing the *midinettes* from their less picturesque workshops and placing them in an unregulated public space in which they could see and, more crucially, be seen.

In these texts, the *midinettes* are commonly depicted in joyous groupings: laughter, song, and birdlike flocking draw the narrators' attention to these young women as they leave their workshops and take to the boulevards on their lunch hour. The opening vignette of the art critic Arsène Alexandre's lyrical nonfiction work *Les reines de l'aiguille* (1902) (a self-described "étude parisienne" illustrated with etchings of attractive workingwomen) emphasizes the jubilant cacophony of the *midinettes*' invasion of public space in a scene often-repeated in pop-cultural products in this period:

> From noon to one o'clock, in the neighborhoods of the Opéra and the Madeleine, an unbelievable activity resumes, a frenetic swarm. . . . The seamstresses, exiting the workshops in waves at the stroke of noon, scatter noisily in search of food. They overflow with gaiety, the result of a first relaxation of their overexcited nerves, though not yet to the extreme. The street is, at this time, a little like their home; they feel at ease there and so fine that, for the most part, they come outside without jackets and hats.[19]

A joyful swarming, a headlong rush, an excess of gaiety—these workingwomen transform the boulevard into their home ("la rue . . . un peu comme un chez-elles"). They are relaxed and temptingly underdressed—a Parisian attraction that leavens capitalist productivity with girlish animation.

Georges Montorgueil, a writer who made a career of describing the Parisian picturesque, included a similar scene in his collection of vignettes *La vie des boulevards, Madeleine-Bastille* (1896), in which Paris's workingwomen are likened to a delightful swarm of bees:

> Between noon and one o'clock, a humming like a swarming bee-hive. The industrious bees with their slender corselets spread out around the neighborhood and forage for the nectar of their noon meal. These are the collaborators with whom Caprice associates to fashion marvelous pieces; the diligent workingwomen, daughters of Parisian taste, volunteer in the battalion of Fashion. In small groups,

---

18 Albert, "Les midinettes parisiennes à la Belle Epoque," 67.

19 Arsène Alexandre, *Les reines de l'aiguille: Modistes et couturières (Etude parisienne)* (Paris, 1902), 17. Lisa Tiersten uses Alexandre as an example of social critics in this period who drew attention to the plight of the garment worker by criticizing the consumer rapaciousness of bourgeois Parisiennes (*Marianne in the Market: Envisioning Consumer Society in Fin-de-Siècle France* [Los Angeles, 2001]).

they strut through the crowd with their playful youth and the imper-
tinent laugh of their white teeth, untroubled by the glances they
receive.[20]

Montorgueil here joins together several components of the *midinette*
ideal: diligence, taste, laughter, and youthful allure. The young women
are also slender-waisted creatures who delicately collect bits of "nectar"
rather than consuming a substantial meal.

Montorgueil was far from the only writer to compare lunching
workers to bees. Alexandre insisted that these women favored eating in boisterous groups, "a need to stay in groups, like the sparrows
of Paris. . . . Such is the necessity of collective labor and the effect of
habit, as much with seamstresses as with bees."[21] Jean Béarnais's 1929
pulp novel *Nouvelle Mimi Pinson: Roman d'amour inédit* employs an analo-
gous image: "The couture houses release their swarms of *midinettes*. The
little fairies of Parisian couture hurry off to lunch."[22] Comparisons to
sparrows, bees, and fairies all presented these workingwomen as interchangeable, unmenacingly diminutive, and possessed of undersized
appetites.

Most writers who took the lunching *midinette* as their subject emphasized the women's airy joyfulness.[23] André Vernières's didactic novel
Camille Frison, ouvrière de la couture (1908), while devoting many pages
to the moral temptations of the *midinette*'s noon break, also viewed the
lunch hour through the insistently rosy lens of a connoisseur. The male
narrator explores the Rue de la Paix at noon with a friend:

> All is gaiety around us. Before going back up to the workshop, the
> female laborer likes to get some air. . . . Their complexions are glow-
> ing, their gestures exuberant, and their gait unrestrained. At one
> window, we see some disheveled models who blow kisses to their
> comrades passing by below. From one end of the street to the other,
> it's like a great burst of laughter under the balmy April sun, a cele-
> bration where hearts warm and wills soften.[24]

Here the trope of the gay working Parisienne attains hyperbolic
heights. Written at a time when labor disputes gripped public attention, it is politically telling that observers insisted on recording the garment laborer's workday as "a great burst of laughter" and a "celebration." Sweatshops are transformed into bordellos, with half-dressed

---

20 Georges Montorgueil, *La vie des boulevards, Madeleine-Bastille* (Paris, 1896), 21–22.
21 Alexandre, *Les reines de l'aiguille*, 22.
22 Jean Béarnais, *Nouvelle Mimi Pinson: Roman d'amour inédit* (Montrouge, 1929), 1.
23 Monjaret et al. note the appealing scene of the lunching *midinette* in Parisian parks,
immortalized in a series of photographs from the first decades of the twentieth century ("Les jar-
dins et leurs usages féminins," in *Le Paris des "Midinettes,"* 395–98).
24 André Vernières, *Camille Frison, ouvrière de la couture* (Paris, 1908), 49.

lovelies leaning out the window blowing kisses and others in the street softening wills and warming hearts with their flushed faces and exuberant gaits. Decades later Stéphane Manier's novel *Midinettes* (1933) opens with a chapter titled "Midi" in which the author likewise brightens at the sight of young female workers on their lunch hour around the Place Vendôme and the Tuileries: "I hear laughter, yes, emanating from the bars, the delicatessens, the bakeries. . . . Nothing but gaiety in this young corps of female laborers *en liberté*."[25] In *Les reines de l'aiguille* Alexandre spends pages detailing the lunch hour in the Tuileries, noting the picnicking workers' "delirious laughter" as they jump rope, read, and chat: "The spectacle, then, of these low-cost feasts is exquisite. The garden is delightfully warm."[26]

Urban chroniclers and fiction writers accentuated the childlike playfulness of the garment trade workers on their lunch break. Alexandre claimed to have witnessed lunching *midinettes* regularly playing schoolyard games: "The last crumbs shaken from their skirts, they begin spontaneous foot races and games of tag. Some, and not the youngest among them, suddenly pull jump ropes out of their pockets, to the applause of the others. And the soldiers are drafted to turn the handles for them and whistle at them, around the flying dresses and rhythmic jumps."[27] Playing tag and jumping rope while their skirts flutter merrily about them, these women seem anything but cogs in the industrial machine. What is more, they are joined in their game by soldiers: an attractive vision of female labor and the forces of order sharing public space just a year after female garment workers had taken to the streets of Paris in a thirty-five-day strike during which government troops were used against strikers.[28]

The primary narrative interest of these scenes and reportage was to posit the lunch hour as a liminal moment in the *midinette*'s day in which she was vulnerable to sexual dissipation by way of working-class and (more often) middle-class men. Much of the lighter *midinette* fiction and entertainment featured male admirers who exploit the lunch pause to flirt with attractive, young garment workers.[29] In his 1897 study *La Parisienne* Montorgueil specified the varieties of lunchtime *midinette* seduction: "It's Don Juan's hour. We can lock up the milliner with a bouquet of violets, but we conquer the laundress only with a

---

25 Stéphane Manier, *Midinettes* (Paris, 1933), 12.
26 Alexandre, *Les reines de l'aiguille*, 20–21.
27 Ibid., 21.
28 Coffin, *Politics of Women's Work*, 178–83.
29 Maurice Ordonneau and Arthur Verneil, for example, set the opening act of their vaudeville operetta *Mimi Pinson* (1882) during a noon break in which Parisian university students and amorous aristocrats surround groups of lunching workingwomen (*Mimi Pinson: Vaudeville-opérette en trois actes* [Paris, 1882]).

gloria [a sugared coffee with brandy]."[30] Alexandre described the amorous "intruders" who could usually be found circling the *midinettes* in the Tuileries: "From time to time, administrative *sous-officiers* escaped from the offices of the Ministry of War come to prowl around the groups [of *midinettes*]. Showing off their decorations, they engage comically in attempts at flirtation that sometimes seem to succeed."[31]

The male narrator of Vernières's novel *Camille Frison* is introduced to the pleasures of the *midinettes'* noontime display by a colleague—a man who first met his own seamstress wife at a restaurant: "You will see all of the couture industry parade before you, and it is a true spectacle, you know!" In practicing a kind of erotically charged ethnographic observation, the two men lunch in the environs of couture workshops and then "stroll about [*flâner*] the Rue de la Paix." Seated at the restaurant before noon to await the *midinettes*, the colleague serving as his friend's "guide" explains that "the workingwomen of couture . . . have a certain number of common traits, and when you have observed one, you will know them all."[32] Thus, in this dehumanizing pseudoscientific aside, the *midinettes* are again presented as interchangeable and alluringly knowable. The two friends are charmed as the lunching *midinettes* around them discuss fashion and love letters. They notice that "at one nearby table, some men have saved a place for a young female guest, who soon arrives, and sits across from their faces beaming with satisfaction . . . a rendezvous that will be followed by an absence from the workshop."[33] Another workingwoman is drawn into a tête-à-tête with male diners when they notice her eyeing their dish of mussels and offer her a taste:

> And the workingwoman, without being asked twice, puts her fingers into the dish. They find this an excuse for some banter, an occasion to engage in conversation. Now they are speaking quickly. They laugh readily. They are at their best. So, invitations—to go to the country on Sunday, or the theater, depending on the weather—are proffered, on the off chance, and timidly refused, which only leads ultimately to them being accepted. Then, when the time comes to pay the bill, the young men cry:
> —Leave that alone, mesdemoiselles![34]

The narrator's guide indicates that this is simply "how things happen at the restaurant" for Parisian garment workers and their admirers.[35]

30 Georges Montorgueil, *La Parisienne peinte par elle-même* (Paris, 1897), 87. On *gloria*, see William Walton, *Paris from the Earliest Period to the Present Day*, vol. 4 (Philadelphia, 1899), 187–88.

31 Alexandre, *Les reines de l'aiguille*, 21.

32 Vernières, *Camille Frison*, 29.

33 Ibid., 33.

34 Ibid., 34.

35 Ibid.

A visceral desire for food leads, during the meal, to a softening of this young woman's moral resolve (unlike her immediate acceptance of the food, she needs to be asked multiple times to agree to an outing).

One finds countless scenes of this ilk throughout *midinette* literature, in which the lunch hour—the park, the restaurant-bar, or, most dangerous, the unsavory *gargote* (cheap restaurant or dive)—is a site of predatory courtship.[36] Louis Artus's 1911 play *Les midinettes* (whose entire second act takes place in a Paris park during lunch) constructs an amusing subplot in the person of Monsieur Lherminier, an elegant older gentleman who moves between the high society salons of his family and peers and the Jardin des Tuileries, where he courts *midinettes*.[37] Lherminier is smitten with a "little milliner" named Julie, but he flirts with all of the young workingwomen in the park: "You cannot imagine the pleasure the 'little twentysomethings' that come here cause me, the pleasure for my eyes, my heart . . . and the rest. I think of them constantly. . . . I dream of them. I write of them."[38] He illustrates this lyrical inspiration one afternoon in the park by serenading the picnicking *midinettes*. In this lascivious (but ostensibly charming) number, Lherminier defends a chic old gentleman who follows the young women "from the workshop to the restaurant":

> Walking behind your boots
> That have been recently resoled,
> He is just a little indecent
> Seeing your childish figures
> And shivers just a little in thinking about them.[39]

Here the lunch break is imagined as a time for female workers to present themselves for amorous encounters ("When you show him your nimble legs, / Raising your thin petticoat / With a slightly cheeky gesture"). The *midinettes*' pursuer covets their youth, energy, and slender bodies—and includes their poverty in the erotic catalog of their attributes (with their recently resoled boots). The last stanzas of the song make plain that their pursuer's intentions are not platonic: "At night, after the caresses, / He will speak gently" (before leaving "furtively" at dawn). The *midinette*, in her now empty bed, is told, "You will be gay!"[40]

The stage directions describe the lunching *midinettes* as "very inter-

[36] As Rebecca Spang demonstrates, the image of the restaurant as an "urban reference point" and a site of "erotic gastronomy" in popular literature dated back to the early nineteenth century and the invention of the modern restaurant itself (*The Invention of the Restaurant: Paris and Modern Gastronomic Culture* [Cambridge, MA, 2000], 215).

[37] Louis Artus, *Les midinettes: Comédie en quatre actes* (Paris, 1912). First performed at the Théâtre des Variétés, Jan. 31, 1911.

[38] Ibid., 84.

[39] Ibid., 85–86.

[40] Ibid., 86.

ested" in Lherminier's song, so beguiled that they join him in singing the refrain as they nod their heads, becoming, Lherminier says, his very own "Conservatoire de Mimi Pinson."[41] The women applaud and laugh when the song ends. The good-natured tone of the piece offers a sense of just how familiar such a scene would have been: Lherminier, the fictive milliners, and presumably the audience seem to take for granted that young garment workers are cheerful and ready sexual prey, as interested in liaisons with wealthy older men as in matrimony with their humble peers. As confirmation of this assumption, Lherminier's object of desire, Julie the milliner, spends the play equivocating between two men she meets on her lunch hour: an honest laborer named Grabure, who hopes to marry her, and Pierre, a bourgeois writer and the husband of one of her clients. The joyful denouement of the play finds Julie and Pierre kissing in the park, having decided to begin an "amourette"—a casual love affair—even as Pierre assures her that he will never leave his wife.[42]

Even when marriage is the conclusion of the lunching *midinette's* seduction, it often is preceded by a fall from virtue and/or many trials. *Couturière sans aiguilles*, a vaudeville operetta from 1905, closes with the engagement of its protagonists, the seamstress Juliette and her suitor Agénor (a saxophonist at a café-concert); nevertheless, the couple reminisces about their first, lustful encounter in a restaurant at lunchtime. They sing to one another, "And this is how / In a restaurant / Between the *saucisson* and the cream / We become lovers."[43] Though the affair leads to a marriage proposal, much of the operetta celebrates the sexual promiscuity of the atelier, where young garment workers candidly discuss lovers. The seamstress Clarisse is taunted by her coworkers because she misses lunch for a dalliance with a wealthy octogenarian, while the women as a group hail the lunch hour as a time for "Lovers that makes us blush."[44]

One chaste young seamstress, Denise Savray in de Lannoy's 1919 novel *Modiste et grande dame*, tries valiantly to avoid a restaurant seduction by taking the metro home every lunch hour to eat with her family.[45] Fate intervenes, however, when she is injured crossing the street dur-

41 Mimi Pinson was a prototypical *midinette*—a fictional character from an 1846 poem by Alfred de Musset. This line specifically refers to a philanthropic effort by Gustave Charpentier to provide workingwomen with song, dance, and music lessons through his Conservatoire de Mimi Pinson. See Tilburg, "Mimi Pinson Goes to War"; and Mary Ellen Poole, "Gustave Charpentier and the Conservatoire Populaire de Mimi Pinson," *Nineteenth-Century Music* 20, no. 3 (1997): 231–52.

42 Artus, *Les midinettes*, 121.

43 Georges Sibre and Albert Verse, *Couturière sans aiguilles: Vaudeville-opérette en un acte* (Paris, 1905), 13. First performed at the Bobino, directed by Eugène Dambreville, with music by J. Deschaux, date unknown.

44 Ibid., 6–7.

45 Pierre de Lannoy, *Modiste et grande dame: Roman inédit* (Paris, 1919).

ing a gas explosion and is taken to a nearby café to be resuscitated. The restaurant is so perilous a place for the virtue of young workingwomen that even when brought there semiconscious, Denise promptly meets (and eventually makes a miserable marriage with) a dashing count.

Jean Béarnais's *Nouvelle Mimi Pinson* follows the travails of an orphan seamstress named Mimi and her suitor Jean, a Montmartrois painter.[46] Their first outing takes place during her lunch hour. While Mimi is accustomed to eating sparingly at a modest café with her friends, Jean takes her to a fine restaurant, where she dines lavishly. The couple proceeds to lunch together regularly, Jean proposes, and Mimi moves to Montmartre to live with him in anticipation of their marriage. Under pressure from his family, Jean, who, we learn, is actually a wealthy aristocrat, soon abandons Mimi without explanation to marry his appropriately upper-class cousin. While Jean eventually divorces his cousin-wife and returns to Mimi, much of the novel concerns the moral precariousness of Mimi's position, all beginning with flirtatious (and relatively copious) restaurant lunches.

In *midinette* literature, substantial or luxurious meals were often a marker of moral corruption or sexual engagement: Mimi's fateful grand lunch with Jean, the young woman dipping her fingers into the plate of mussels, the consummation of Julie and Agénor's love over *saucisson* and cream. Broadly speaking, however, the chroniclers of the Parisian *midinette* in many cases went to great lengths to convince readers that their attractive subjects were ordinarily willful undereaters and not especially hungry. Undereating is referenced repeatedly in these essays, novels, songs, and plays as part and parcel of the appealing, featherbrained frivolity of Parisian garment workers.

As historians of the body and gender have demonstrated, delicate appetites and disordered eating were, by the early twentieth century, (mis)understood even by many physicians as signs of "coquettishness" and as part of a trend toward a more slender silhouette for upper and middle-class women.[47] Though the *midinette* likewise was idealized for her small stature and thin waist, her undereating in favor of fashion was understood to result from a lack of appetite and a desire to economize for fashionable things rather than from the drive for modish thinness

46 Béarnais, *Nouvelle Mimi Pinson*, 3.

47 See Edward Shorter, "The First Great Increase in Anorexia Nervosa," *Journal of Social History* 21, no. 1 (1987): 69–96. Shorter notes that at the turn of the century "references to anorexia in aid of modish thinness and romantic acceptance begin to proliferate" (82). Middle- and upperclass women treated for anorexia nervosa in the first decade of the twentieth century evinced a desire to be more fashionably trim. Mary Lynn Stewart and Nancy Janovicek trace the fashion industry's particular investment in promoting a slender frame in the decades straddling World War I ("Slimming the Female Body? Re-evaluating Dress, Corsets, and Physical Culture in France, 1890s–1930s," *Fashion Theory: The Journal of Dress, Body and Culture* 5, no. 2 [2001]: 173–93).

that preoccupied some middle-class women. These related but distinct images reveal how much is missed when scholars focus almost exclusively on middle-class women in histories of the body.

Susan Bordo demonstrates that Victorian fiction tended to use female hunger as a "code for female desire," just one more voracious and threatening appetite of female sexuality.[48] Thus, for the *midinette* to be obviously undereating yet not particularly hungry provided an ideal, desirable, but not excessively desiring body for consumption by the bourgeois viewer/reader/lover. What is more, this vision of the *midinette* blurred generic conventions in nineteenth-century literature, where delicate appetites were the purview of virtuous upper-class ladies. By mapping slight appetites onto working bodies, pop-cultural narratives erased the privation of actual workers, at a time when this privation was itself the subject of government inquiries, reform efforts, and labor campaigns. In such narratives, therefore, the well-documented hunger of workingwomen was transfigured, as if by enchantment, into coquettish undereating.

Montorgueil rhapsodized about the working Parisienne's noneating in *Midi: Le déjeuner des petites ouvrières* (1899), a book that contains remarkably few references to actual eating.[49] He reproached "moralists" who agonized over the hunger of these women and who claimed that the joyous comportment of the *midinettes* was a "ruse" that hid the misery of an underfed life:[50]

> The laughter of the workingwomen rings true. And their joy is not an act. The mediocrity of their meals causes them neither sadness nor embarrassment. "One should not live to eat, said Harpagnon, but rather eat to live." [These women] are not so sure of that: they live, or believe they do, and do not eat. . . . Their appetite is so frail that the most fragile emotion can cut it. Propose some pleasure to them unexpectedly and their appetite, as if by magic, disappears. In this way the theater has always, for the People, been at the expense of dinner.[51]

Here was the common refrain of the *midinette*'s enthusiasts: these were workingwomen who lived for and *on* pleasure — not food. As an example of this, Montorgueil recounted his time spent with Ernestine Curot, a seventeen-year-old workingwoman elected as the "Muse of Paris" in 1898. As one of the competition's judges, Montorgueil was charged with taking Curot and two of her female companions to the famed couturier

48 Susan Bordo, *Unbearable Weight: Feminism, Western Culture, and the Body* (Berkeley, CA, 1993), 206.
49 Montorgueil, *Midi*.
50 Ibid., 68.
51 Ibid., 69.

Charles Worth to be dressed for a fete at the Hotel de Ville, accompanying them to the fete, and escorting them home afterward. At the end of this busy day, during which Montorgueil never saw the young women eat, he suggested that they should at last have dinner:

> The Muse looked at me with an almost ironic face: "Eat? But, Monsieur," she said, "we don't eat when we go to the theater!" I insisted, I invoked the physical necessity, the fatigue of this long day, the depleted strength that they needed to replenish. I preached in vain:
> —When we go to the theater, we do not eat.
> They did not eat. They went to the theater.[52]

Casting aside the wise words of their bourgeois escort, these young workers happily forgo meals in favor of entertainment—and Montorgueil is amused by their flippancy. Alfred Desfossez's 1904 play *Les midinettes*, whose entire first act is set in a "restau des midinettes," features an equally blithe *midinette* named Zuzut, who, when given some money by a male admirer to eat more substantially, announces she will instead use the money to go to the theater.[53] Here, as in many texts featuring *midinettes*, benevolent bourgeois paternalism confronts the worrisome if adorable lifestyle of the garment worker, with systemic malnourishment in the garment trades neatly transformed into a girlish lifestyle choice.

When *midinettes* are portrayed eating at all, it is often to highlight the charming lightness of their meals. Desfossez's band of lunching *midinettes* eats sparingly and frivolously: fries, pickles, pastries, *crèmes au chocolat*. In *Midi* Montorgueil referred to workingwomen's meals as "un repas d'oiseau," and in *La vie des boulevards*, as light fare: "fries or artichoke" and "some cherries."[54] A lengthy lunch scene in the moralizing novel *Camille Frison* likewise represented *midinettes* as impractical eaters and capricious consumers:

> Some bought oranges from a street cart, others candy from the grocer, brightly colored cards, or complimentary theater tickets from the tobacco shop. Still others crowded around the ambulant pastry salesman. Further along, some waited, bowls in hand, in front of a shop where fries bubbled in the frying pan. . . . There were some who entered the dairy shop, the baker's, the delicatessen, to lay in hasty provisions before launching themselves into the commotion of a bar where they ordered only a white wine or a coffee.[55]

---

52 Ibid., 74–75.
53 Alfred Desfossez, *Les midinettes: Drame en 5 actes et 7 tableaux* (Paris, 1904), 5, 7. Premiered at the Théâtre des Fantaisies Saint-Martin, Jan. 1, 1904, and performed later at the Théâtre de Belleville, Jan. 31, 1904, and at the Théâtre Montparnasse, May 14, 1904.
54 Montorgueil, *Midi*, 38; Montorgueil, *La vie des boulevards*, 21–22.
55 Vernières, *Camille Frison*, 38–39.

Oranges, fries, candy, wine, and coffee—hardly the makings of a nourishing meal, but a list perfectly calibrated to evoke the gay impulses of the ideal *midinette*. A contemporary song, "La marche des ouvrières," celebrates an equally insubstantial lunch:

> Do you hear noon ringing?
> It's time for your lunch;
> The fried potato's bubblin'
> And the brie's runnin' at the dairy.
> Go get your beakful
> In a nice paper cone.
> And drink a dewdrop
> At the neighborhood Wallace.[56]

Some fries, a bit of cheese, and a drop of water from a public fountain—here is another sparse *midinette* lunch, no more than a birdlike "beakful," but one that evokes pleasure rather than pathos. *Midinette* lunches were depicted in this way consistently—meals of small quantity, often composed of snacks or sugary treats.

Alexandre's extended chapter on the *midinettes*' lunch hour veers between romanticizing the lightness of the women's consumption and playing up the tragic insufficiency of their collations—two closely related responses, I suggest. Alexandre depicts the plaintive undereaters ("huddled in their cloaks, they melancholically eat the humble and austere nourishment they hold in the fold of a newspaper spread open over their knees")[57] and later refers to the "mouse-sized stomachs of the little Parisiennes." He admits that "it is incontestable that in Paris, the workingwoman at four francs a day finds nowhere to feed herself adequately." Yet, on the very next page, he concludes, "This life is essentially pleasant and emits a potent perfume of kindness, of affectionate temperament, and instinctive delicacy."[58] He approves of the "pensive or cheerful young women" who descend from their workshops to buy a pleasantly insubstantial lunch from a seasonal fruit and vegetable cart: "delicious fruits and crudités . . . cherries, apples, pink radishes."[59]

Montorgueil similarly notes the misery of these women's diets ("the 'petite main' makes a sum so modest that we ask ourselves by what miracle she is able to live. To this question one workingwoman responded: 'Why, we do not eat our fill'") and on the very next page assures readers that nonetheless "this distress" is hidden by a "mask of

---

56 A. Poupay, "La marche des ouvrières," quoted ibid., 48. "Wallace du quartier" references cast-iron public drinking fountains that appeared in Paris in the late nineteenth century.

57 Alexandre, *Les reines de l'aiguille*, 19–20.

58 Ibid., 24, 25.

59 Ibid., 18.

insouciance and gaiety" provided by youth and taste.[60] These women, he insists, "remain piquant and so desirable that they would make some conquests of old men along their way if they were not all horrified by banal vice."[61] Montorgueil adds that the "frugal meal" of fries, artichokes, and cherries was seasoned with "the salt of playful remarks and shot through with more laughter than the copious feasts of modish cabarets."[62] Thus the "lugubrious" portrait painted by the reformers he cites is immediately banished by images of alluring women and quaint picnics.[63] Some workingwomen, Montorgueil continued, even found spare change for an occasional coffee or vanilla ice cream. In this way undereating and a frivolous diet are both denounced and eroticized.

Explaining the *midinette*'s undereating as a choice made in the service of an instinctive attachment to fashion and coquetry further eroticized the malnourished garment worker. As an example of his thesis that workingwomen's *coquetterie* deadened their hunger, Montorgueil pointed again to the behavior of Curot and her friends: "Did they eat during these blissful days [?] . . . Eat! Sure, they were considering it. Considering their beautiful gowns, yes, which they saw were lined with silk, and so, they confided to one another, later they could unstitch the lining and make two dresses out of one."[64] Indeed, not eating, Montorgueil revealed, was "the secret to not jeopardizing either the delicate gracefulness of her body or the return on her earnings."[65] Once more, the Parisian garment worker is seen to prioritize what observers like Montorgueil wished she would—fashion. As a result, the reality of the sweated laborer, malnourished because of a meager salary, is neatly elided in favor of a chic coquette who chooses not to eat her fill in order to revel in the pleasures of Parisian couture.

Vernières's *Camille Frison* features a young garment worker who spends her lunch hour at a restaurant describing the "ravishing little embroidered collar" at Galeries Lafayette that she will soon buy: "She had gone without meat for eight days to have enough money."[66] In Béarnais's *Nouvelle Mimi Pinson* the entire staff of a Parisian couture workshop curbs its eating to allow for fashion expenditures: "They had the habit of meeting up at a little café on the Rue Caumartin where they would lunch frugally on charcuterie and a café-crème. These meager meals enabled them to save up to buy powder, rouge and, on

---

60 Montorgueil, *La vie des boulevards*, 186, 187.
61 Ibid., 187.
62 Ibid., 186, 188.
63 Ibid., 187.
64 Montorgueil, *Midi*, 71.
65 Ibid., 76.
66 Vernières, *Camille Frison*, 35.

occasion, a little, elegant outfit."[67] One seamstress, Jeanne, considers taking a lover to sate both her physical hunger and her appetite for fashion: "I've had enough of being honorable, of depriving myself to preserve this elegance that they envy in us, to live this life of relentless privation."[68] Downgrading her wardrobe does not occur to Jeanne as a solution. As in many renderings of Mimi Pinson, Jeanne's concern for appearance and taste for fashion are represented as an instinctive drive—far more urgent than a steady diet. Manier's *Midinettes* features Yvette, a twenty-six-year-old *second main* in a Parisian couture house who also sacrifices meals for her love of fashion: "To stay coquette, to save money, Yvette only eats once a day, at lunch, at an inexpensive restaurant."[69] In this way novelists like Manier and Béarnais assuaged social fears about the wretchedness of sweated labor (by depicting workers' undereating as a coquettish sacrifice for apparel and makeup) and reaffirmed cultural expectations about the impeccable tastefulness of Paris's workingwomen.

Indeed, many scenes of the *midinette* lunch hour involve no eating whatsoever but instead depict garment workers covetously touring the boulevards' shop windows. The (purported) *midinette* columnist "Gaby" from *Le journal de Mimi Pinson* described her own lunch hours thus: "I love to *flâner*. . . . My nose is pressed up against the shop windows of the boutiques in the neighborhood. . . . It amuses me so just to look—without even really seeing at times—the loads of things that are in there!"[70] Béarnais's novel opens with *midinettes* rushing toward lunch who pause "in front of the sumptuous jewelry shops and admire the expensive necklaces, the rings that will never grace their fingers, the diamonds that will be worn at dreamlike parties by those who don the gowns fashioned by the skillful little hands."[71] These young women are not fomenting revolution as they examine the luxury goods produced by their labor but beyond their reach. Rather, they are lighthearted *flâneuses* whose consumerist desires affirm the capitalist economy of which they are the bottom rung.

As Rita Felski and others point out, workingwomen's taste for luxury was often portrayed as the first step in a descent toward sexual promiscuity.[72] To be sure, many of these stories understood appetites

67 Béarnais, *Nouvelle Mimi Pinson*, 2–3.

68 Ibid., 3.

69 Manier, *Midinettes*, 38: "Pour rester coquette, faire des économies, Yvette ne mange qu'une fois par jour, à déjeuner, dans un restaurant à bon marché."

70 Gaby, "Babil de Trottin," *Le journal de Mimi Pinson, à l'atelier et dans la famille*, Aug. 10, 1908, 2.

71 Béarnais, *Nouvelle Mimi Pinson*, 1.

72 Rita Felski, *The Gender of Modernity* (Cambridge, MA, 1995), 72.

(for fashion, for food, for sex) as interrelated and corrupting. Béarnais's Mimi, before agreeing to her first meal with her soon-to-be-lover Jean, considers the example of her coworker Mado, who, thanks to a wealthy lover, is always fashionably dressed ("du dernier chic") and eats her lunch "in restaurants, à la carte."[73] Many philanthropists and reformers parroted the pop-cultural contention that the *midinette*'s frivolous and underdeveloped appetite for food complemented other, more highly developed (and morally treacherous) appetites.

Lunch Reform and the *Midinette*

Alongside these picturesque representations, the female worker's lunch drew increasing attention in the belle epoque as a target of reform. Turn-of-the-century reformers generally agreed that the lunch break imperiled young Parisian workingwomen and so proposed initiatives to create lunchrooms, both secular and confessional, where *midinettes* could safely enjoy a wholesome meal for a modest sum.[74] Such initiatives, while engendered primarily by concern for the insufficient salaries and diet of the Parisian female workforce, were also motivated by interlaced fantasies and concerns about the moral susceptibility of the garment trade worker.

One of the first workingwomen's lunchrooms was established in the 1890s by the Union Chrétienne des Ateliers de Femmes—a group composed of garment trade *patronnes* and society ladies—at the place du Marché Saint-Honoré.[75] A short-lived Catholic restaurant, on the Rue Jean-Jacques Rousseau, and another, the Restaurant de Dames Seules on the Rue de Richelieu, followed. This latter space included a reading room and library, a prix fixe restaurant, and a second, à la carte restaurant.[76] In 1893 a group of Protestant society ladies opened the Foyer de l'Ouvrière, a kitchen on Rue d'Aboukir in the neighborhood of some of the most poorly paid of the needle trades—military caps and hat manufacture.[77] Given the popularity of this endeavor,

---

73 Béarnais, *Nouvelle Mimi Pinson*, 3.

74 Albert, "Les midinettes parisiennes à la Belle Epoque," 61–74. Albert is primarily interested in the *midinette*'s lunch hour and in restaurant reform as part of a broader interest in workingwomen's consumption in this period, but she focuses on noncomestible consumption.

75 This first effort faced several difficulties, such as finding an affordable location close to garment trade workplaces and developing a menu that was both appealing and modestly priced. For information on these early endeavors, see Comte d'Haussonville, *Salaires et misères de femmes* (Paris, 1900).

76 Ibid., 48. Charles Benoist refers to the lending library at this establishment in *Les ouvrières de l'aiguille à Paris* (Paris, 1895), 233–34.

77 Haussonville noted that high prices inevitably meant that the principal clientele comprised *demoiselles de magasins* and that the *directrice* was too forceful in pushing a "certaine influence religieuse" (*Salaires et misères de femmes*, 52). The founding of the Rue d'Aboukir site is dated 1893 in Maurice Bonneff, "Fin de saison—fin de travail," *L'action*, July 18, 1908.

other locales opened in subsequent years—on the Rue Réaumur, Rue de la Victoire, Rue du Faubourg-Saint-Denis, Rue de Charonne, and Rue de Richelieu.[78] The Rue du Bac saw the establishment of a multi-confessional restaurant run by Jewish, Catholic, and Protestant ladies. In 1905 an alliance of public school teachers and labor representatives (including Clémence Jusselin, the secretary of the Chambre Syndicale des Ouvrières Lingères in Paris) founded "Les Midinettes": Restaurants Coopératifs d'Ouvrières.[79] This project, which sought over time to make workingwomen the primary stakeholders in the cooperative, modeled itself after successful networks of workers' restaurants in Geneva and in Lyon (established in 1890 and 1892, respectively).[80] Another Parisian establishment opened on the Rue Béranger offering a "pension complet"—meals and lodging for workingwomen at a cost of between seven and twelve francs per week.[81] The Cercle du Travail Féminin on the Boulevard des Capucines promoted itself as a "center of entertainment and friendship" for workingwomen without any confessional or political association. Its services included a restaurant, as well as affordable seaside vacations for subscribers. By 1908 the Cercle boasted 900 members and provided "carefully prepared" lunches in its restaurant for around 250 women for less than eighty centimes each.[82]

In addition to lunchrooms, some reformers focused on supporting businesses that provided employees with adequate lunching facilities on site—principally in the form of kitchens where workers could prepare and heat their own meals. The Ligue Social d'Acheteurs gave high marks to workshops that provided stoves and lunching spaces.[83] In 1906 the Rue Saint-Honoré saw the opening of the Réchaud, where for about ten centimes workingwomen could cook their own meals. The organizers provided supplements of vegetables, salad, and wine for a small price. By 1908 some 120 female garment workers from the neighborhoods of the Rue de la Paix and the Place Vendôme ate there every day.[84]

---

78 Ibid.

79 *"Les Midinettes": Restaurants coopératifs d'ouvrières; Société anonyme à capital et à personnel variables* (Paris, 1905). This initiative is mentioned in Louise Compain, *La femme dans les organisations ouvrières* (Paris, 1910). Compain refers to a soon-to-be-opened *restaurant de midinettes* that has raised ten thousand francs in donations. Whether this is the same initiative as that incorporated in 1905 is difficult to say, though Jusselin is mentioned prominently in both places.

80 *"Les Midinettes": Restaurants coopératifs d'ouvrières*, 6.

81 Bonneff, "Fin de saison—fin de travail."

82 Ibid.

83 *Bulletin de la Ligue sociale d'acheteurs* (nov. 1904, 1er trimestre 1905), 7–8. Benoist observed that most of the diners were young women, as older and married women preferred to economize even further by remaining at the workshop to eat (*Les ouvrières de l'aiguille à Paris*, 234). The Ligue Sociale d'Acheteurs was founded in 1902 to raise awareness among bourgeois Parisian shoppers about the working conditions of those employed in the garment businesses they patronized.

84 Bonneff, "Fin de saison—fin de travail."

In his social investigation *Les ouvrières de l'aiguille à Paris* (1895), Charles Benoist estimated that, in the high season, twelve hundred to fifteen hundred lunches were served weekly in "restaurants-bibliothèques" for workingwomen in the needle trades. With a Parisian working population of some eighty-eight thousand *ouvrières couturières*, wrote Benoist, clearly more such venues were needed.[85] Indeed, by 1912 the number of lunchrooms and soup kitchens expressly serving workingwomen in Paris swelled to thirty-five—with names like the Repas de Midinette and Restaurant du Syndicat de l'Aiguille.[86]

The menus of workingwomen's lunchrooms offered a corrective to the widespread association of *midinettes* and frivolous eating. While the popular imagination envisioned *midinettes* lunching on a "beakful" of sweets and snacks, diners at the Foyer de l'Ouvrière enjoyed complete meals consisting of a meat dish, vegetable, and bread for only eleven sous.[87] The Restaurant de Dames Seules offered a ninety-centime *menu fixe* (a meat dish, a vegetable dish, a dessert, bread, and wine, beer, or milk), as well as an à la carte selection that included meat, fish, soups, salad, and vegetables.[88]

For some reformers, the economically driven malnourishment of the garment worker was the principal impetus for these lunchroom initiatives. A schoolteacher who helped found the Société des Midinettes (a restaurant cooperative) wrote of a former student, a leather worker, who was "reduced to nibbling a couple of fries or bits of charcuterie, while walking, showered by rain or wind. Isn't this a fortifying nourishment and consumed in conditions that promise a happy effect! . . . After this, you can go ahead and call all the congresses you want to combat the ravages of tuberculosis and to halt the white slave trade!"[89] Maurice Bonneff, a working-class activist who coauthored a number of *enquêtes* into the lives of French workers with his brother Léon, explained that workingwomen lunched outside by necessity, not by dint of a picturesque playfulness, and he quoted a workingwoman herself (rare in these sources):

> First off, the bistros are not much interested in our patronage. We do not order apéritifs. And then, lunch rarely amounts to less than twenty-five sous. That's fine for rich people. To cut costs, sometimes, we order smaller portions. Often, we drink only water. This time, the bistro gets angry, and hits us with a fine. Yes indeed! When we

85 Benoist, *Les ouvrières de l'aiguille à Paris*, 234.
86 Office Central des Oeuvres de Bienfaisance, *Paris charitable et bienfaisant* (Paris, 1912).
87 Bonneff, "Fin de saison—fin de travail."
88 Haussonville, *Salaires et misères de femmes*, 48. The prices on this menu closely approximate those found in sample menus provided in Benoist, *Les ouvrières de l'aiguille à Paris*, 232.
89 *"Les Midinettes": Restaurants coopératifs d'ouvrières*, 5.

ask for the bill, they have us paying ten centimes extra, to punish us for contributing, by way of our sobriety, to the slump in wine sales! They charge us for the silverware too. So much that, despite our rigorous calculations, our desire for economizing, we end up spending wildly: twenty-three sous![90]

Bonneff remarks that this "economy of the little sou" is "infinitely distressing. . . . It gives us a glimpse of an entire life of privation and labor, and the anemia and the tuberculosis that decimate so many workingwomen."[91] In their *enquête* titled *La vie tragique des travailleurs* (1911), unusual among many descriptions of the *midinette* lunch, the Bonneff brothers define these laborers' undereating as a painful economic necessity, rather than as a sacrifice for fashion or a preference for insubstantial meals.[92] They demonstrate that even a modest daily midday meal exceeded the salary of many women in the flower industry. They also note that added money for food could not be gleaned from other parts of the workingwoman's budget—minimal heating and laundry costs and "the already limited costs of clothes."[93] Rather than blaming excessive coquetry and taste for fashion, the Boneffs highlight the inequitable salaries of women compared with men as the root of their pecuniary misery.

Yet many other reformers, even those decrying abusive labor practices, reaffirmed the prevalent notion of female garment workers as frivolous and willful undereaters. In his 1900 investigative report *Salaires et misères de femmes* the Comte d'Haussonville admitted that it was difficult to construct a menu for a workingwomen's restaurant: "Generally, [these girls] have little appetite, despite their twenty years, and this is understandable given the sedentary existence they lead, deprived of fresh air and exercise. Big pieces of meat do not tempt them. They only like small dishes. Some demand dessert and coffee."[94] In her study *Celles qui travaillent* (1913), the novelist (and former *ouvrière*) Simone Bodève concurred that it was a mistake to establish restaurants for workingwomen alone: "Our young women eat little and drink even less. . . . In places where a restaurateur is assured of a male clientele, the food will be both more varied and fresher, simply because its consumption is certain. . . . [To the young workingwoman] eating seems to be an irksome operation; eating a lot is, in her eyes, shameful and indelicate."[95]

---

[90] Quoted in Bonneff, "Fin de saison—fin de travail."

[91] Ibid.

[92] Léon Bonneff and Maurice Bonneff, *La vie tragique des travailleurs: Enquêtes sur la condition économique et morale des ouvriers et ouvrières d'industrie*, 4th ed. (Paris, 1911), 26–27, 330–31.

[93] Ibid., 315–16.

[94] Haussonville, *Salaires et misères de femmes*, 47.

[95] Simone Bodève, *Celles qui travaillent* (Paris, 1913), 128–29.

A certain Dr. Parfait, writing in a magazine aimed at *midinettes* in 1909, emphasized the deleterious health effects of workingwomen's insufficient meals: "The mealtime of the workingwoman—yours, charming lady readers—is perhaps the most interesting and most alarming aspect of her situation, as much from the point of view of the stomach as that of the crowded closeness of the restaurant." Tuberculosis and stomach ailments were a certain result of such undereating, the physician warned. He suggested, however, that these inadequate meals were in no small part the result of workers' appetite for fashion: "Some workingwomen, rather than trying to feed themselves well, prefer to lunch on a ten-centime black coffee and a croissant . . . so that they can buy themselves a bit of ribbon, a cravat, or a bouquet of violets."[96] To convince his working-class readers to heed his advice, Parfait patronizingly framed his admonition as beauty tips: "Remark—and this argument will have more value in your eyes than all the best ones in the world—remark, I say, that frequent congestion of the face often leads to eczema. . . . Eczema that disfigures, that makes the most beautiful woman ugly, and that resists even the most energetic treatments."[97] Tuberculosis and any of the other serious health ailments Parfait enumerates in this article evidently would not concern the gay *midinette* in the way that threats to her beauty might. Here another middle-class male reformer relies on a potent cultural fantasy of *midinette* frivolity even as he tries to combat systemic malnourishment in the garment trades. Bodève similarly explained the undereating of Parisian workingwomen in part as a result of their devotion to fashion. Bodève refers to the lunch hour as the best time to see the *ouvrières parisiennes* "lively and happy": "Those privileged ones that can 'treat themselves' to restaurants lunch on four mouthfuls and a thousand words, then rush off to the department store to try on hat styles."[98] Other workingwomen, led astray by their "vanity," agree to accompany a seducer to a meal simply for "the joy of entering a beautiful restaurant" and later "kill themselves with night work [*veillées*] and privations to have a wardrobe without asking for anything from their lover."[99] Intentional and frivolous undereating in the service of fashion and beauty worked as only one important element in a prevalent vision of the *midinette* as sexually available and desirable yet politically neutered.

The *midinette*'s lunchtime corruption, a scene reiterated across popular literature in this period, bled into government investiga-

96 Dr. Parfait, "Midinette et l'hygiène: Vous mangez trop vite," *Midinette: Journal de la femme et de la jeune fille qui travaillent*, Nov. 12, 1909, 10.
97 Ibid.
98 Bodève, *Celles qui travaillent*, 14.
99 Ibid., 67–68.

tions of conditions in the garment trades. Indeed, turn-of-the-century lunchroom initiatives were driven not only by perceptions of working-women's undereating but also by alarm about the lunch hour as a space of temptation, seduction, and moral peril—a fall from virtue that was itself a staple of romantic representations of these women.[100] In 1901 the Commission Départementale du Travail de la Seine held numerous meetings on the question of the *veillées* (supplementary late evening hours imposed on many workers during the high season). As part of this debate, Stéphanie Bouvard, leader of the *fleuristes-plumassières'* union and one of only two women involved in the commission's deliberations, advocated requiring all employers to provide refectories.[101] Workingwomen, Bouvard argued, often lived too far from their workplace to return home for lunch and earned too little to eat at restaurants. More important, having the *ouvrière* lunch in a designated space at the workshop would "safeguard her morality and remove her from the influences of the street."[102] M. Walckenaer, a mining engineer and member of the commission, was sympathetic to Bouvard's argument: "It is the fear that young women, obliged to go out into the street and to take shelter in cheap cabarets for their meals, find themselves exposed to moral or material dangers more frightful than the inconveniences of their current way of life."[103]

Fear of these unspecified but doubtlessly well-understood "moral dangers" seems to have helped shape reform initiatives. The founding documents of the Société des Midinettes' restaurant cooperative included as justification of its work a vision of the moral dangers of the lunch hour: "And here, then, is my workingwoman, obliged to go eat outside, in the street, in the square, on a bench on the boulevard, exposed to bad weather, to glacial temperatures, to rain, to wind; exposed also to all the repugnant and dangerous promiscuities, so much so that her moral health is as threatened as her physical health."[104] Inclem-

---

100 Spang notes that the restaurant had been perceived, since its inception in the early nineteenth century, as a space of erotic adventure (*Invention of the Restaurant*, 215).

101 "Séance du 22 février 1901," in *La question des veillées devant la Commission départementale du travail du département de la Seine: Extraits des procès-verbaux des séances, 1900–1901* (Paris, 1901), 25. Bouvard served on the commission as a *délégué* of the Bourse du Travail.

102 Ibid., 26.

103 Ibid., 28. The commission could not agree on the proposition, and it was withdrawn. One delegate, M. Antourville from the Bourse du Travail, who disagreed with Bouvard and Walckenaer, insisted that the diminution of health that would result from workers' enclosure inside all day was more perilous than the "influence of the street," which was "not as dangerous as we claim." Furthermore, remaining in the workshop for lunch could be even more threatening from a moral perspective, "especially in the mixed-sex workshops, where the men and women live together from morning till night in a closeness that leads to familiarities and intimacies that are almost impossible to achieve in the street" (ibid., 26). Antourville also feared that employers would take advantage of the policy to keep employees working through the lunch hour.

104 *"Les Midinettes": Restaurants coopératifs d'ouvrières*, 4.

ent weather and moral danger are placed side by side as threats to the lunching *midinette*. Paul Deschanel's 1909 initiative, Réfectoire: Société Mutuelle de Prévoyance Alimentaire des Dames et Demoiselles Couturières, Lingères, Modistes, Brodeuses, afforded women in the garment trades during the low seasons "a wholesome and fortifying meal" but also "a shelter from bad weather and the temptations of the street."[105] The Ligue Sociale d'Acheteurs praised one couture house for offering a stove where employees could heat up their lunch "so as to have them avoid a meal at the corner restaurant where one is always badly fed and exposed to often dangerous encounters."[106]

In *Salaires et misères de femmes* Haussonville described in detail the scenario to be avoided by the creation of workingwomen's lunchrooms:

> While they mull over an economical meal, menu in hand, a gallant from the dairy shop arrives and proposes adding something to their lunch or even paying for the whole thing. If they refuse on account of pride, the gallant does not surrender. He returns the next day and offers some object for their toilette, a silk ribbon or a plated brooch. After all, there's nothing wrong with this. So, each young woman who consents to have something paid for, whether a lunch or a ribbon, is on the path that will lead to her ruin.[107]

Echoing popular *midinette* literature, Haussonville's sociological study neatly joins fashion, food, and moral ruin—and does so with the narrative suspense of a pulp novel. In his 1895 study of the needleworkers of Paris, the journalist, historian, and later politician Charles Benoist composed a similarly lurid scene in which a workingwoman, driven by dreams of copious restaurant lunches and fashion purchases, falls for her seducer:

> She who hardly earns enough to feed herself, who lunches sparingly and hurriedly at noon, and is bent in two over her work, she has a dream: to be able to eat, like this girl or that girl, at a restaurant . . . which she imagines as a place of delights. As soon as she has a couple of sous, she will go. As soon as she has gone, she will be unable to go without it, by vanity and pleasure.
>
> One day not too far off, she will meet a gallant from her class there. . . . She will resist as best she can, but for all sorts of reasons her best is not good enough. First off, she is poor, and second, she is a coquette. . . . She has the curiosity to know and the desire to have:

105 "Pour les ouvrières parisiennes: Une oeuvre utile," *Midinette: Journal de la femme et de la jeune fille qui travaillent*, Nov. 12, 1909, 4.

106 Baronne Georges Brincard, "La Ligue sociale d'acheteurs et les Maisons de la liste blanche," presented to the Assemblée Générale of the Ligue, Apr. 23, 1904; *Bulletin de la Ligue sociale d'acheteurs*, Nov. 1904, 7. In compiling its liste blanche (businesses given a seal of approval because of their fair labor practices), the Ligue specified which fashion houses provided their workers with space and facilities to prepare and enjoy midday meals.

107 Haussonville, *Salaires et misères de femmes*, 21.

> a bagatelle, a bauble, a ribbon. . . . The modest workingwoman gives
> in one night. In a dark alley, she slips through a half-open door into
> a disreputable house. . . . She will not come out again.[108]

Restaurant dining again figures as a gateway temptation leading inexorably to desires for fine things, a seduction, and, in short order, moral ruin. Like many fiction writers and *midinette* enthusiasts, Benoist knits together this imaginary workingwoman's meager diet and her supposed *coquetterie*—and conflates hunger and acquisitiveness as the cause of her fall. The very tone of the passage echoes the melodramatic narrative of much *midinette* fiction—a virtuous but dreamy working-class girl, a gallant encounter, a dark alleyway.

Benoist returns to the restaurant later in his study, reasserting the inevitability of workingwomen's fall after exposure to its temptations. Once these women have the occasion "to lose themselves, they are lost: and such an occasion is offered them at least once a day. Where then? They tell you themselves: at the dive restaurant [*la gargote*]!"[109] Benoist investigates a *gargote* on his own one afternoon, employing the sensational tones of a feuilleton in his description: "In the Paris of elegance, one hundred feet from the Madeleine, a boutique painted bright red. First we see a room where a fat man with a hoarse voice and an apoplectic expression reigns over the gleaming zinc counter. At the back, a second room, from which curls acrid smoke, part grease and part pipe fumes, a thick bluish vapor that clings to you as soon as you enter."[110] Benoist climbs to the second floor, where he finds a number of workingwomen ordering their "semblance of a lunch," all with the "same monotone and weary tone": "If they eat, it is either nothing or less than nothing. The worst poison at the *gargote* does not affect the stomach. Here, in this kind of private dining room, there were no masons or carpenters, as there were downstairs. There were only gentlemen, and what gentlemen!"[111] On the very next page Benoist conjures an imagined milliner: "Hunger does not move her and she waits. While waiting, she calculates . . . three hundred francs per month, an apartment and furnishings. Neither perversity nor passion. Business and, in a manner of speaking, an 'installation.' She adds a liaison to the daily routine of her life, without missing a step, like a flower or a feather on a hat."[112] The fall of this fictive hatmaker, Benoist avows, is brought on not by "material misery" but by an attachment to fine things; another workingwoman is represented as an intentional undereater unmoved

108 Benoist, *Les ouvrières de l'aiguille à Paris*, 118–20.
109 Ibid., 123.
110 Ibid., 123–24.
111 Ibid., 124.
112 Ibid., 125.

by hunger.[113] Later in the same work Benoist places hunger and moral frivolity on a comparable plane of social priority when examining the degradation of the garment trade worker: "One must first combat hunger, then vanity [*la coquetterie*], vanquishing in the *ouvrière* both the human animal and the woman. One must drive Paris out of Paris, deprive the street of all its temptations."[114] The Parisian street is, for Benoist, the site and origin of these women's seemingly unavoidable moral ruin, and the lunch hour the critical space in which their (very literary) fall began: "There, in the street, the novel opens that will draw to a close at the wine bar."[115] Workingwomen's lunchroom initiatives appear in Benoist's study as a weapon against sexual and moral temptation, not simply or even primarily as a space for affordable meals. Thus reform-oriented social scientific inquiries, like their pop-cultural contemporaries, seemed unable to avoid imagining garment workers' lives in melodramatic and romantic literary terms.

Union organizers suggested a different danger for lunching *midinettes*. In the March 22, 1901, meeting of the Commission Départementale du Travail de la Seine, Jusselin reported on the recent strike in the needle trades. The strike had failed in part, she claimed, because certain employers had forced their workers to eat in their workshops (some even providing lunch and a small daily raise for those women who remained) to "prevent workingwomen from coming into contact with strikers."[116] Indeed, police reports throughout this period indicated that the lunch hour was a key moment for police agents' surveillance of workingwomen and their possible contacts with labor agitators.[117] During garment trade strikes in 1917, for example, the Préfecture de Police conducted surveillance of restaurants frequented by *midinettes*, using police spies to assess the influence of syndicalizing young men on lunching workingwomen.[118]

113 Ibid., 127.
114 Ibid., 143.
115 Ibid., 143–44.
116 "Séance du 22 mars 1901," in *La question des veillées*, 28.
117 See, e.g., Report from the Chef du Service des Renseignements Généraux to the Préfet de Police, "Au sujet de lettres anonymes adressées à des ouvrières des Maisons 'LAROCHE' et 'MORIN,'" Sept. 29, 1917. Archives de la Préfecture de Police de Paris, BA 1376, Grèves de l'habillement, 1917 à 1918.
118 Report from the Ministre de l'Intérieur (Direction de la Sûreté Générale) to the Préfet de Police, Sept. 11, 1917, no. 2432. Archives de la Préfecture de Police de Paris, BA 1376, Grèves de l'habillement, 1917 à 1918. One report referenced a sixteen-year-old *brodeuse* who claimed to have witnessed young men in the restaurants pressuring workingwomen to strike. A subsequent report indicated that an agent sent to frequent these restaurants was unable to find either this *brodeuse* or any evidence of syndicalizing in the restaurants. Report from the Chef du Service des Renseignements Généraux to the Préfet de Police, "Au sujet d'une certaine effervesence qui se serait manifestée parmi les midinettes: Modistes, brodeuses, couturières, travaillant dans le quartier de l'Opéra," Sept. 28, 1917. Archives de la Préfecture de Police de Paris, BA 1376, Grèves de l'habillement, 1917 à 1918.

The *Midinette en Grève*

Despite a profusion of reportage and fiction that denied hunger in the garment trades, female garment workers demanded increased lunch allowances and lunch facilities throughout the various strikes in their trade from 1901 to 1917. The organ of the hatmakers' union, *L'ouvrier chapelier*, published a letter from a workingwoman in the garment trades in 1914 that gave some sense of the appalling lunch conditions in such ateliers—and the way that "lunch reform" was in some cases more concerned with controlling *midinettes* during their breaks than providing a sustaining meal: "The house provides lunch, but in such a deplorable and insufficient fashion that everyone is obliged to buy themselves something else with their own money and at exorbitant prices. . . . Lunch is obligatory for everyone and no one can leave during those hours."[119] This garment worker counters visions of a gaily undereating *midinette*, placing the blame for light meals squarely on workers' meager salaries rather than girlish lack of appetite or fashionable outlay.

Yet, when workingwomen in the Parisian garment trades took to the streets in these years, even the socialist press seemed to leaven their militancy by recycling the image of the cheerily lunching *midinette*. During the *grève des midinettes* of September 1910, several newspapers described the striking women as carefree lunchers. When protesting women were hemmed in by police agents on September 28, *Humanité* reported: "The *midinettes* then headed out of Paris and organized, in small, smiling groups, light tea parties on the grass of the city walls."[120] During a significant garment trade strike in May 1917, *Humanité* again tagged the popular trope of the lunching *midinette*:

> Noon.
>   A long cortege advances along the *grands boulevards*. It is the *midinettes* of Paris, with their blouses adorned with lilacs and lilies of the valley. They run, they jump, they sing, they laugh. Yet this is neither the feast of Sainte-Catherine nor the Mi-Carême: it is the strike.[121]

Thus even this socialist newspaper views female labor militancy in the Parisian garment trades through an unmistakably nostalgic lens.

By the end of World War I, as Parisian garment workers joined massive strike mobilizations, labor leaders and socialist journalists

119 "Chez les modistes," *L'ouvrier chapelier*, May 1, 1914. The letter was penned, according to the editors, by "une de nos actives camarades du Syndicat" (one of our friends active in the union) at the Maison Lewis.

120 "La grève de Reaumur: Dinette sur les fortifs, bagarres à Montmartre," *L'humanité*, Sept. 28, 1910, Archives Nationales, F/7/13740. The same scene was recorded in the *Petite république* that day.

121 "La grève des midinettes parisiennes," *L'humanité*, May 16, 1917.

underscored the purportedly novel activism of female garment trade
workers by suggesting that the romantic image of the undereating *midinette* now was outdated (disregarding the significant and well-publicized
strikes by female garment workers in the first decade of the century).
In May 1917 one left-leaning journalist, covering the garment strikes
that spring, noted that the movement seemed to have won over "all the
workshops where the fairies of the needle have so long toiled without
demanding anything":

> This is no longer the time when Jenny l'Ouvrière and Mimi Pinson
> contented themselves with a lunch of a cone of fries and a dinner of
> a cutlet of brie seasoned with a couple of sentimental refrains from
> the "masterpieces" of Paul Delmet or some other equally mushy
> novelist.
>   The war, which has changed many things, modified all of that.
> And it is not a pity.[122]

This passage does several things at once. It applauds the (seemingly)
newfound activism of workingwomen in the garment trades, but it does
so by reaffirming a romantic vision of these women as formerly frivolous (reading popular romantic literature, singing, not striking, undereating). The author uses the literary prototypes of Jenny l'Ouvrière
and Mimi Pinson as useful references for readers to situate the current
labor unrest in its proper historical context: *midinettes* once were flip-
pant and unengaged; since the war, they no longer accept their exploitation. Thus even keen supporters of garment trade activism reified a
pop-cultural representation of workingwomen as dainty eaters, senti-
mental consumers, and quiescent citizens. This is a pointed illustration
of the way that the *midinette* archetype could bolster and obscure political action. Here striking garment workers are depicted as heroically
overcoming their historical lethargy, giving the 1917 actions increased
weight while eclipsing the very real contributions of female labor activists in the decade before and ignoring the role that such images might
have played in suppressing garment trade activism in years past.

Mary Lynn Stewart suggests that by the 1930s garment workers
"encountered less criticism . . . about inappropriate clothing and
sexual behavior" and attributes this shift to "increased labor organization and militancy." I offer that a pervasive pop-cultural investment in

---

122 "Les grèves féminines parisiennes: Et on s'en fout . . . On f'ra la s'maine anglaise," press
clipping, May 24, 1917, Archives Nationales, F/22/170, Grèves, 1908, 1916, 1918. These strikes,
which seem to have begun with workers in the Maison Jenny, ultimately included thousands of
workingwomen demanding the *semaine anglaise* (a workweek that included an obligatory half-day
off on Saturday afternoon, instead of only Sunday off) and a daily allowance to help with the cost-
of-living increases of the war years. Paul Delmet (1862–1904) was a composer of popular Parisian
songs at the turn of the century.

a nostalgic notion of Parisian garment workers as attractive coquettes was stimulated in the decades straddling the war as a means of managing this increased labor action by Parisian women.[123] Focus on the moral perils of the lunch hour, while grounded in a picturesque fantasy of the *midinette*, may have made female labor militancy more palatable. Indeed, by 1917 many employers were providing midday meals for their employees, indicating some progress in this regard since the first significant *midinette* strikes in 1901.[124] The preceding analysis, however, also suggests that the ubiquitous appearance of an adorably undereating young workingwoman somewhat neutered the perceived threat of working (female) bodies across the political spectrum at precisely a time when visions of proletarian misery were poised to bring significant change in France. What is more, the lunching *midinette* was an especially potent and commercially attractive version of the *femme nouvelle*— a young woman who bolstered the consumer economy with both her labor and her acquisitiveness by a seemingly effortless denial of troubling female hunger and desire.

123 Stewart, *Dressing Modern Frenchwomen*, 99.

124 "Les grèves féminines parisiennes." See also "Les ouvrières en grève," *L'humanité*, May 24, 1917.

La Capitale de la Faim: Black Market
Restaurants in Paris, 1940–1944

Kenneth Mouré

Abstract   *Black market restaurants thrived in Occupied Paris. German authorities castigated the French for their failure to shut them down, claiming that profiteers consumed luxurious fare in restaurants at the expense of hungry Parisians waiting in marketplace queues. Paris restaurants merit closer attention for the evidence they provide on the conflicts and relative powers in Franco-German "collaboration," for the glaring inequities in food distribution exemplified by these restaurants that discredited Vichy food management policies, and for the creativity of Parisian restaurant owners in finding methods of alternate supply and service for their clients. The restaurants provide material for a case study to highlight the development of black markets and the frustration of control efforts, the reasons for popular sentiments of injustice in food supply, and the critically important role of German demands in the development of black market activity.*

Keywords   marché noir, *restaurants, economic controls, food supply, Occupation*

Food is a weapon of war.[1] Access to food through rations, coupons, queues, friends, and black markets rapidly became the most important concern in Parisians' daily lives during the German Occupation. Restaurants, a key part of food distribution in a city dependent on supplies from rural France, underwent acute crises. Some flourished; most struggled to survive. Restaurant experience during the Occupation provides a revealing perspective on food problems in Occupied France: how and why black market activity thrived, the structure of

Kenneth Mouré is professor of history at the University of Alberta. Since publication of his *The Gold Standard Illusion: France, the Bank of France, and the International Gold Standard 1914–1939* (2002) he has been working on economic controls, food supply, and black markets in wartime France, with recent articles published in the *Historical Journal*, the *Journal of Contemporary History*, *French History*, and *French Politics, Culture and Society*.

   This article was first presented as a conference paper for a panel honoring the work of Dominique Veillon at the Western Society for French History annual conference in Portland, Oregon, in 2011. The author would like to thank Sara Norquay, Erika Rappaport, and Jack Talbott for their helpful comments and to thank Bertram Gordon, Erica J. Peters, and the editors of and referees for *French Historical Studies* for their valuable guidance in revising the article for this special issue on food in French history.

   1 See Lizzie Collingham, *The Taste of War: World War Two and the Battle for Food* (London, 2011), which focuses on Britain, Germany, the United States, and Japan. See also Gesine Gerhard, "Food and Genocide: Nazi Agrarian Politics in the Occupied Territories of the Soviet Union," *Contemporary European History* 18, no. 1 (2009): 45–65; and Gerhard, "Food as a Weapon: Agricultural Sciences and the Building of a Greater German Empire," *Food, Culture and Society* 14, no. 3 (2011): 335–51.

French Historical Studies, Vol. 38, No. 2 (April 2015)   DOI 10.1215/00161071-2842590

unequal access to scarce goods and the social divisions this caused, and the prevailing German influence on how the food economy was administered. The inequities in access to food supplies show the unbalanced structure of Franco-German "collaboration" and the French complicity in serving German demands.

Germans appreciated Parisian haute cuisine. Paris had been the locus for a major transformation of the cooking, serving, and evaluation of fine dining for a paying public in the eighteenth and nineteenth centuries, creating the standards for a new cuisine and a new culture of dining in public that would influence culinary practice throughout Europe and the world. The concepts, the customs, and the language of haute cuisine were distinctly French, from the "invention of the restaurant" and the organization of the professional kitchen to the critical language and the standards of practice for preparing food, designing menus, and reviewing food experience.[2] When the Germans arrived in Paris in 1940, food and sex were foremost in the minds of many soldiers, and the German authorities had to regulate access to restaurants and brothels, including the overlap between the two kinds of service.[3] Given food rationing in Germany, it is indicative of their respect for French food that a guide, translated for soldiers in 1943, told them regarding Paris restaurants that Germans could "live as God in France."[4]

Reichsmarschall Hermann Göring found French cuisine excellent, too excellent in fact for the French. He complained in 1942 that the French were eating too well, particularly in luxury restaurants: "Mais je n'ai pas envie que les Français puissent y mettre les pieds. L'excellente cuisine de chez Maxim's doit nous être réservé. Trois ou quatre de ces boîtes pour les officiers et pour les soldats allemands, c'est parfait, mais rien pour les Français" (But I don't want the French to set foot there. The excellent cuisine chez Maxim's should be reserved for us. Three or four of these places for German soldiers and officers, that's fine, but nothing for the French). Germans dominating the most pres-

2 See Priscilla Parkhurst Ferguson, *Accounting for Taste: The Triumph of French Cuisine* (Chicago, 2004); Susan Pinkard, *A Revolution in Taste: The Rise of French Cuisine, 1650–1800* (Cambridge, 2009); Rebecca L. Spang, *The Invention of the Restaurant: Paris and Modern Gastronomic Culture* (Cambridge, MA, 2000); Amy B. Trubek, *Haute Cuisine: How the French Invented the Culinary Profession* (Philadelphia, 2000); and, on the development of Michelin guides and their star rating system for restaurants in the 1930s, Stephen L. Harp, *Marketing Michelin: Advertising and Culture in Twentieth-Century France* (Baltimore, MD, 2001), 245–56.

3 Allan Mitchell, *Nazi Paris: The History of the German Occupation, 1940–1944* (New York, 2008), 14–16; Henri Michel, *Paris allemande* (Paris, 1981), 48, 82; Insa Meinen, *Wehrmacht et prostitution sous l'Occupation (1940–1945)* (Paris, 2006).

4 Pierre Andrieu in Dore Ogrizek, ed., *Paris, Frankreich und Provinzen* (1943), quoted in Bertram M. Gordon, "*Ist Gott Französisch?* Germans, Tourism and Occupied France, 1940–1944," *Modern and Contemporary France* 4, no. 3 (1996): 288. The phrase was popularized by Friedrich Sieburg, *Gott in Frankreich? Ein Versuch* (Frankfurt am Main, 1929), published in translation as *Dieu est-il français?* (Paris, 1930).

tigious French restaurants would demonstrate the victory of German power over French culture. And their restaurants, he claimed, were full of black market *trafiquants* feeding on their gains from overcharging Germans. It reminded him of Berlin in 1919, when war profiteers gorged in fine restaurants while the people starved, "avec cette difference que le peuple français n'a pas faim" (with this difference, that the French people aren't hungry).[5] But French citizens were hungry. The German writer Ernst Jünger, who often dined in the best restaurants during his long sojourn in Paris, had a better sense of the inequities in access to food. He commented on a lunch at the Tour d'Argent, in July 1942: "On a l'impression que les personnes attablées là-haut, consommant les soles et les fameux canards, voient à leurs pieds, avec une satisfaction diabolique, comme des gargouilles, l'océan gris des toits sous lesquels vivotent les affamés. En de telles époques, manger, manger bien et beaucoup, donne un sentiment de puissance" (You get the impression that the people at the tables up there, dining on sole and the famous ducks, look down with a diabolical satisfaction, like gargoyles, on the gray ocean of roofs under which the hungry struggle to survive. In such times, to eat, to eat well and abundantly, gives a feeling of power).[6]

The difference between luxury cuisine in the best restaurants and the quotidian fare for most Parisians was vast, and was a matter of power. For Charles Braibant, director of the Ministry of Marine's library, Paris in 1943 was "la capitale de la faim" (the capital of hunger). In his diary he commented, "Nous sommes tous de pauvres gens en ce moment, à part des collaborateurs et les trafiquants du marché noir" (We're all poor folk now, except for the collaborators and the black marketeers).[7] Jean Galtier-Boissière noted rising meal prices in his journal, including a restaurant on the Rue Cherche-Midi in October 1942 where he saw a table set for twelve: "Lorsque les convives s'installent, faces épanouies de profiteurs et belles femmes au luxe voyant, nous reconnaissons dans l'amphitryon: Jacques Doriot. Nous sommes loin des campagnes du *Cri du peuple* contre le marché noir et les restaurants à cinq cents francs par tête!" (When the guests settle in, the beaming faces of profiteers and beautiful women bathed in luxury, we recognize among them: Jacques Doriot. We're far from the campaigns in *Le cri du peuple* against the black market and restaurants at five hundred francs per person!).[8] Police reports on public opinion noted the

5 Göring talk to military commanders, Aug. 6, 1942, reproduced as "Göring et la 'collaboration': Un beau document," *Cahiers d'histoire de la guerre*, no. 4 (1950): 79.

6 Ernst Jünger, *Premier journal parisien: Journal II, 1941–1943* (Paris, 1980), 148.

7 Charles Braibant, *La guerre à Paris* (Paris, 1945), 262, 374.

8 Jean Galtier-Boissière, *Journal, 1940–1950* (Paris, 1992), 113.

frustrations of Parisians waiting in queues, with food shortages, rising prices, and an obvious flow of scarce and luxury foods to restaurants where the rich and the black market profiteers ate lavish meals. On June 16, 1941, for example, they observed that the middle and working classes saw consumers as divided in two groups: the wealthy, who could eat normally by means of the black market, and the rest, who could not afford essentials. Philippe Pétain's claims of equality in the face of restrictions were scorned.[9]

Those who could eat in the finest restaurants were visible exceptions to the "shared sacrifice" that rationing was supposed to provide: the collaborators and *trafiquants* mentioned by Göring, Braibant, and Galtier-Boissière; the German occupation forces for whom Göring wanted fine dining; and the very wealthy, whether French or foreign. Most Parisians spent long hours queuing for food and supplemented their rations by any means they could—trips to the country to buy food, packages sent by relatives and friends, barter and bargaining for extras, *le système D* (from *se débrouiller*, to improvise, to make do).[10] At the Hotel Majestic, headquarters for the Wehrmacht's economic administration, German officials decried black market restaurants as a scandal, increasing the suffering of ordinary Parisians who waited for rationed food in market queues. They rebuked French officials for their ineffectual control of restaurants, where French *trafiquants* and businessmen filled their plates with no concern for ration quantities or prices. Yet these officials did little for the ordinary Parisians: much of this black market system thrived under their protection.

The Germans claimed there were black market restaurants everywhere in Paris, diverting food from public markets. French officials knew that price and rationing offenses were common practice in restaurants but disagreed on the origins of the problem and the measures needed to enforce compliance. Paris restaurants fostered a Franco-German conflict over food distribution and administrative authority that has received little historical attention.[11] The availability of food

---

9 Paris, Archives de la Préfecture de Police (hereafter APP), Situation de Paris, June 16, 1941.

10 Kenneth Mouré and Paula Schwartz, "On Vit Mal: Food Shortages and Popular Culture in Occupied France, 1940–1944," *Food, Culture and Society* 10, no. 2 (2007): 261–95; Mouré, "Food Rationing and the Black Market in France (1940–1944)," *French History* 24, no. 2 (2010): 262–82.

11 See Eric Alary et al., *Les Français au quotidien, 1939–1949* (Paris, 2006), 259–64; Alfred Sauvy, *La vie économique des Français de 1939 à 1945* (Paris, 1978), 132–33; and Hervé Le Boterf, *La vie parisienne sous l'Occupation, 1940–1944 (Paris bei Nacht)*, vol. 2 (Paris, 1975), 107–50, with many factual errors. Fabrice Grenard treats food supply scandals with no specific attention to the black market restaurants in *Les scandales du ravitaillement: Détournements, corruption, affaires étouffées en France, de l'Occupation à la guerre froide* (Paris, 2012) and gives minor attention to restaurants in *La France du marché noir (1940–1949)* (Paris, 2008), 37–39. See also the limited coverage in Paul Sanders, *Histoire du marché noir, 1940–1946* (Paris, 2001), 140–43; and Richard Vinen, *The Unfree French: Life under the Occupation* (New Haven, CT, 2006), 216. Restaurants receive only passing men-

and the consumer practices to find, buy, and consume (or hoard) food are fundamental to "the practice of everyday life" and the politics of consumer purchases and use of goods.[12] Food acquisition, politics, and everyday life are particularly important in the popular responses to shortages, challenging the authority and the legitimacy of the state in situations of conflict and war.[13] In Occupied France food scarcity, consumer strategies to obtain food in addition to ration quantities, and popular protests against shortages, particularly by women, have been significant in regional studies attentive to the politics of everyday life.[14] Restaurants played an important role in urban food culture for the numbers they served, their visibility, and their priority for official supplies. In black market restaurants, with their daily practices structured to evade state controls, the prices they charged excluded most Parisians.

Paris restaurants merit closer attention for four reasons. First, restaurant controls were a matter for recurrent conflict between German authorities and French administrators and demonstrate the power imbalance and the hostility in negotiating "collaboration." Second, the complexity of restaurant regulation and enforcement shows the difficulties, indeed the near impossibility, of managing an effective regulatory regime for food in Occupied France. Third, the importance of food for survival, the inequities in access, and the differences between the luxury menus in the best Paris restaurants and the paltry fare available to ordinary Parisians illustrate how food was a cause for deep economic discontent, discrediting the Vichy regime. Social tensions increased, support for Vichy eroded, and the shortages and inequities incited powerful resentments. Fourth, the menus and the systems for alternate supply in black market restaurants show the importance of German

---

tion in Mitchell, *Nazi Paris*. Restaurants in other European countries in wartime have received little attention but did offer privileged access to scarce food supplies and functioned as important venues for black market activity.

12 Michel de Certeau, *The Practice of Everyday Life*, trans. Steven Randall (Berkeley, CA, 1984).

13 This is true particularly for World War I. For Germany, see Belinda J. Davis, *Home Fires Burning: Food, Politics, and Everyday Life in World War I Berlin* (Chapel Hill, NC, 2000); for Austria, Maureen Healy, *Vienna and the Fall of the Habsburg Empire: Total War and Everyday Life in World War I* (Cambridge, 2004). Russia during the war and the early years of the Bolshevik Revolution has been well covered; see esp. Mary McAulay, *Bread and Justice: State and Society in Petrograd, 1917–1922* (Oxford, 1991). For later experience in the Soviet Union, see Sheila Fitzpatrick, *Everyday Stalinism: Ordinary Life in Extraordinary Times; Soviet Russia in the 1930s* (Oxford, 1999); and Julie Hessler, *A Social History of Soviet Trade: Trade Policy, Retail Practices, and Consumption, 1917–1953* (Princeton, NJ, 2004).

14 Dominique Veillon, *Vivre et survivre en France, 1939–1947* (Paris, 1995); Robert Zaretsky, *Nîmes at War: Religion, Politics, and Public Opinion in the Gard, 1938–1944* (University Park, PA, 1995); Miranda Pollard, *Reign of Virtue: Mobilizing Gender in Vichy France* (Chicago, 1998); Lynne Taylor, *Between Resistance and Collaboration: Popular Protest in Northern France, 1940–45* (London, 1999); Robert Gildea, *Marianne in Chains: In Search of the Occupation of France 1940–45* (London, 2002); Shannon Fogg, *The Politics of Everyday Life in Vichy France: Foreigners, Undesirables, and Strangers* (Cambridge, 2009).

demand and the resourcefulness of Paris *restaurateurs* in finding food
and evading controls, for motives ranging from practical strategies for
survival to unprincipled greed for profit.

The Restaurant Control Regime

Paris restaurants before the war served four to five hundred thousand
meals per day. In February 1940 the state limited the number of servings and the quantities of meat and butter served in restaurants, but it
was in the summer and autumn of 1940 that restrictions became essential to manage food shortages. Meat deliveries to the Paris slaughter-
house at La Villette fell precipitously after the French defeat. A November 1940 evaluation stated bluntly with regard to meat supplies that
"les Restaurants ne peuvent plus s'approvisionner, doivent ou simpli-
fier dangereusement leurs menus ou s'adresser au marché noir" (Restaurants can no longer get provisions and must either severely restrict
their menus or resort to the black market).[15] The invasion and the German occupation disrupted the harvest, imports, transport, and stor-
age. Fixed prices in Paris in 1940 were lower than those that farmers
could get in other markets or by selling the food they produced at
the farm. The ministry of industrial production suggested a regime of
higher prices in Paris, but this would have required a huge price control staff. Price and enforcement policy developed on an ad hoc basis,
dealing with problems as they became obvious, with limited resources.
The key issues were the purchase and transport of food to cities, price
inequities, and departmental authorities hoarding supplies to meet
local needs.

French officials assumed that shortages would be temporary. The
national food rationing system imposed in September 1940 acqui-
esced to German demands in exchange for a promise to restore French
authority over food stocks and distribution.[16] Shortages, fixed prices,
transport difficulties, and the German requisitions and purchases from
a declining output fostered an extensive black market. Direct purchases
by German soldiers in the first months of Occupation were encouraged as a form of victory celebration and to buy up French consumer
amenities that had become rare in Germany. German purchasing benefited from a deliberate undervaluation of the franc (twenty francs per
mark when its purchasing parity was twelve) and charging tribute as
"occupation costs"—initially four hundred million francs (twenty mil-

---

[15] Paris, Archives Nationales (hereafter AN), AJ 41 2147, "Situation des restaurants à Paris,"
report by Colonel de Mazerat, sent by Minister of Industrial Production to Minister of Agriculture
and Food Supply, Nov. 8, 1940.

[16] Mouré, "Food Rationing," 265–68.

lion marks) per day. German soldiers received forty francs per day to spend on French goods; shopkeepers and farmers were required to sell to them.[17] Prefect reports and diaries in 1940 tell of massive purchasing of meat, dairy products, and clothing scarce in Germany: stories of twelve-egg omelets and of lingerie stores having their shelves stripped bare.[18]

Initial measures in June 1940 froze prices and limited restaurant meals to three courses, with set days on which no meat or alcohol could be served.[19] Fresh cream and butter could be served in cooked foods only; coffee could not be served after three p.m. To clarify the differences in the prices, quantities, and qualities of menus offered in restaurants, a decree of May 2, 1941, established four categories of restaurant and fixed the prices, the content, and the quality of courses in all meals. The prices ranged from a maximum of eighteen francs for the lowest-quality, category D restaurants, to a maximum of fifty francs in category A establishments. Better than A, a category "exceptionnel" (E) was added on July 25 at German demand, to allow menus charging up to seventy-five francs.[20] In addition, a few select Paris restaurants were designated as "hors catégorie" (HC), with no limits on their menus and prices; these restaurants were supposed to serve both German and French customers.[21] All restaurants (except HC establishments) were required to post their menus in advance of the meals, to keep a record of each day's menus, and to provide customers with written bills specifying the content and the cost of the meal they had consumed. This would provide written proof for the clients and the controllers that the rules had been observed. All restaurants were required to collect tickets for the rationed foods consumed.[22]

Obtaining food was the major problem for all categories of restaurant. Official supplies offered little choice. A restaurant owner

17 Louis Franck, *French Price Control from Blum to Pétain* (Washington, DC, 1942), 54.

18 In AN, AJ 41 388, Oct. 19, 1940, for example, the prefect talks of massive purchases of meat and dairy goods; comments in diaries on German soldiers buying all they can include Gitou Vallotton and Annie Vallotton, *C'était au jour le jour: Carnets (1939–1944)* (Paris, 1995), 100.

19 APP, BA 1806, decree of June 18, 1940.

20 Savigny-le-Temple, Centre des Archives Economiques et Financières (hereafter CAEF), B 49757, records Ministry of Finance discussions of the restaurant categories with German officials. The price ranges permitted for each class were for class D, up to 18 frs; class C, 18 frs 10 to 25 frs; class B, 25 frs 10 to 35 frs; class A, 35 frs 10 to 50 frs; and class E, 50 frs 10 to 75 frs. The German request for category E restaurants is in "Extrait du résumé des pourparlers de 6 au 12 juin," AN, AJ 41 184. On January 31, 1942, twenty-six restaurants in Paris were classed as *exceptionnel*, including the Ritz; AN, AJ 40 784, Guillard and Serre to Gerhardt, Feb. 3, 1942.

21 AN, AJ 41 184, and AN, AJ 40 785, for the documentation on creation of this category of restaurant.

22 In Britain restaurant meals did not require ration tickets and until March 1942 were not subject to price controls. They offered an important supplement to the rations in Britain, as well as opportunities for black market profit. Ina Zweinger-Bargielowska, *Austerity in Britain: Rationing, Controls, and Consumption, 1939–1955* (Oxford, 2000), 166–67.

explained the difficulties in detail in 1943, using the example of a category A restaurant that served one hundred dinners each day, thus twenty-six hundred dinners in the month. In May 1943, official supplies would provide one hundred kilos of potatoes, sixty eggs, one hundred kilos of cauliflower, ten kilos of *conserve de tomates*, two allotments of fifteen kilos of fish, and nine kilos of meat per week. This would be sufficient to feed nine hundred diners; the owner would need to find other sources to feed the remaining seventeen hundred.[23] The price controls made it impossible for owners to raise meal prices when their food costs increased, a matter about which they made frequent complaint.[24] Restaurant survival required purchasing from unofficial sources, at black market prices, and then disguising the extra charges needed to cover costs. The most common practice was to give two bills for each meal, an official bill charging the legal price, and a second bill with additional costs and extra-to-menu supplements. Some restaurants gave a two-part bill with the extra charge portion destroyed after payment. They also overcharged for alcohol to cover the higher costs of the food.[25] Liliane Schroeder, dining with her mother in a category A restaurant in 1941, was able to order extra *haricots blancs* with her meal; the bill charged them for liqueurs, and they were told, "Les liqueurs, c'est les haricots" (The liqueurs, that's the beans).[26] Controls were ignored or evaded from the start. In February 1941 the contrast was already stark between the unrestricted meals served to the nouveaux riches in black market restaurants and the meager rations handed to housewives after standing in queues for hours.[27]

Restaurant owners had to find food outside official supply depots and develop methods to circumvent the legislation on menus, quantities, and prices.[28] The most frequent restaurant offenses were for overcharging, serving food not listed on the menu, serving larger portions than allowed, possession of food stocks with no bill of sale (meat, sugar, and butter were the most common), and serving meat on days and at times not permitted. An extended restaurant control operation

23 CAEF, B 49756, exposé de M. René Laffin, 1943.
24 CAEF, B 49756, contains many notes on this in 1943 and 1944.
25 AN, AJ 40 784, De Sailly to Directors, July 2, 1942, Annexe IV.
26 Liliane Schroeder, *Journal d'Occupation: Paris, 1940–1944* (Paris, 2000), 94.
27 Galtier-Boissière, *Journal*, Feb. 13, 1941. He noted that for Germans and their friends there were no restrictions: "Les beefsteaks interdits sont dissimulés sous des œufs sur le plat. Clientèle de nouveaux riches. . . . Le richard triomphe dans *l'Ordre nouveau*. Avec du fric, beaucoup de fric, on peut toujours s'en fourrer jusque là, pendant que les ménagères font des heures de queue sous la neige, pour décrocher un tronçon de rutabaga" (Forbidden beef steaks are hidden under eggs on the plate. A clientele of nouveaux riches. . . . The fat cat triumphs in the New Order. With dough, lots of dough, you can stuff yourself to the gills, while housewives spend hours in line in the snow to get a chunk of turnip).
28 CAEF, B 49516, "Rapport mensuel sur l'activité du Service départemental de Contrôle Economique de la Seine pendant le mois de décembre 1943."

in early 1941 found infractions in nearly half the restaurants checked. Most were restaurant owners trying to satisfy their clients by offering foods "necessary to their commerce," bought on the black market. They charged extra to cover their increased costs and often drew little profit.[29] Paris police observed in November 1941 that if rationing measures were strictly observed, many restaurants would have to close.[30] Illicit practices were widespread, but proof for most offenses was difficult, as restaurants did not keep accurate records of commerce for which they could be fined or shut down and learned to store black market supplies off restaurant premises.[31]

Responsibility for restaurant supervision was shared by three agencies. The Paris police (*répression des fraudes*) paid increasing attention to price and ration violations, noting of their increased surveillance in April 1941 that they had found 2,176 infractions in recent weeks and would pay particular attention to *restaurants de luxe*.[32] The Service des Contrôle des Prix, an arm of the Ministry of Finance that became the Contrôle Economique in 1942, monitored prices and rationed quantities.[33] The Ravitaillement Général held responsibility for food supply and ration infractions. The staff available for verifications was not large: there were more than ten thousand restaurants in Paris and its suburbs, and the police and the Contrôle Economique normally had only a few agents attending to restaurant controls.

The restaurant owners, staff, and clients shared a common interest in providing meals that violated price and rationing rules and resisted the enforcement of controls. Routine failure to post accurate menus or to keep record of meals served and supplies purchased meant that controllers often fined owners for the poor state of their record keeping rather than for the offenses they had failed to document. Owners and staff developed strategies to protect their commerce: to stall controllers when they arrived, to hide black market purchases, to take meat from customers' plates or remove kitchen supplies from the premises. At least one restaurant kept a guard at the door to delay the entry of controllers. Because infractions for serving controlled items and for overcharging for the meals happened sequentially, controllers found they

29 CAEF, B 49757, note dated 1941 on control operations in the Paris region beginning Mar. 31.

30 APP, BA 1808, note of Nov. 29, 1941.

31 CAEF, B 49598, contains reports on the difficulties in finding evidence in known black market restaurants in 1943.

32 APP, Situation de Paris, Apr. 21, 1941.

33 On the history of the Contrôle Economique, see Fabrice Grenard, "L'administration du contrôle économique en France, 1940–1950," *Revue d'histoire moderne et contemporaine* 57, no. 2 (2010): 132–57. I use the name Contrôle Economique as shorthand for its changing official titles (it was the Direction Générale du Contrôle Economique [DGCE] from June 1942 to February 1944 and from November 1944 to April 1946).

Figure 1 "Today, I'd advise sticking to the regular menu." *Devant le marché noir* (Paris, 1943), collection of Dominique Veillon

could catch only one or the other category of offense. By sudden entry into a restaurant they could catch some offenses in the act, but evidence was needed for the menus offered, the quantities of food served, and the prices charged at the end of the meal. The full range of offenses could be observed and punished only if the controller was present as a seemingly legitimate customer during the entire meal (fig. 1).

Although German authorities demanded tight control of Paris restaurants, they provided little support and resisted enforcement in establishments serving German diners. They insisted on the cate-

gory "exceptionnel" for restaurants authorized to charge from fifty to eighty francs per meal, as well as that the category of luxury restaurants be exempt from controls in serving high German officials and their distinguished guests.[34] In May 1941 Elmar Michel, head of the Wehrmacht economic administration at the Hôtel Majestic, proposed the creation of ten to fifteen such restaurants, which he claimed would be in the interest of both French and German clients. The proposal was contested throughout the summer, with French officials objecting to the lack of controls and asking how these restaurants could be supplied without increasing the demands on insufficient food supplies and encouraging the growth of the black market. They finally agreed to allow six luxury restaurants exempt from quantity and price controls to serve Germans and their guests. The initial list included Maxim's, Lucas Carton, Lapérouse, La Tour d'Argent, Drouant, and the Ritz.[35] Controllers' duties would be limited to verification that each restaurant reported the number of clients it served and that ration tickets were collected.[36] The two sides argued over who would supply these restaurants to prevent an increase in black market activity. The French finally agreed to do so on a trial basis. They insisted that high profits in these restaurants in the absence of price controls should be compensated by a "special contribution" of 10 percent of the restaurants' receipts to the Secours National.[37]

HC restaurants served meals that could run to more than one thousand francs per person, made available a wide range of luxury foods, and showed contempt for the control regime.[38] Maxim's customers were said to consume more than ten thousand bottles of champagne per week. The Ritz played host to Table Ronde lunches that brought together German and French economic elites once every three weeks from February 1941 to October 1942, intended to foster economic collaboration (and known to Ritz staff as "déjeuners de la collaboration"—collaboration lunches). French and German guests were seated alternately at two round tables; they were charged 200, and later 250, francs for the meal (for "simple fare," according to one guest), and they were expected to give ration tickets for the food they consumed.

34 AN, AJ 41 184, discussions of May 28 and 30, 1941. Initially Germans wanted one hundred to two hundred restaurants in the E category; at the end of June they had reduced this request to fifty, and the French were willing to allow twenty-five; they compromised at forty: "Compte-rendu: Réglementation des prix des restaurants," June 27, 1941. Likewise the Germans, who at first had asked for a maximum price per meal of eighty francs, compromised at seventy-five.

35 AN, AJ 41 184, Michel to Barnaud, Oct. 7, 1941.

36 CAEF, B 49757, Secrétaire d'Etat de Ravitaillement to Président du Comité d'Organisation Professionnelle de l'Industrie Hotelière, Nov. 10, 1941.

37 AN, AJ 41 184, first discussed in conversations on Oct. 18, 1941.

38 AN, AJ 40 785, contains prices for menu items and wine in the HC restaurants in July 1943.

French guests were often unwilling or unable to do so, and the organizers arranged for the necessary coupons to be supplied by the Hôtel Majestic.[39]

Beyond these six, the Germans shielded many well-known restaurants and clubs whose service they wanted, and which they permitted to remain open beyond normal restaurant hours. One such was Marcel Jamet's renowned brothel, the One Two Two. Although not requisitioned by the Germans, it was patronized by them and by the French Gestapo. Jamet had no trouble obtaining German permits for vehicles, fuel, and the transport of rationed food and alcohol: "Le capitaine (Radecke), qui adorait la bonne cuisine, n'était que trop heureux de nous rendre ce service qui lui permettrait de venir gueuletonner au 122" (Captain Radecke, who adored good food, was only too happy to do us this favor, which would allow him to come and eat to his heart's content at the 122). Food and liquor were abundant. Fabienne Jamet claimed she never drank so much "real" coffee as during the Occupation.[40] The Hotel Claridge, off-limits to French clients until July 1942, was found on July 30 to serve meals averaging three hundred francs per person, to serve butter and desserts not permitted in restaurants, and to have nearly seven hundred kilos of meat lacking the health stamp provided in state slaughterhouses. The German official who accompanied the French inspectors informed them the next day that there would be no penalties and no report written on the control operation.[41] At La Coupole on the Boulevard du Montparnasse, the dining rooms upstairs served four hundred Germans a day, with a separate entrance and provisioning by German services.[42]

The exemption for the six HC restaurants ended in June 1942. It had been criticized from the outset, particularly by other restaurants.[43] French authorities complained that in addition to these six, another eleven Paris restaurants escaped their control because Germans obstructed French control efforts and allowed open violation of

39 AN, F 12 9559, report by Sûreté inspector René Gatel, June 14, 1945; report by Bellec, Feb. 28, 1946; and interviews with guests who had attended the lunches. See also Annie Lacroix-Riz, *Industriels et banquiers sous l'Occupation: La collaboration économique avec le Reich et Vichy* (Paris, 1999), 438–41; and Philippe Burrin, *France under the Germans: Collaboration and Compromise*, trans. Janet Lloyd (New York, 1996), 258–59.

40 Fabienne Jamet, *One Two Two* (Paris, 1975), 125, 132.

41 AN, AJ 40 784, Secrétaire d'Etat de Ravitaillement to Dr. Reinhardt, Sept. 2, 1942.

42 Françoise Planiol, *La Coupole: 60 ans de Montparnasse* (Paris, 1986), 143–44.

43 AN, F 37 5, Comité Economique Interministériel, Dec. 19, 1941; and APP, Situation de Paris, Nov. 24, 1941, where the police noted that restaurant owners complained that these would increase inequities and black market activity. The police also reported that the Parti Communiste Français urged women to demonstrate in front of these restaurants and to take food from them for their children, but I have seen no reports of such demonstrations taking place. APP, BA 2093, note of Jan. 20, 1942.

the laws governing restaurant service.[44] The Germans proposed adding three restaurants to the HC group, now referred to as *restaurants libres* (free restaurants). The French feared that ending the HC privileges would simply diffuse German patronage, rendering control of other restaurants impossible. Facing strong French opposition, Michel decided that the six HC restaurants should return to the *catégorie exceptionnelle* effective July 15, 1942. He had refused to allow any public notice of the creation of the HC restaurants in October 1941. Now he required that the press give special attention to the end to their special HC status, well aware of the strong popular discontent caused by the privilege it accorded.[45] The dispute shows the appreciation on both sides that restaurant consumption demonstrated too visibly the privileges and the inequities that structured access to food.

The HC restaurants had received priority in the allocation of food arriving in Paris, causing resentment from other restaurant owners, as well as the public. In exchange for ending the HC category, Michel insisted that *catégorie exceptionnelle* restaurants be allowed to increase their maximum price to one hundred francs per meal. French authorities opposed this measure unless it would allow increased prices in all restaurants, as the rising food costs hurt all. Michel was interested in facilitating dining by Germans in the higher-quality restaurants, not French consumption.[46] Exceptional status under German control was restored to four restaurants in October 1942[47] and suspended again in April 1943. But their privileges did not need official exemption: German interference took place whenever controllers tried to enforce the rules being broken in serving Germans. The HC restaurants were the most visible sign of a deeper problem. Rations and price controls were adjusted to facilitate German exploitation and privilege rather than to promote equitable access to food.

The contrast between the lavish fare in black market restaurants and the miserable yield from official rations after long hours in queues added to public discontent with the Vichy regime. Police reporting on conversations in market queues in 1942 and 1943 regularly detailed the negative impact of inequities in access to food and the visible privileges in restaurants. Collective enterprises providing some public service

44 CAEF, B 49757; DGCE, "Note pour Monsieur l'Administrateur," Aug. 20, 1942; and DGCE, "Rapport au ministre sur les vérifications opérées par les Services de Contrôle Economique dans les restaurants parisiens," Aug. 28, 1942.
45 AN, AJ 41 184, summary of talks on May 4–6, 1942, and Michel to French authorities, June 18, 1942.
46 AN, AJ 41 184, Michel note of Aug. 4, 1942; Barnaud opposed increasing the category E prices in a letter to Michel on July 16, 1942.
47 CAEF, B 49757, Michel to Ministers of National Economy and Agriculture, Apr. 6, 1943. The four were Maxim's, La Tour d'Argent, Lapérouse, and Au Caneton.

were given priority in allocations of food that arrived in Paris. Hospitals, factory canteens, and restaurants all received their food allocations before supplies were delivered to markets for retailers and individual consumers. Police reports on the resentments this caused include, for example, comment on June 1, 1942, that consumers were unhappy with the way in which collectivities benefited from priority in distributing food supplies. Canteens, cooperatives, hospitals, and restaurants were serving meat, tripe, or fish at every meal, while the latter were *quasi-introuvables* (all but unfindable) from most retailers. "De sévères critiques sont toujours formulées contre les services du Ravitaillement et les Autorités Allemandes que l'on tient pour responsables, de la pénurie de produits alimentaires" (They consistently voice harsh criticisms of the food supply service and the German authorities, which they hold responsible for the food shortages).[48]

Evading Control

Which restaurants would be subject to control verifications, initially a matter of reputation and chance, was decided increasingly by evidence of black market traffic, as well as by denunciations submitted by a public angry about inequities and injustice.[49] Even the diners in black market restaurants were not necessarily happy customers, discontented with the shortages (increasingly seen as a result of poor state policy) and restaurant controls. The customers wanted better meals, were willing to pay, and resented state interference. The Germans demanded increased surveillance in 1942; it was implemented with full awareness that owners had become adept at hiding illicit traffic and that customers, if they were not German, should be subject to harsh penalties for their part in the "intolerable abuses" of the rationing system.[50]

The restaurants at the lowest price levels, categories C and D, had neither the resources nor the customer affluence to afford substantial black market activity, but they were nonetheless found to violate their price limits to cover food costs.[51] Their small-scale contraventions

---

48 APP, Situation de Paris, June 1, 1942.

49 Denunciations were an important part of state efforts to suppress black market activity. On denunciations under authoritarian governments, see Robert Gellately and Sheila Fitzpatrick, eds., *Accusatory Practices: Denunciation in Modern European History, 1789–1989* (Chicago, 1997). For France, see Laurent Joly, ed., *La délation dans la France des années noires* (Paris, 2012), esp. Fabrice Grenard, "La dénonciation dans la répression du marché noir," 139–61.

50 CAEF, B 49888, Note de service no. 297, "Contrôle des restaurants," May 31, 1943.

51 CAEF, B 49723, contains cases from 1943 for C and D class restaurants, charging from 120 to 300 francs for meals in C class restaurants authorized to charge up to 25 francs; CAEF, B 49757, "Rapport sur les vérifications effectuées dans les restaurants de Paris et de sa banlieue," July 13, 1942, explains that the limited means of their clients meant that these restaurants used the black market rarely and on a small scale.

— On n'aurait pas dû écrire les menus sur le dos des cartes d'avant guerre... (Dessin d'André François.)

Figure 2 "We shouldn't have written the menus on the backs of ones from prewar." *Ric et Rac*, Mar. 5, 1943. © The British Library Board, MF247N, 1943, p. 29

had little visibility and little impact. The better restaurants had greater potential for profit through the quality and quantity of black market foods they could offer, and some prided themselves on maintaining a "prewar menu." The phrase evoked an abundance and a quality desired by all, affordable by few, and prewar standards were a recurrent point of reference for wartime deprivation, from restaurant tables to school classrooms to newspaper cartoons (fig. 2).[52] Controllers caught only a fraction of the black market traffic, but enough to make clear the most common strategies for maintaining a prewar menu through black market purchasing. Those in favor with the Germans obtained access to food supplies through German officials, as had the Table Ronde lunches at the Ritz. Many restaurants purchased direct from producers to obtain sufficient meat, vegetables, dairy products, and alcohol to serve their clients. Transport was essential: many businesses, factories, and trucking firms used their vehicles for direct purchase, buying for their own kitchens, selling to their own staff and to restaurants.

The Banque de France was caught in such activity in July 1943. A Banque de France truck with authorization to transport used currency

[52] Pierre Audiat, *Paris pendant la guerre* (Paris, 1946), 244; Roger Vailland, *Playing for Keeps*, trans. G. Hopkins (Boston, 1948), 54; Benoîte Groult and Flora Groult, *Journal à quatre mains* (1962; Paris, 2002), 149, 418. For comparisons of wartime shortages with prewar abundance in schools, see Lucie Aubrac, *Outwitting the Gestapo*, trans. Konrad Bieber (Lincoln, 1994), 24–25; and Raymond Ruffin, *Journal d'un J3* (Paris, 1979), 70–72, 96–97.

notes back to Paris was stopped near Poitiers and found to be hauling 10 tons of sugar and 864 liters of eau-de-vie. The transport papers had been signed by the director of the Banque's staff buffet, which was now serving more than three times its prewar number of staff lunches. The press suggested that the Banque de France regularly purchased food in the countryside to sell at a huge profit in Paris. According to one account, the Banque was "l'une des plus importantes organisations de marché noir en France" (one of the most important black market organizations in France).[53] The central bank did not deserve this status, but the use of its trucks indicates a pervasive practice in French business. Canteens to serve office staff were common in many government administrations; René Laffin claimed the Banque was typical of a stream of illicit traffic supplying canteens for government offices that included the Ministry of Finance and the Prefecture of Police in Paris.[54] Truck drivers carrying food for cooperatives and canteens had the access to vehicles, fuel, and permits to buy and transport food that they could easily divert to destinations other than those authorized.[55]

Such transport was easier for the restaurants with a German clientele in the Occupation administration, the Wehrmacht, the SS, or the Organization Todt. They could obtain scarce goods, meat in particular, often purchased by military personnel and delivered by army trucks. A post-Liberation analysis of the vehicles and methods used to carry black market food to Paris noted that the new methods employed since the Liberation were the successors in supplying a black market "autrefois alimenté en grande partie par les camions allemands" (previously supplied mainly by German trucks).[56] Because the German trucks were not subject to French control, they left little trace in the records of the control administration. In April 1942 four controllers stopped a German truck carrying fifteen hundred kilos of pork and nine hundred kilos of mutton from the illicit slaughter of thirty hogs and twenty-eight sheep in the Seine-et-Marne. Although driven by a German soldier, the truck had been rented by French *trafiquants* to transport meat to Paris for distribution to restaurants.[57] A restaurant on the Rue de Berri was found to have 1,400 kilos of beef, 480 kilos of veal, and 11,000 eggs on

53 Paris, Archives de la Banque de France, 1060200101/71, and extensive press reports in CAEF, B 49602; quotation from *Aujourd'hui*, July 5, 1943.

54 CAEF, B 49756, exposé de René Laffin. For Vichy ministries' use of the black market to supply their staff, see Grenard, *Les scandales du ravitaillement*, 99–113.

55 Paris, Institut d'Histoire du Temps Présent, ARC 091, Fonds Victor Guillermin. Agendas and brief reference to this traffic are in Anne Thomazeau, "Un ingénieur français et son entreprise: Les hauts fourneaux de La Chiers pendant la Seconde Guerre mondiale" (mémoire de maîtrise en histoire contemporaine, Université de Paris X, 2001).

56 CAEF, B 57660, Cruse, "Note pour le ministre," May 5, 1945.

57 CAEF, B 49503, Commissaire Tissot report of Apr. 20, 1942.

the premises; the restaurant was closed for six months. The owner was interned by French authorities but then released by the Germans.[58] In January 1944 the gendarmerie stopped an army truck carrying three thousand kilos of meat in Aubervilliers, north of Paris. The driver was a French butcher delivering meat to Paris restaurants.[59] Restaurants were rarely mentioned in arrest records for the illegal transport of meat through the Department of the Seine-et-Oise, which encircled Paris (the Department of the Seine). The low numbers reflect the protection this traffic obtained from German authorities, not an absence of such traffic.[60] Officials estimated that 30 percent of the meat supply in France was slaughtered illicitly and sold on the black market by 1943; the Germans were major purchasers on the black market in addition to their official requisitions. In the intensified sweep to catch restaurant violations in the summer of 1942, the majority of the infractions involved meat consumption, the meat acquired illegally, most often with help from the German army.[61] Restaurants took advantage of the opportunities offered. When Parisians went without meat rations because markets were empty in September 1943, it took two weeks for meat to disappear from some restaurants.[62]

Most Paris restaurants in categories A, B, and E obtained substantial food supplies on the black market.[63] Although German connections were the most useful, French suppliers were employed in several ways, including sending family parcels, direct purchases in the countryside, and restaurant connections to rural producers. The use of *colis familiaux*, parcels to supply "family" needs, was widespread.[64] The parcels transported tons of food each day from rural producers to the cities, including to urban restaurants, using a variety of ruses to disguise the contents, volume, and purpose of the traffic: mislabeling contents, sending parcels from different post offices and train stations,

58 CAEF, B 49508, report of the Gouvernement Militaire de Paris, fifth bureau, June 27, 1945.

59 CAEF, B 49516, "Rapport mensuel sur l'activité du Service départemental du Contrôle Economique de la Seine pendant le mois de janvier 1944." Similar cases are cited in CAEF, B 49757, "Rapport sur l'action du Service dans le contrôle des restaurants," May 1, 1943.

60 On meat traffic in the Seine-et-Oise, see Noëmie Fossé, "Les acteurs du trafic et de la répression: Le marché noir de la viande et du bétail en Seine-et-Oise, 1940–1944" (mémoire de master 2 recherche en histoire, Université Paris VIII, 2008), 129–32.

61 CAEF, B 49757, "Rapport sur l'action," May 1, 1943. Of 2,895 restaurants found in violation, there were 1,504 food supply infractions, of which 1,479 were for serving meat or purchases of meat without proper receipts.

62 Braibant, *La guerre à Paris*, 285–86.

63 CAEF, B 49516, "Rapport mensuel . . . décembre 1943."

64 Sylvain Leteux, "Le commerce de la viande à Paris sous Vichy: Qui tire profit de la situation?," in *Les entreprises de biens de consommation sous l'Occupation*, ed. Sabine Effosse, Marc de Ferrière le Vayer, and Hervé Joly (Tours, 2010), 94–96; for more information on family parcels, see Veillon, *Vivre et survivre*, 173–76; Grenard, *La France du marché noir*, 111–13; Fogg, *Politics of Everyday Life*, 32–39.

and addressing them to restaurant employees or to residents in the restaurant's neighborhood.[65] The volume of traffic was immense. Alfred Sauvy estimated that 13.5 million *colis* sent in 1942 transported 279,900 metric tons of food;[66] his estimate appears to have been for *colis* of three to fifty kilos. Half as much again was shipped in smaller *paquets* of up to three kilos, mailed from rich agricultural regions.[67] The parcel traffic by post mainly carried food, with little regard for the rules (butter, in particular, was often shipped in this way).[68] Post office statistics show Paris receiving forty-five million such parcels in 1942 and seventy million in 1944.[69] Most were addressed to individuals, but they could serve as conduits to restaurants, as in the case of a restaurant on the Rue du Bac supplied by parcels from Saint-Saviol containing twenty to thirty kilos of meat, addressed to several of the café's waiters.[70] The Contrôle Economique noted in 1942 that parcels addressed to restaurant owners and their staff often supplied restaurants rather than feed the families of the addressees. Closer supervision was deemed essential to avoid "les abus constatés chez les restaurateurs" (the abuses recorded in restaurants).[71]

The examples from traffic caught by controllers provide a fragmentary glimpse of the variety of means employed. A woman arrested in August 1945 as the likely carrier of goods abandoned at the train station in Brive admitted to having made trips each month between Paris and Brive since 1941, and although she claimed the food she transported was for her personal consumption, her past record of carrying packages and her denial that the suitcases and packages that triggered her arrest belonged to her convinced the police that she was "une habituée du trafic clandestin" (a regular in illicit traffic), particularly for tobacco and pork.[72] An official working for the egg and poultry dis-

---

65 CAEF, B 49510, letter of Oct. 17, 1943.

66 Sauvy, *La vie économique des Français*, 134–35.

67 Kenneth Mouré, "'The Antechamber of the Black Market': *Colis familiaux* in Occupied France" (paper presented to the Western Society for French History, Banff, AB, Oct. 2012).

68 Sending butter by mail was forbidden in October 1942 but continued on a large scale. Some wrapped butter in cabbage leaves or packed it in ceramic pots surrounded by vegetables to insulate it; in hot weather, melting butter from parcels made a mess in rail and post office sorting depots. André Paul, "Histoire des PTT pendant la Deuxième Guerre mondiale (1939–1945)," 285–86 (manuscript, Bibliothèque Historique des Postes et Télécommunications, Paris); and Xavier de Guerpel, *1939–1945: Une certaine vie de château au bocage Normand; Témoignage d'un agriculteur* (Condé-sur-Noireau, 1973), 118.

69 AN, F 90 21627; in the last three months of 1943, *colis familiaux* received in Paris train stations numbered 5,444,358; CAEF, B 57659, letter to Taittinger.

70 CAEF, B 49529, Contrôle Economique notes, Aug. 1943; restaurant provisioning also reported in B 49511.

71 AN, AJ 40 784, Chef du Service de Contrôle Economique to MM. les Directeurs régionaux et départementaux, July 2, 1942.

72 Tulle, Archives Départementales de la Corrèze, 550 W 635, Commissaire de Police de Brive to the Directeur Départemental du Contrôle Economique, Aug. 10, 1945. The goods seized

tribution system was investigated in March 1942 for having used his position to divert eggs to restaurants, including having shipped 58,680 eggs (since the previous June) to one Paris restaurant on the Boulevard des Capucines.[73] A restaurant on the Rue de Sèvres relied on the family connections of its proprietress in Brittany for its meat supply.[74] A butcher on the Rue Marbeuf who supplied meat to Paris restaurants and to hotels requisitioned by the Germans had a farm in Calvados and German transport papers to authorize the transport of meat to Paris.[75] The scale of traffic evident in the cases of those caught suggests this traffic was very large and that much went undetected.

In June 1942 German authorities insisted that the French crack down on black market restaurants. German officials had suspended restaurant checks in Paris for six weeks in May–June 1942, probably because of conflict between French controllers and German diners. When controls resumed, the French were instructed to follow a German model of "massive" verifications, checking all restaurants in specific neighborhoods. Elmar Michel insisted on this in conjunction with the end to privilege for HC restaurants. In recent months, he claimed, black market offenses in restaurants had increased in number and severity. This could no longer be tolerated. With the ending of HC privileges, French authorities must act "avec la plus grande énergie" (with the greatest vigor) against all restaurants violating price and rationing regulations.[76]

The German method used massive sweeps through particular neighborhoods, checking all restaurants, using teams of controllers who would descend without warning on the targeted quarter, hoping to catch staff and clients off guard. Regions were divided into sectors with about thirty restaurants in each; teams of three agents would be deployed to check two or three restaurants. Each team would have a policeman, an economic controller, and a food supply official. To prevent collusion among agents and warning of restaurant owners, team composition would change each time, and the lists of restaurants to be checked were issued in a sealed envelope an hour before the operation was to begin, to be opened thirty minutes before the first inspection. The operations could involve up to two hundred agents.[77] The initial

included one rabbit, eight kilos of fresh meat, twenty kilos of lard, thirty liters of wine, nine kilos of oil, and fifteen kilos of tobacco.

[73] Rennes, Archives Départementales d'Ille-et-Vilaine, 118 W 74, Secrétaire d'Etat de Ravitaillement to Préfet Régional in Rennes, Mar. 9, 1942, and "Enquête" to investigate charges.

[74] Paris, Archives de Paris, Perotin, 3314/71/1/8 16, case no. 339.

[75] Ibid., case no. 342.

[76] CAEF, B 49757, Michel to Délégué Général aux Relations Economiques Franco-allemandes, June 18, 1942.

[77] CAEF, B 49757, DGCE note, n.d. [likely June 1942].

results, checking nearly 700 restaurants in Paris and its suburbs, found 190 in violation of regulations, mainly food supply offenses, particularly serving meat on days it was forbidden, serving larger quantities than permitted, and charging higher prices. Most infractions were in A and B category restaurants. These restaurants had wealthier clients, including commercial travelers who could locate, purchase, and deliver goods to the restaurants, and thus had better connections to sources of supply, as well as higher revenue. Given the high proportion of meat offenses (25 to 30 percent of restaurants served meat on *jours interdits*), the control service concluded that the black market offered great opportunities for purchasing meat.[78] News of the crackdown was published to broadcast the range and importance of the enforcement measures, as well as the names of the restaurants found in violation.

The initial results demonstrated widespread black market activity. Dr. Gerhard, an administrator under Michel, criticized French control efforts in August: abundant food for the rich in Paris restaurants, in contrast to the meager supplies available to the working classes waiting in market queues, was "scandalous" and had reached the ears of the Führer and Reichsmarschall Göring. If the French could not end these abuses, the German police would take charge.[79] Jean de Sailly, director of the Contrôle Economique, replied that the difference between respect for regulations in the Unoccupied Zone and the abuse in the Occupied Zone indicated that the problem was one of enforcement. The suspension of restaurant inspections in Paris by German order from May 4 to June 28, 1942, had caused an immediate surge in black market practice from which it was difficult to recover. German interventions obstructed French controllers and protected the networks of supply and the practice of abundant servings in restaurants known for their "bon repas," setting a poor example for the rest of Paris. De Sailly cited twenty recent examples, including Maxim's and the Hotel Claridge, and the impact of German protection in encouraging other restaurants to imitate the control violations, upsetting public opinion. To restore order, de Sailly proposed reducing the number of restaurants in Paris and its environs, tightening the requirements for provisioning, and establishing clear authority for enforcement by French officials.[80] Gerhard agreed, and Michel issued a memo to German authorities on August 31 to emphasize the need for cooperation with French authori-

---

78 CAEF, B 49757, "Rapport sur les vérifications," July 13, 1942.
79 CAEF, B 49757, "Rapport au ministre," Aug. 28, 1942.
80 Ibid.; his recommendation of restaurant closures and tougher sanctions repeated those suggested to him by the Contrôle Economique chief administrator for the Department of the Seine in July.

ties in tightening control and reporting and punishing the abuses in black market restaurants.[81]

The massive sweeps increased. From July 1942 to April 1943 French teams conducted seventy-four such sweeps to punish violations in Paris-area restaurants. They visited 17,569 restaurants. Nearly 3,000 were found in violation of controls, and 649 were punished with closures for periods ranging from one to three months (555 cases), with only 6 for longer than nine months. The initial results had been promising, with more than 30 percent of the restaurants checked in July and August found in contravention of rules. This rate fell off sharply as the number of restaurants checked increased. They had checked 342 restaurants in July and 450 in August. In September they checked 2,263; in October, 2,043; in November, 3,054. The percentage of restaurants in violation fell to 16–19 percent.[82] This decline reflected the scale of operations and the tactics restaurants found to resist control. No one claimed these results to be a success. Rather, black market supply to restaurants was recognized as extensive in response to customer demands that could not be met with official supplies. The sweeps could identify contraventions but did nothing to solve problems in the systems of supply.

The Contrôle Economique concluded that selective targeting of suspect restaurants was more effective in terms of the manpower deployed, public relations, and restaurant practice. The massive sweeps required calling in agents unfamiliar with restaurant controls and practices and training inexperienced agents and resulted in inept fieldwork and difficulty in concealing the impending sweeps. The interference in restaurants where regulations were observed gave controllers a bad public image. And the restaurants developed tactics to resist. Restaurant owners and staff quickly alerted customers and neighborhood cafés and took action to hide violations. "Il suffit qu'un seul restaurateur soit prévenu pour qu'immédiatement il alerte par téléphone tous ses collègues, et le contrôle massif s'avère inopérant" (It just takes one restaurant owner being warned for him immediately to warn all his colleagues by telephone, and the massive sweep is no longer effective). Some owners closed their restaurants if black market supplies could not be removed or concealed. The controllers reported 2,676 restaurants closed when they arrived, often with a sign posted on the door to claim: "Fermé pour manque de ravitaillement" (Closed for lack of food). All manner of actions were used to conceal infractions: delaying the con-

---

[81] AN, AJ 40 784, Michel memorandum, Aug. 31, 1942.
[82] CAEF, B 49757, "Rapport sur l'action," May 1, 1943.

trollers upon their entry into the restaurant, destruction of bills and receipts, hiding of supplies including moving them out of the restaurant (agents unfamiliar with the premises did not know how or where to guard against this), and concealing or rapidly consuming illicit helpings, with black market steaks gulped in haste or pocketed to eat later.[83]

In place of *contrôles massifs*, the Contrôle Economique advocated a return to targeted interventions in suspect restaurants. These had proved more successful when both practices were in use in early 1943; it had saved on manpower and increased the rate of violations found.[84] Rather than erupt into restaurants to catch infractions in progress, they suggested that controllers eat in the restaurants to observe what was served and how it was billed and paid. They also recommended requiring complete bills (inviting clients, via the press, to insist on this) and measures to punish the restaurant staff and customers, not just the owners, as they were complicit in the violations.[85]

Despite these recommendations, black market restaurants prospered. The German commitment to retreat from large-scale black market purchasing in 1943 reduced military purchases of supplies and luxuries without having a discernible impact on their restaurant use. Michel tried to link the German shift away from black market purchasing to harsher repression by the French, but closer coordination between French and German authorities and an end to German protection were essential to curb the restaurant activity. German authorities used their change in purchasing to blame the French for the continuing black market activity. There were at least two hundred restaurants in Paris, they asserted in April 1943, where one could eat as much as one wished. It was unacceptable for French civilians to violate controls with impunity when the German military would be subject to strict penalties. French controllers, they claimed, routinely warned the restaurants subject to control.[86] They insisted that their crackdown on German traffic must be matched by increased penalties for French offenders, including the death penalty for serving meat from the clandestine slaughter of livestock. In Paris restaurants "le marché noir est pratiqué sur une grande échelle" (the black market is practiced on a grand scale), and it was scandalous that this had not been suppressed.[87] After ten months of action by German design to suppress this activity, these complaints tes-

83 Ibid.

84 For the period surveyed, the large-scale sweeps checked 764 restaurants and found 134 in violation (17.5 percent); targeted raids checked 54 restaurants, with 15 found in violation (27.8 percent).

85 CAEF, B 49757, "Rapport sur l'action," May 1, 1943.

86 AN, F 37 4, "Entretien du 2 avril 1943 à l'Hôtel Majestic."

87 AN, AJ 41 98, "Entretien au Majestic du 6 mai 1943," and "Entretien du 29 avril 1943 au Majestic."

tified to the persistence of German demand for quality restaurant meals and to the role of continuing shortages and the inequities in wealth and privilege that sustained the black market restaurants.

The Disintegration of Control

The difficulties in controlling restaurants increased as official supplies contracted, black market networks grew, and rations were reduced in late 1943 and early 1944. As the Contrôle Economique observed in May 1943, the black market restaurant problem was fundamentally one of access to food: "Tous se plaignent de ne pouvoir satisfaire leur clientèle en raison des difficultés rencontrées pour leur ravitaillement" (All complain that they cannot satisfy their clients because of the difficulties in getting supplies). Category C and D restaurants often closed in evenings for lack of food and asked for higher allocations of potatoes, dried vegetables, and pasta. Category A and B restaurants relied on black market purchases to meet their customers' needs. All categories lied about the number of meals they served to increase their official allocations, which were never sufficient to feed the number of diners they reported. To collect more supplies, restaurants routinely claimed to serve more meals than they actually did. Those claiming to serve 400, 220, and 450 meals had in fact served 120, 80, and 95.[88] Owners agreed that only greater equity in supply and the ability to charge prices to cover their costs would allow them to function legally. Those serving the Germans continued to benefit from better access to supplies and protection from French controllers. Prefecture of Police reports showed violations caught and punished in about 30 percent of the restaurants they checked, demonstrating their continued success in targeting likely offenders.[89]

Below the category D restaurants, there was a notable effort to feed working-class Parisians. The state encouraged the development of workplace canteens that received permission for direct purchasing in the countryside and priority in food allocations. Abuse of these privileges was usually not in the canteens themselves, which were tightly controlled and provided minimal fare for workers, but in the opportunity for their drivers and managers to use their food access for additional black market activity. In December 1942 the state created *restaurants communitaires* to feed workers unable to afford restaurants. Thirty-two "rescos" opened in the Paris region in December 1942 and eight in Paris suburbs; by July 1943 there were three hundred rescos,

---

88 CAEF, B 49757, "Rapport sur l'action," May 1, 1943.
89 APP, B 1810, Direction de la Police Economique, weekly reports, Jan.–July 1944.

serving more than half a million meals a week and providing nearly 1.4 million cooked meals to take away.[90] They were intended for workers earning up to three thousand francs per month and charged on a sliding scale according to income, with dinners ranging from eight to sixteen francs.[91] They were closely watched to prevent abuse of their purchasing privileges.[92]

In the meantime, the state's attitude toward the restaurants, treating owners as crooks, turned commerce against the state. The Contrôle Economique in particular was despised, frequently criticized in the press, and denounced by restaurant owner René Laffin as "un véritable repaire de Racketters, de souteneurs, et de maître chanteurs" (a veritable den of racketeers, procurers, and blackmailers).[93] The public and the press, confused by the variety of control agencies, believed that controllers benefited from preferential treatment in restaurants. Food supply fraud by state officials, particularly in the Ravitaillement Général administration and in restaurant controls, was widely suspected and often reported in the press.[94]

Restaurants and controllers faced greater challenges in 1944. The German war effort on the Eastern Front increased demand for French resources. Allied bombing disrupted domestic supply and transport; black market networks increased their ability to pull supplies from official markets, and control efforts faltered with fewer resources to contain increasing black market activity.[95] In March 1944 most Paris restaurants closed for two or three days a week because of shortages. In April meat supplies to Paris were virtually nonexistent, fuel shortages threatened to close restaurants for three days a week, wood supplies were sufficient for only one-third of Paris bakeries, and municipal distress plans were developed to feed the millions of Parisians who would have no fuel to cook food in their homes.[96]

The Allied invasion on June 6 further disrupted food supply. The railways and the post office could not move food supplies from Normandy and Brittany, and rail and road traffic was endangered through-

90 APP, BA 1808, notes of May 11, 1943, and July 17, 1943; numbers of meals from note of Apr. 20, 1943. Audiat cites slightly lower numbers based on daily averages in *Paris pendant la guerre*, 243.

91 APP, BA 1808, "Comment fonctionnent les restaurants communautaires." The three-thousand-franc limit was for a single worker, with the limit raised by five hundred francs for each dependent.

92 CAEF, B 49888, Note de service no. 315, July 1, 1943; and APP, BA 1808, Apr. 22, 1943, note of seven rescos losing their status in Paris for having trafficked in food intended for clients.

93 CAEF, B 49756, "Exposé de M. René Laffin."

94 See Grenard, *Les scandales du ravitaillement*.

95 Grenard characterizes the Vichy administration as "totalement débordée" in *La France du marché noir*, 227–29.

96 APP, BA 1807, "Plan de détresse," and APP, Situation de Paris, Apr. 3 and 17, 1944.

out northern France. Trucks used to haul food were requisitioned for military use, as were fuel supplies (the city of Paris emergency plan for maintaining its food supply needed four to five thousand trucks to replace rail supplies). Family parcels that supplemented official rations could no longer be sent from departments in northern and western France.[97] Parisians did benefit from goods bought in the country-side and resold at black market prices in Paris by retreating German forces.[98] The city's distress plan called for the suspension of control enforcement; the director of the Contrôle Economique argued against this.[99] But controls were impossible to enforce; the need for food took precedence over following rules designed to distribute an organized food supply.[100] Black market restaurants continued their commerce, particularly when supplied and protected by German officials or the French Gestapo, who ignored controls and threatened the few control-lers who interfered with their meals.[101]

Liberation

Within days of Liberation, the Paris restaurants that benefited from German protection were targeted for closing. Enforcement had been virtually impossible through the summer; Contrôle Economique direc-tor Jean de Sailly wanted to reassert control and to track down and punish traffickers and profiteers. Controls were particularly impor-tant for food and necessities. He urged that every effort be made to gather evidence on wartime offenders protected by the Germans.[102] The price control administration for the Department of the Seine (the Paris region) began compiling a list of persons and establishments that had worked for German services, with details on the infractions and the German protection that shielded them from French prosecution. De Sailly sent the minister for the national economy an initial list of *tra-fiquants* who had German protection, urging rapid action, as it would become more difficult to punish them in the future. Those who had benefited financially from the Occupation, particularly in serving the Germans, were disguising their commerce and hiding their profits. Given the number of such cases and the need for prompt action, de

        97 CAEF, B 57659, "Note sur les prix au marché noir dans la région parisienne entre le 1er mai et le 25 juin 1944," June 29, 1944.
        98 Edmond Dubois, *Paris sans lumière, 1939–1945: Témoignages* (Lausanne, 1946), 197.
        99 CAEF, B 57659, "Note pour le ministre," July 1, 1944.
        100 CAEF, B 9860, Direction Générale du Contrôle Economique, *Rapport sur l'activité de la DGCE au cours de l'année 1944.*
        101 CAEF, B 49508, case of Restaurant Maury, Feb. 1944.
        102 CAEF, B 57659, Directeur Général de Contrôle des Prix to Directeurs régionaux de Con-trôle des Prix, Aug. 31, 1944.

Sailly proposed that he send successive lists, beginning with those who were "indiscutablement coupable ou dont l'attitude peut être considérée comme particulièrement scandaleuse" (indisputably guilty or whose attitude was particularly scandalous).[103]

On September 2 he sent the first in a series of lists of restaurants and businesses guilty of black market infractions and protected by the Germans. Because most of the restaurants had paid fines for ration infractions but had not been closed thanks to German interference, new legislation was needed to inflict a second penalty for the same offense.[104] The restaurants were closed for periods ranging from three months to two years, effective immediately. Some reopened under different auspices, as restaurants and clubs serving Allied soldiers or refugees. By the end of the year, de Sailly had cited more than one hundred restaurants and businesses for closure in the Paris region. The luxury restaurants that had briefly been *hors catégorie* were not included. These restaurants under German control, de Sailly explained, had been out of bounds to French controllers and thus had not been charged with black market offenses. While it might seem unfair to close restaurants over whom German authority had been indirect while leaving open those under official German control, these restaurants enjoyed a certain notoriety and contributed "à assurer la reputation de la capitale" (to assure the reputation of the capital).[105] The minister of food supply claimed the restaurants offered visitors "le témoignage du gout français" (the evidence of French taste) and would play the same role in food as did *maisons de grande couture* in the recovery of French fashion.[106]

Reestablishing control brought new problems, as supplies did not improve much, while public expectations rose and the salary increases to compensate workers for wage stagnation under Vichy (by 40 percent in September 1944) raised consumer demand.[107] De Sailly emphasized the importance of the controls on food transactions and warned of the need to resume controls gently, with tact and attention to the educational role of price controls.[108] Closing the restaurants protected

103 CAEF, B 49477, head of Contrôle des Prix in the Department of the Seine to Director of Contrôle des Prix, and the first list of forty restaurants, cabarets, and cafés to be closed, listing their offenses and the German protection provided; B 57659, DGCE, "Note pour Monsieur le Secrétaire Général à l'Economie Nationale," Aug. 30, 1944.

104 CAEF, B 49477, Jean de Sailly, "Note au ministre," Sept. 16, 1944, and decree to close restaurants issued Sept. 23, 1944.

105 CAEF, B 57659, "Note pour le ministre," Sept. 29, 1944.

106 Angoulême, Archives Départementales de la Charente, 2 W 95, Ministère du Ravitaillement, "Bulletin d'information no. 5," Dec. 27, 1944.

107 Michel-Pierre Chélini, *Inflation, état et opinion en France de 1944 à 1952* (Paris, 1998), 312–18.

108 CAEF, B 57659, Director General of Contrôle des Prix to regional directors of Contrôle des Prix, Aug. 31, 1944.

by the Germans had the support of the provisional government. More difficult was the need to control who could eat in restaurants. Allied servicemen had their own supply system and were not supposed to eat in French restaurants. But restaurants and cafés were a common destination for troops and the locus for a new black market in US Army goods.[109] The ban was widely violated, and controllers attempting to enforce it were ignored or threatened. The director of price controls in Paris and the director of the Police Economique both reported they were powerless to enforce the ban. The best they could do was notify the Allied command of the restaurants where abuses were common and hope that military police would intervene.[110]

Black market restaurants thrived in the post-Liberation circumstances of continuing shortages, restricted access to food and transport, and state controls weakened by reduced staff and resources. In the food economy, the Ravitaillement Général and Contrôle Economique were seen as creations of Vichy, now trying to sabotage the Liberation. The continued price, rationing, and control regimes were characterized as "Vichy continues."[111] This view, and the expectations that food availability would return to normal after the Germans were gone, increased conflict between controllers and those buying and selling goods. In a long analysis of restaurant supervision in August 1945, the Police Economique noted that the most common offenses had not changed: price infractions, unauthorized transport, and coupon and billing violations. But the black market restaurants were more difficult to catch, as they were suspicious of customers they did not know, admitting only customers they knew and trusted.[112] Traffic in meat, sugar, and wine continued with new opportunities to divert imported goods, creating scandals when abuses by officials were publicized in the press. By mid-1946 controls on restaurants had become all but unenforceable, although price and portion controls remained on the books. Price controls, even modified to allow supplements that raised the licit price for category A restaurant meals to two hundred francs, could not accommodate the rapid rise in food prices during the postwar inflation.[113] A slow improvement in food supplies, less emphasis on routine price vio-

109 Noëmie Fossé, "Les trafiquants de la Libération: Le commerce illégal des produits US Army en Seine-et-Oise; Vols, recels et marché noir" (paper presented to the Western Society for French History, Banff, AB, Oct. 2012).

110 CAEF, B 57659, "Note pour Monsieur l'Administrateur," Nov. 20, 1944, and "Note pour le ministre," Nov. 25, 1944.

111 Jacques Debû-Bridel, *Histoire du marché noir (1939–1947)* (Paris, 1947), 85; Grenard, *La France du marché noir*, 266–73.

112 CAEF, 5 A 28, "Activité de la Direction de la Police Economique pour la période du 1er au 15 août 1945," Aug. 16, 1945, and CAEF, B 49757, "Rapport au ministre," Aug. 28, 1945.

113 CAEF, B 49756, "Rapport sur la réglementation des restaurants," Aug. 20, 1946, and new regulations in a decree of Sept. 19, 1946, DGCE note no. 31.2414, Oct. 18, 1946.

lations, and the removal of the German layer of official interference all reduced the need for controls and enforcement. Increasing food supplies moderated inequities and in that way lessened the visibility of restaurants as a symbol for injustice in food allocation.

Conclusions

In a Paris that was for most citizens "the capital of hunger," black market restaurants allowed a privileged elite to eat very well. This elite included not just the Germans but the rich, the nouveaux riches, and the influential, including French officials, collaborators, and black market profiteers. The best restaurants offered sumptuous fare to those with money and power. German connections were a vital part of restaurant supply networks and protection from French controllers. Restaurants exempted from controls charged high prices and bought black market goods without concern for the law. The handful of restaurants where controllers had no power had been exempted to avoid disturbing their German clientele, but their diners were often French. In one of the short periods when these restaurants' immunity from control was suspended, French controllers visited several. They found that Maxim's, in particular, paid no attention to restaurant rules and that clients were predominantly French; "des gens qui paraissent appartenir à ce monde des affaires, né des circonstances économiques de l'heure présente" (people who seem to belong to the world of business born of the current economic circumstances).[114]

The "current economic circumstances" were German domination and an economy of exploitation. The people belonging to this business world were the collaborators and *trafiquants* evoked by many French observers, and by German officials all the way up the hierarchy from Paris-based administrators like Gerhard and Michel to Hermann Göring in Berlin. These luxury restaurants thrived under German protection from the controls the French were rebuked for failing to enforce. They were often supplied by German army purchasing and transport when they served German clients, and by a range of improvised supply systems for French clients who could afford to pay for better menus. A Contrôle Economique check on dinners served in Maxim's, Lapérouse, and La Tour d'Argent in October 1942 found the clientele to be mostly French. The menu at La Tour d'Argent followed rationing rules for menus and tickets and charged higher prices for alcohol. At Maxim's, customers rarely consulted a menu: "Chaque consommateur commande selon son désir, sans considération du nombre de plats, ni de la

---

114 APP, BA 1808, report of Oct. 30, 1942.

nature des mets servis; c'est ainsi que les enquêteurs ont vu apporter à certains clients du gigot de mouton, des steaks et de la volaille" (Each consumer orders what they wish, with no consideration for the number of courses or the nature of the food served; investigators have seen some clients be served leg of mutton, steaks, and poultry). Cheese and desserts followed, with liqueurs (on a day *sans alcool*), and the meal finished with pure coffee, unadulterated, and sugar.[115] Another Contrôle Economique report noted that clients did not patronize Lucas Carton for the *menu affiché*; the official menu had "nothing in common" with the meals served to customers eating partridge, poultry, and trout.[116]

But it is the restaurants below this level, the A and B restaurants serving a French clientele, that provide the more interesting perspective on restaurant experience, the black market, and adaptation in an economy of penury. Clients included not just collaborators and profiteers but *résistants* as well, who needed food as badly as others and often used restaurants for rendezvous. Jean Moulin authorized Daniel Cordier to use Resistance funds for the food they needed when Cordier observed that his men could not afford black market prices.[117] Most of these restaurants bought food and liquor on the black market and charged higher prices to cover their costs, with opportunities to add significant profit. Rationing did not allow adequate supply; price controls did not allow increased prices. The most common violations reflect the combined impact of black market prices and consumer demand in conditions of inadequate supply: higher prices by any means that might escape control, meat in greater quantities than rationing allowed, and food stocks purchased from unknown sellers without receipts. The combination of controls and German interference created a hierarchical system that relied on black market activity, ran without risk at the highest levels, and increased inequities in a system intended to provide equal access to scarce supplies. Food diverted from official channels by black market prices went to the wealthy and the privileged, leaving ordinary citizens to share greater sacrifice. This structural inequity was the product of German exploitation and French collaboration in a hierarchy based on prices, wealth, and privilege.

That privilege is evident in diaries from the period. Those without enough to eat were obsessed by the food they needed and craved, an obsession that "'occupied' minds and bodies."[118] The contrast between

---

[115] CAEF, B 49508, report by Contrôle Economique inspector Savarit, Oct. 30, 1942.

[116] CAEF, B 49598, Contrôle Economique "Enquête effectuée," Apr. 19, 1944.

[117] Daniel Cordier, *Alias Caracalla* (Paris, 2009), 536. *Résistants* enjoyed black market restaurants when they could; for examples, see ibid., 579, 1010; and Roger Vaillant, *Drôle de jeu* (Paris, 1944).

[118] Mouré and Schwartz, "On Vit Mal," 273.

the diaries of ordinary Parisians and those of German visitors like Ernst Jünger and Gerhard Heller, who moved comfortably between the best Paris restaurants and private functions offering menus worthy of prewar cuisine, is striking. Heller commented of the Thursday receptions hosted by Florence Gould, wife of Frank Jay Gould, that "sa table ignorait les restrictions" (her table paid no attention to the restrictions) and that some French guests "supportaient mal, étant donné leur régime habituel, ces copieux repas, ces vins excellents, le champagne et cette rareté, le vrai café" (could not tolerate, given their usual diet, these copious meals, these excellent wines, the champagne, and this rarity, real coffee).[119] Parisians regularly reported on food shortages and restaurant meals for their composition and price, whereas the privileged, who could take for granted their access to sufficient food, dropped the names of restaurants and hosts with rare comments on just what and how well they ate. Parisian *lycée* student Micheline Bood, who often recorded her food concerns, captured this difference inadvertently. Returning from the countryside in December 1942, where she had eaten well, and bringing thirty kilos of food over which her mother and sister exclaimed with delight, she observed, "C'est curieux, mais quand on mange bien, on ne fait plus du tout attention à la nourriture" (It's strange, but when you eat well, you no longer pay any attention to the food).[120] Those short of food, whether in conversations in market queues or recording the lives they observed around them in diaries, were acutely conscious of what they ate, what it cost, and what they lacked. The disappearance of desired foods from markets, the access to extras through friends, the prices in restaurants, and the abundance and luxury in black market restaurants were part of the culture of penury and the daily sense of deprivation that occupied their lives. Ernst Jünger's casual observation that eating well gave a feeling of power was particularly apparent to those without.

The black market restaurants in Paris serving "prewar menus" to Occupation authorities and to the French economic and political elites were the highest and most powerful tier in a system of restaurant supply based on the control system imposed by the Germans and run by the French. The visibility and cultural significance of restaurants made them targets for control, dispute, and popular discontent. The German program to ration French food and create restricted access to fine dining for their officials and collaborators structured a hierarchy

---

119 Gerhard Heller, *Un allemand à Paris, 1940–1944* (Paris, 1981), 62; Jünger, *Premier journal parisien*; Arno Breker, *Paris, Hitler et moi* (Paris, 1970).
120 Micheline Bood, *Les années doubles: Journal d'une lycéenne sous l'Occupation* (Paris, 1974), 179.

of privileges based on power. French officials protested but nonetheless collaborated in running a system that built inequality and corruption into the organization of food distribution.

Black market restaurants were the most visible and provocative embodiment of this inequality. Popular anger with hunger in proximity to abundance is clear in Marcel Aymé's 1943 story "En attendant," in which customers queuing for food outside a grocery store in Mont-martre tell their stories of hardship. One mother laments that the rich are eating more than ever:

> Ils se forcent même à manger, peur d'en laisser aux malheureux. J'invente pas. . . . Tous assassins, tueurs d'enfants, voilà ce que c'est. Marchez, la guerre, ça durera pas toujours. Quand les Allemands ils partiront, on aura des comptes à régler. Tous ceux qui auront la gueule fraîche et le ventre sur la ceinture, on aura deux mots à leur dire. Pour chacun de mes gosses qu'ils m'auront assassiné, il m'en faudra dix. A coups de galoche dans la gueule, que je les ruerai, et je mettrai du temps, je veux qu'ils souffrent.

> [They even force themselves to eat, for fear of leaving anything for the unfortunate. I'm not making this up. . . . They're murderers, child killers, that's what they are. Well, the war, it won't last forever. When the Germans leave, we'll settle scores. All of them with fresh faces and paunches hanging over their belts, we'll show them. For every one of my children they've killed, I'll get ten of them. With boots to their faces, that's how I'll do them in, and I'll take my time; I want them to suffer.][121]

For the many Parisians who could rarely afford black market food, the contrast between the black market abundance in select restaurants and the ordinary citizens' hunger in the street displayed the failure of Vichy's promise to provide "equality of sacrifice." They saw the Germans, the collaborators, and the rich eating better than ever.

---

[121] Marcel Aymé, "En attendant," in *Le passe-muraille* (Paris, 1943), 213.

News

CALL FOR PAPERS: ARCHIVES AND ARCHIVAL PRACTICE IN FRENCH HISTORY

French Historical Studies seeks articles for a special issue, to appear in the spring of 2017, on archives and archival practice in French history. Recent transnational scholarship on archives has alerted us to the ways in which archives are not neutral sites but ones where knowledge is constructed and negotiated. Discussions about whether or not cultural history has lured historians away from the archives have missed an underlying reality: historians of France and the French empire now use a wider range of public and private holdings beyond national, departmental, defense, and colonial archives. These archives often require different strategies for entry and use. To note only the most obvious differences: finding aids have not always been compiled by trained archivists, and classificatory schemes vary considerably, depending on organizations' needs. Access to outsiders and the communication of documents may be limited or restricted. Technology is also transforming both the archive itself and access to the archive.

We invite articles that situate these issues in the context of French history and historiography. More than just tales from the archives, articles will reflect authors' experiences in archives that illuminate both archival practice and ways of doing French history. We invite authors to consider, among the various nontraditional archives, church and missionary archives, corporate archives, associations' archives, mayors' office and communal records, hospital archives and medical records, private papers, and colonial archives outside Aix. We also welcome articles on nontraditional ways of using traditional archives, on the impact of digitization and other technologies on archival practice, and on the encounter between historians and archivists.

Queries about submission and other matters regarding this special issue should be addressed to the guest editors, Sarah Curtis (scurtis@sfsu.edu) and Stephen Harp (sharp@uakron.edu).

To submit an article, please visit www.editorialmanager/fhs. After registering, follow the submission instructions under "Instructions for Authors" on the website. Articles may be either in English or in French but must conform to *French Historical Studies* style (for details, see www.dukepress.edu/fhs) and must be accompanied by titles and 150-word abstracts in both languages. Manuscripts should be between 6,000 and 8,000 words excluding footnotes, and no longer than 10,000 words including footnotes. For illustrations, written permission must be obtained by the author from the relevant persons or institutions for both print and online publication. The deadline for submissions is July 15, 2015.

French Historical Studies, Vol. 38, No. 2 (April 2015)   DOI 10.1215/00161071-2842602
Copyright 2015 by Society for French Historical Studies

Recent Books and Dissertations on French History

Compiled by Sarah Sussman

GENERAL AND MISCELLANEOUS

Abel, Véronique, Marc Bouiron, and Florence Parent. *Fouilles à Marseille: Objets quotidiens médiévaux et modernes.* Arles: Errance, 2014. 409p. €39.00.

Agnès, Frédérique, and Isabelle Lefort. *100 ans de combats pour la liberté des femmes.* Paris: Flammarion, 2014. 546p. €29.95.

Albertone, Manuela. *National Identity and the Agrarian Republic: The Transatlantic Commerce of Ideas between America and France (1750–1830).* Farnham: Ashgate, 2014. 324p. $144.95.

Arboit, Gérald. *Des services secrets pour la France: Du Dépôt de la guerre à la DGSE (1856–2013).* Paris: Centre National de la Recherche Scientifique, 2014. 444p. €25.00.

Bady, Jean-Pierre, Marie Cornu, Jérôme Fromageau, Jean-Michel Leniaud, and Vincent Negri, eds. *1913: Genèse d'une loi sur les monuments historiques.* Paris: Documentation Française, 2013. 602p. €39.00.

Baecque, Antoine de. *La traversée des Alpes: Essai d'histoire marchée.* Paris: Gallimard, 2014. 423p. €24.50.

Bensacq-Tixier, Nicole. *La France en Chine de Sun Yat-sen à Mao Zedong, 1918–1953.* Rennes: Presses Universitaires de Rennes, 2014. 751p. €28.00.

Bergeron, Andrée. *Une mémoire pour demain: 30 ans de culture scientifique, technique et industrielle en France—Deuxièmes rencontres Michel Crozon.* Paris: Harmattan, 2014. 202p. €20.00.

Berlière, Jean-Marc, Jonas Campion, Luigi Lacché, and Xavier Rousseaux, eds. *Justices militaires et guerres mondiales Europe, 1914–1950/Military Justices and World Wars: Europe, 1914–1950.* Louvain-La-Neuve: Presses Universitaires de Louvain, 2013. 423p. €30.00.

Blier, Gérard. *Les villes du Poitou-Charentes: Histoire parallèle de l'antiquité à nos jours.* Saintes: Croît Vif, 2014. 241p. €22.00.

Bonin, Hubert. *Banque et identité commerciale: La Société Générale, 1864–2014.* Villeneuve d'Ascq: Presses Universitaires du Septentrion, 2014. 290p. €24.00.

Cardot, Monique. *La forge de Froncles dans l'histoire, XXème siècle.* Clichy-la-Garenne: Cardot, 2013. 340p. €35.00.

Carroy, Jacqueline, Nathalie Richard, and François Vatin, eds. *L'homme des sciences de l'homme: Une histoire transdisciplinaire.* Nanterre: Presses Universitaires de Paris Ouest, 2013. 269p. €21.00.

Carteret, Xavier. *Michel Adanson (1727–1806) et la méthode naturelle de classification botanique.* Paris: Champion, 2014. 527p. €95.00.

Chastagnaret, Gérard, and Laurence Américi, eds. *La mosaïque des racines: Pouvoirs, cultures et sociétés en France et en Méditerranée, XVIe–XXIe siècle; Mélanges en l'honneur du professeur Gérard Chastagnaret.* Aix-en-Provence: Presses Universitaires de Provence, 2014. 327p. €25.00.

French Historical Studies, Vol. 38, No. 2 (April 2015)   DOI 10.1215/00161071-2842614

Conord, Fabien. *Le Tour de France à l'heure nationale, 1930–1968.* Paris: Presses Universitaires de France, 2014. 356p. €23.00.

Corvol, Andrée, Groupe d'Histoire des Forêts Françaises, et al., eds. *Regards sur la forêt.* Paris: Harmattan, 2014. 477p. €44.00.

Coste, Laurent, Stéphane Minvielle, and François-Charles Mougel, eds. *Le concept d'élites en Europe de l'antiquité à nos jours.* Pessac: Maison des Sciences de l'Homme d'Aquitaine, 2014. 406p. €27.00.

Damaggio, Jean-Paul. *Elections municipales à Montauban, 1904–2008: Une commune laboratoire.* Angeville: Brochure, 2013. 297p. €20.00.

Davoust, Jean-François, and Igor Martinache. *Du sport ouvrier au sport oublié? Histoire mêlée de la CGT et du sport.* Montreuil: CGT, 2013. 218p. €10.00.

DeJean, Joan E. *How Paris Became Paris: The Invention of the Modern City.* New York: Bloomsbury, 2014. 307p. $30.00.

Deladerrière, François, and Franck Roubeau. *Ugine, une ruée vers l'acier.* Arles: Actes Sud, 2014. 140p. €35.00.

Enckell, Marianne, Guillaume Davranche, Rolf Dupuy, Anthony Lorry, Anne Steiner, Hugues Lenoir, and Claude Pennetier, eds. *Les anarchistes: Dictionnaire biographique du mouvement libertaire francophone.* Paris: Atelier, 2014. 527p. €50.00.

Fauvel, Maryse. *Exposer l'"autre": Essai sur la Cité nationale de l'histoire de l'immigration et le Musée du quai Branly.* Paris: Harmattan, 2014. 228p. €23.00.

Favreau, Robert, and Jean Glénisson. *Histoire de l'Aunis et de la Saintonge.* Vol. 2. La Crèche: Geste, 2014. 567p. €60.00.

Flauraud, Vincent, Nathalie Ponsard, Jean-Yves Gouttebel, and Pierre Juquin. *Histoire et mémoire des mouvements syndicaux au XXe siècle: Enjeux et héritages.* Nancy: Arbre Bleu, 2013. 399p. €22.00.

François, Stéphane. *Au-delà des vents du Nord: L'extrême droite française, le pôle Nord et les Indo-Européens.* Lyon: Presses Universitaires de Lyon, 2014. 319p. €20.00.

Fuligni, Bruno, and Sergio Aquindo. *Tour du monde des terres françaises oubliées.* Paris: Trésor, 2014. 143p. €17.00.

Fureix, Emmanuel. *Le siècle des possibles, 1814–1914.* Paris: Presses Universitaires de France, 2014. 240p. €14.00.

Galloro, Piero-Dominique, and Ahmed Boubeker. *Histoires et mémoires des immigrations en Lorraine.* Nancy: Presses Universitaires de Lorraine, 2014. 398p. €20.00.

Georges, Olivier. *Pierre-Marie Gerlier, le cardinal militant, 1880–1965.* Paris: Desclée de Brouwer, 2014. 474p. €35.00.

Glasson, Denis. *Les cantonniers des routes: Une histoire d'émancipation.* Paris: Harmattan, 2014. 365p. €37.50.

Griset, Pascal, ed. *Les ingénieurs des télécommunications dans la France contemporaine: Réseaux, innovations et territoires, XIXe–XXe siècles; Colloque des 21 et 22 octobre 2010.* Paris: Comité pour l'Histoire Economique et Financière de la France, 2013. 376p. €35.00.

Groupe d'Information et de Soutien des Immigrés. *Mémoire des luttes de l'immigration en France.* Paris: GISTI, 2014. 215p. €16.00.

Hamoneau, Didier. *Les racines musulmanes de la France: Des Sarrasins aux Ottomans.* Beirut: Dar Albouraq, 2014. 364p. €18.00.

Iancu, Michaël. *Les Juifs de Montpellier et des terres d'Oc: Figures médiévales, modernes et contemporaines.* Paris: Cerf, 2014. 191p. €25.00.

Jeanneney, Jean-Noël, and Jean-François Sirinelli. *René Rémond, historien.* Paris: Sciences Po, 2014. 152p. €15.00.

Kahan, Alan S. *Alexis de Tocqueville.* New York: Bloomsbury Academic, 2013. 168p. $29.95.

Kasdi, Mohamed. *Les entrepreneurs du coton: Innovation et développement économique, France du Nord, 1700–1830.* Villeneuve-d'Ascq: Presses Universitaires du Septentrion, 2014. 370p. €32.00.

Le Douget, Annick. *Violence au village: La société rurale finistérienne face à la justice (1815–1914).* Rennes: Presses Universitaires de Rennes, 2014. 334p. €21.00.

Lenhard, Philipp. *Volk oder Religion? Die Entstehung moderner jüdischer Ethnizität in Frankreich und Deutschland, 1782–1848.* Göttingen: Vandenhoeck und Ruprecht, 2014. 413p. €79.99.

Le Roux, Thomas, Claire Barillé, Jean-François Belhoste, and Florence Bourillon. *Les Paris de l'industrie, 1750–1920: Paris au risque de l'industrie.* Grâne: Créaphis, 2013. 155p. €25.00.

Lévy, Michel-André. *Louis I, II, III, XIV: L'étonnante histoire de la numérotation des rois de France.* Waterloo: Jourdan, 2014. 266p. €19.90.

Marcel-Ponthier, Marylène, and Lucien Dupuis. *Aiguebelle dans la Drôme: L'histoire longue et mouvementée d'une abbaye cistercienne et de ses filles, Bouchet, Bonlieu, Maube.* Montélimar: Marcel-Ponthier, 2010. 235p. €24.00.

Martin, Boris. *L'iconoclaste: L'histoire véritable d'Auguste François, consul, photographe, explorateur, misanthrope, incorruptible et ennemi des intrigants.* Paris: Pacifique, 2014. 205p. €38.50.

Monnier, Gérard, and Evelyne Cohen. *La République et ses symboles: Un territoire de signes.* Paris: Publications de la Sorbonne, 2013. 482p. €40.00.

Muller, Annalena. "Forming and Re-forming Fontevraud: Monasticism, Geopolitics, and the *Querelle des Frères* (c. 100–1643)." PhD diss., Yale University, 2014.

Nivet, Philippe. *Guerre et patrimoine artistique à l'époque contemporaine: Actes du colloque d'Amiens des 16–18 mars 2011.* Amiens: Encrage, 2013. 450p. €35.00.

Pauquet, Alain. *Une histoire de la citoyenneté politique en France: 30 documents d'archives du XVIIIe siècle à nos jours.* Paris: Harmattan, 2014. 166p. €17.00.

Pénicaud, Blandine, and Vincent Vidal-Naquet. *Les révolutions de l'amour: Sexe, couple et bouleversements des moeurs de 1914 à nos jours.* Paris: Perrin, 2014. 426p. €23.00.

Pineau, Frédéric. *La Croix-Rouge française: 150 ans d'histoire.* Paris: Autrement, 2014. 222p. €32.00.

Pizzorni-Itié, Florence. *L'histoire du fort Saint-Jean.* Marseille: Musée des Civilisations de l'Europe et de la Méditerranée, 2014. 138p. €15.00.

Price, Roger. *A Concise History of France.* 3rd ed. Cambridge: Cambridge University Press, 2014. 528p. $28.99 paper.

Quilliet, Bernard. *Lacépède savant, musicien, philanthrope et franc-maçon.* Paris: Tallandier, 2013. 431p. €26.90.

Renaudeau, Olivier, Dominique Prévot, and Baptiste Christian. *Mousquetaires! Paris, Musée de l'armée, Ministère de la Défense, du 2 avril au 14 juillet 2014.* Paris: Gallimard, 2014. 271p. €35.00.

Sternhell, Zeev, and Nicolas Weill. *Histoire et lumières: Changer le monde par la raison; Entretiens avec Nicolas Weill.* Paris: Michel, 2014. 365p. €24.00.

Tartakowsky, Danielle. *Les droites et la rue: Histoire d'une ambivalence, de 1880 à nos jours.* Paris: Découverte, 2013. 221p. €18.00.

Vaisse, Pierre. *Deux façons d'écrire l'histoire: Le legs Caillebotte.* Paris: Ophrys, 2014. 120p. €18.00.

Viart, Jean-Paul. *Panorama des présidents de la République.* Paris: Larousse, 2013. 255p. €9.00.

Viret, Jérôme Luther. *Le sol et le sang: La famille et la reproduction sociale en France du Moyen Age au XIXe siècle.* Paris: Centre National de la Recherche Scientifique, 2014. 491p. €25.00.

Vray, Nicole. *Femmes, églises et société, du XVIe au XIXe siècle.* Paris: Desclée de Brouwer, 2014. 244p. €21.00.

Wing, Thomas Chapman. "The Future Looks Backward: Projection and the Historical Imagination in Nineteenth-Century France." PhD diss., Yale University, 2013.

Yarrington, Jonna M. "*Droits* and *Frontières*: Sugar and the Edge of France, 1800–1860." PhD diss., University of Arizona, 2014.

Zuber, Valentine. *Le culte des droits de l'homme.* Paris: Gallimard, 2014. 405p. €26.00.

MEDIEVAL AND RENAISSANCE

Albano, Joseph. *Anne de France, roi femme: Le génie oublié.* Toulon: Presses du Midi, 2014. 256p. €18.00.

Bernet, Anne. *Brunehaut: Epouse de Sigebert Ier.* Paris: Pygmalion, 2014. 477p. €24.00.

Berthe, Pierre-Marie. *Les procureurs français à la cour pontificale d'Avignon, 1309–1376.* Paris: Ecole des Chartes, 2014. 1,004p. €55.00.

Billoré, Maïté. *Dans le secret des archives: Justice, ville et culture au Moyen Age; Sources et commentaires.* Rennes: Presses Universitaires de Rennes, 2014. 399p. €22.00.

Bouyer, Mathias. *La principauté barroise, 1301–1420: L'émergence d'un état dans l'espace lorrain.* Paris: Harmattan, 2014. 733p. €65.00.

Bucheit, Nicolas. *Les commanderies hospitalières: Réseaux et territoires en Basse-Alsace, XIIIe–XIVe siècles.* Paris: Comité des Travaux Historiques et Scientifiques, 2014. 348p. €29.00.

Chartier, Alain. *L'abusé en cour: Le curial.* Paris: Champion, 2014. 150p. €25.00.

Claverie, Pierre-Vincent. *La conquête du Roussillon par Pierre le Cérémonieux (1341–1345).* Canet: Trabucaire, 2014. 302p. €20.00.

Cooper, Stephen. *Agincourt: Myth and Reality, 1415–2015.* Barnsley: Pen and Sword Military, 2014. 256p. £19.99.

Dehoux, Esther. *Saints guerriers: Georges, Guillaume, Maurice et Michel dans la France médiévale, XIe–XIIIe siècle.* Rennes: Presses Universitaires de Rennes, 2014. 327p. €21.00.

Dejoux, Marie. *Les enquêtes de Saint Louis: Gouverner et sauver son âme.* Paris: Presses Universitaires de France, 2014. 475p. €27.00.

Fabry-Tehranchi, Irène. *L'humain et l'animal dans la France médiévale (XIIe–XVe s.)/Human and Animal in Medieval France (12th–15th C.).* Amsterdam: Rodopi, 2014. 231p. €50.00.

Galland, Bruno. *Philippe Auguste: Le bâtisseur du royaume.* Paris: Belin, 2014. 211p. €21.00.

Gaude-Ferragu, Murielle. *La reine au Moyen Age: Le pouvoir au féminin, XIVe–XVe siècle, France.* Paris: Tallandier, 2014. 344p. €23.90.

Girault, Pierre-Gilles. *Les funérailles d'Anne de Bretagne, reine de France: L'hermine regrettée.* Montreuil: Gourcuff Gradenigo, 2014. 95p. €14.00.

Isabelle of France. *The Rules of Isabelle of France: An English Translation with Introductory Study.* Ed. and trans. Sean L. Field. St. Bonaventure, NY: Franciscan Institute Publications, 2013. $24.95.

Laffont, Pierre-Yves, Yvon Pellerin, and Claudy Lebreton. *Les élites et leurs résidences en Bretagne au Moyen Age: Actes du colloque organisé par le conseil général des Côtes-d'Armor (Guingamp et Dinan, 28 et 29 mai 2010).* Rennes: Presses Universitaires de Rennes, 2014. 238p. €29.00.

Mériaux, Charles. *La naissance de la France: Les royaumes des Francs (Ve–VIIe siècle).* Paris: Belin, 2014. 216p. €16.00.

Michon, Cédric, and Loris Petris. *Le cardinal Jean Du Bellay: Diplomatie et culture dans l'Europe de la Renaissance.* Tours: Presses Universitaires François Rabelais de Tours, 2013. 400p. €35.00.

Minois, Georges. *Philippe le Bel.* Paris: Perrin, 2014. 797p. €28.00.

———. *Poitiers, 19 septembre 1356.* Paris: Tallandier, 2014. 235p. €19.00.

Moufflet, Jean-François. *Sous le sceau du roi Saint-Louis de Poissy à Tunis, 1214–1270.* Paris: Mare et Martin, 2014. 80p. €15.00.

Nimmegeers, Nathanaël, and Alain Dubreucq. *Evêques entre Bourgogne et Provence, Ve–XIe siècle: La province ecclésiastique de Vienne au haut Moyen Age.* Rennes: Presses Universitaires de Rennes, 2014. 402p. €24.00.

Spitzbarth, Anne-Brigitte. *Ambassades et ambassadeurs de Philippe le Bon, troisième Duc Valois de Bourgogne (1419–1467).* Turnhout: Brepols, 2013. 664p. €99.00.

Stoclet, Alain J. *Fils du Martel: La naissance, l'éducation et la jeunesse de Pépin, dit "Le Bref" (v. 714–v. 741).* Turnhout: Brepols, 2013. 386p. €82.00.

Stouff, Louis. *Arles au Moyen Age finissant.* Aix-en-Provence: Presses Universitaires de Provence, 2014. 374p. €30.00.

1550–1770

Abou El-Seoud, Iman. *Complicité et sédition dans la littérature pamphlétaire de l'Ancien Régime: Images du lecteur et de l'auteur.* Paris: Manuscrit, 2013. 403p. €35.90.

Aubert, Gauthier. *Les révoltes du papier timbré, 1675: Essai d'histoire événementielle.* Rennes: Presses Universitaires de Rennes, 2014. 718p. €29.00.

Beaurepaire, Pierre-Yves, Aurélie Boissière, and Jules Grandin. *La communication en Europe de l'âge classique au siècle des Lumières.* Paris: Belin, 2014. 364p. €33.00.

Bernard, Pauline. "Une institution d'Ancien Régime: La maréchaussée dans le Lyonnais au début du XVIIIe siècle." PhD diss., Ecole des Hautes Etudes en Sciences Sociales, 2014.

Bernat, Chrystel, and Frédéric Gabriel. *Critique du zèle: Fidélités et radicalités confessionnelles; France, XVIe–XVIIIe siècle.* Paris: Beauchesne, 2013. 308p. €44.00.

Bijon, Jean. *Madame Dupin: Une féministe à Chenonceau au siècle des Lumières.* Joue les Tours: Simarre, 2014. 240p. €20.00.

Blond, Stéphane. *L'atlas de Trudaine: Pouvoirs, cartes et savoirs techniques au siècle des Lumières.* Paris: Comité des Travaux Historiques et Scientifiques, 2014. 416p. €54.00.

Briffaud, Serge, Emmanuelle Heaulmé, and Olivier Damée. *Chantilly au temps de Le Nôtre: Un paysage en projet.* Florence: Olschki, 2013. 224p. €34.00.

Castelluccio, Stéphane. *Le prince et le marchand: Le commerce de luxe chez les marchands; Merciers parisiens pendant le règne de Louis XIV.* Paris: SPM, 2014. 878p. €80.00.

Corvisier–de Villèle, Marie-Anne, Bertrand Fonck, and Claude Ponnou, eds. *Champs de bataille du Grand Siècle: Catalogue des cartes de l'"Atlas historique" jusqu'à la fin du règne de Louis XIV.* Paris: Archives et Culture, 2013. 383p. €39.00.

Coutelle, Antoine. *Poitiers au XVIIe siècle: Les pratiques culturelles d'une élite urbaine.* Rennes: Presses Universitaires de Rennes, 2014. 468p. €24.00.

Crouch, Christian Ayne. *Nobility Lost: French and Canadian Martial Cultures, Indians, and the End of New France.* Ithaca, NY: Cornell University Press, 2014. 250p. $35.00.

Dahlinger, James H. *Saving France in the 1580s: Writings of Etienne Pasquier.* New York: Lang, 2013. 132p. $74.95.

Daussy, Hugues. *Le parti huguenot: Chronique d'une désillusion (1557–1572).* Geneva: Droz, 2014. 888p. €79.90.

Desan, Philippe. *Montaigne: Une biographie politique.* Paris: Jacob, 2014. 727p. €29.00.

Di Biase, Sante. *Alla ricerca di un nuovo equilibrio: I rapporti diplomatici tra la Repubblica di Venezia e il regno di Francia tra XVI e XVII secolo.* Rome: Aracne, 2014. 584p. €33.00.

Durand, Stéphane, Arlette Jouanna, Elie Pélaquier, Jean-Pierre Donnadieu, and Henri Michel, eds. *Des Etats dans l'Etat: Les Etats de Languedoc de la Fronde à la Révolution.* Geneva: Droz, 2014. 983p. €49.80.

Felton, Marie-Claude. *Maîtres de leurs ouvrages: L'édition à compte d'auteur à Paris au XVIIIe siècle.* Oxford: Voltaire Foundation, 2014. 353p. $75.00.

Fonck, Bertrand. *Le maréchal de Luxembourg et le commandement des armées sous Louis XIV.* Seyssel: Champ Vallon, 2014. 641p. €29.00.

Gasper, Julia. *The Marquis d'Argens: A Philosophical Life.* Lanham, MD: Lexington, 2014. 297p. $80.00.

Grata, Giulia. *Des lettres pour gouverner: Antoine Perrenot de Granvelle et l'Italie de Charles-Quint dans les Manuscrits Trumbull de Besançon.* Besançon: Presses Universitaires de Franche-Comté, 2014. 454p. €35.00.

Kennedy, Gregory M. W. *Something of a Peasant Paradise? Comparing Rural Societies in Acadie and the Loudunais, 1604–1755.* Montreal: McGill-Queen's University Press, 2014. 272p. $80.00.

Kerjan, Daniel. *Les débuts de la franc-maçonnerie française de la Grande Loge au Grand Orient, 1688–1793.* Paris: Dervy, 2014. 353p. €23.00.

Knecht, Robert J. *Hero or Tyrant? Henry III, King of France, 1574–89.* Farnham: Ashgate, 2014. 370p. $199.95/£75.00.

Kwass, Michael. *Contraband: Louis Mandrin and the Making of a Global Underground.* Cambridge, MA: Harvard University Press, 2014. 472p. $49.95.

Lajaumont, Stéphane, and Michel Cassan. *"Un pas de deux": Clercs et paroissiens en Limousin (vers 1660–1789)*. Limoges: Presses Universitaires de Limoges, 2014. 529p. €38.00.

Lazer, Stephen. "The State with Two Centers: The French Monarchy and the Dukes of Pfalz-Zweibrücken in Early Modern Alsace, 1648–1789." PhD diss., University of Miami, 2014.

Leleu-Desseaux, Fabienne. *Assister ou soigner au XVIIIe siècle: L'exemple d'Amiens*. Amiens: Ancrage, 2014. 264p. €29.00.

Lemarchand, Laurent. *Paris ou Versailles? La monarchie absolue entre deux capitales (1715–1723)*. Paris: Comité des Travaux Historiques et Scientifiques, 2014. 401p. €28.00.

Le Pelletier de La Houssaye, Félix, Antoine Cathala-Coture, and Patric Ferté, eds. *La grande généralité de Montauban sous Louis XIV: Quercy, Rouergue, Gascogne, Pays de Foix; D'après le Mémoire pour l'instruction du duc de Bourgogne (1699) et son complément par A. Cathala-Coture (1713)*. Paris: Comité des Travaux Historiques et Scientifiques, 2014. 2 vols. 556p., 676p. €100.00.

Leroux, Anne-Laure. *La naissance de la presse au XVIIe siècle: Le Mercure français*. Paris: Harmattan, 2013. 145p. €14.00.

Markovits, Rahul. *Civiliser l'Europe: Politiques du théâtre français au XVIIIe siècle*. Paris: Fayard, 2014. 400p. €24.00.

Meistersheim, Anne. *Théodore de Neuhoff: Roi de Corse, prince des chimères*. Bastia: Musée de la Ville de Bastia, 2013. 273p. €28.00.

Mentzer, Raymond A. *Les registres des consistoires des églises réformées de France, XVIe–XVIIe siècles: Un inventaire*. Geneva: Droz, 2014. 170p. €60.00.

Merger, Charles. *Des voyageuses à la découverte du Pacifique: Passagères de Bougainville, La Pérouse et d'Entrecasteaux, au siècle des Lumières*. Paris: Harmattan, 2014. 267p. €27.50.

Micallef, Fabrice. *Un désordre européen: La compétition internationale autour des "affaires de Provence" (1580–1598)*. Paris: Publications de la Sorbonne, 2014. 455p. €27.00.

Milstein, Joanna. *The Gondi: Family Strategy and Survival in Early Modern France*. Farnham: Ashgate, 2014. 243p. £63.00.

Monahan, W. Gregory. *Let God Arise: The War and Rebellion of the Camisards*. Oxford: Oxford University Press, 2014. 384p. $115.00.

Morin, Christophe. *Marigny: Ministre des arts au château de Menars*. Milan: Silvana, 2012. 125p. €28.00.

Rameix, Solange. *Justifier la guerre: Censure et propagande dans l'Europe du XVIIe siècle (France-Angleterre)*. Rennes: Presses Universitaires de Rennes, 2014. 373p. €21.00.

Rousseau, Michel. *Quand Louis XIV brûlait le Palatinat . . . : La guerre de la Ligue d'Augsburg et la presse*. Paris: Harmattan, 2014. 225p. €35.00.

Rule, John C., and Ben S. Trotter. *A World of Paper: Louis XIV, Colbert de Torcy, and the Rise of the Information State*. Montreal: McGill-Queen's University Press, 2014. 829p. CAD$49.95.

Stanley, Sharon A. *The French Enlightenment and the Emergence of Modern Cynicism*. Cambridge: Cambridge University Press, 2014. 235p. $94.00 cloth, $34.99 paper.

Sternberg, Giora. *Status Interaction during the Reign of Louis XIV*. Oxford: Oxford University Press, 2014. 320p. $99.00.

Szulman, Eric. *La navigation intérieure sous l'Ancien Régime: Naissance d'une politique publique*. Rennes: Presses Universitaires de Rennes, 2014. 376p. €22.00.

Taillefer, Michel. *Etudes sur la sociabilité à Toulouse et dans le Midi toulousain de l'Ancien Régime à la Révolution*. Toulouse: Presses Universitaires du Mirail, 2014. 524p. €35.00.

Teague, Savanna Rae. "Wretched Excess? Conspicuous Consumption amongst the Aristocracy in Eighteenth Century France." PhD diss., Middle Tennessee State University, 2013.

Terrall, Mary. *Catching Nature in the Act: Réaumur and the Practice of Natural History in the Eighteenth Century*. Chicago: University of Chicago Press, 2014. 275p. $40.00.

Turner, Anthony. *Globes, lunettes et graphomètres: Alexandre de La Rochefoucauld et les sciences*. Paris: Amandier, 2014. 137p. €20.00.

Vaugelade, Daniel. *Louis Alexandre de La Rochefoucauld, 1743–1792: Un aristocrate au service de la science*. Paris: Amandier, 2014. 335p. €22.00.

Vignal Souleyreau, Marie-Catherine. *Le trésor pillé du roi: Correspondance du cardinal de Richelieu, année 1634.* 2 vols. Paris: Harmattan, 2013. 664p., 534p. €57.00, €50.00.

Vittet, Jean, and Marc Walter. *Les Gobelins au siècle des Lumières: Un âge d'or de la manufacture royale.* Paris: Swan, 2014. 359p. €109.00.

Walshaw, Jill Maciak. *A Show of Hands for the Republic: Opinion, Information, and Repression in Eighteenth-Century Rural France.* Rochester, NY: University of Rochester Press, 2014. 322p. $99.00.

Warlin, Jean-Fred. *J.-P. Tercier, l'éminence grise de Louis XV: Un conseiller de l'ombre au siècle des Lumières.* Paris: Harmattan, 2014. 638p. €55.50.

Wicquefort, Abraham de. *Les gazettes parisiennes de l'année 1653, suivies de L'état de la France en 1654.* Ed. Philippe Mauran. Paris: Champion, 2014. 456p. €85.00.

FRENCH REVOLUTION AND NAPOLEONIC ERA

Andress, David, ed. *Experiencing the French Revolution.* Oxford: Voltaire Foundation, 2013. 332p. $106.00.

Artarit, Jean. *Fontenay-le-Comte sous la Révolution: Les malentendus de la liberté.* La Roche-sur-Yon: Centre Vendéen de Recherches Historiques, 2014. 490p. €24.00.

Baillot, Anne. *France-Allemagne: Figures de l'intellectuel, entre révolution et réaction, 1780–1848.* Villeneuve-d'Ascq: Presses Universitaires du Septentrion, 2014. 208p. €22.00.

Bertaud, Jean-Paul. *Napoléon et les Français, 1799–1815.* Paris: Colin, 2014. 543p. €24.50.

Bodinier, Gilbert. *Les officiers du Consulat et de l'Empire.* Saint-Cloud: Soteca, 2014. 798p. €39.00.

Boudon, Jacques-Olivier. *Napoléon et la campagne de France, 1814.* Paris: Colin, 2013. 365p. €20.00.

Branda, Pierre. *La guerre secrète de Napoléon: Ile d'Elbe, 1814–1815.* Paris: Perrin, 2014. 474p. €24.00.

Brasme, Pierre. *Dictionnaire des révolutionnaires français.* Paris: Centre National de la Recherche Scientifique, 2014. 507p. €12.00.

Byrnes, Joseph F. *Priests of the French Revolution: Saints and Renegades in a New Political Era.* University Park: Pennsylvania State University Press, 2014. 344p. $74.95.

Chappey, Jean-Luc, Carole Christen, and Igor Moullier. *Joseph-Marie de Gérando (1772–1842): Connaître et réformer la société.* Rennes: Presses Universitaires de Rennes, 2014. 342p. €20.00.

Cohendet, Sophie-Henriette, and Sandrine Fillipetti. *Mémoires sur Napoléon et Marie-Louise, 1810–1814.* Paris: Mercure de France, 2014. 321p. €8.00.

Cuccia, Phillip R. *Napoleon in Italy: The Sieges of Mantua, 1796–1799.* Norman: University of Oklahoma Press, 2014. 314p. $32.95.

Daniel, Max. *1792: Le diable s'appelait André Pomme.* Puteaux: Net, 2013. 160p. €13.00.

Dean, Rodney J. *L'assemblée constituante et la reforme ecclésiastique, 1790.* Paris: Picard, 2014. 798p. €45.00.

Edelstein, Melvin Allen. *The French Revolution and the Birth of Electoral Democracy.* Farnham: Ashgate, 2014. 327p. $154.95.

Evrard, Sébastien. *L'or de Napoléon: Sa stratégie patrimoniale (1806–1814).* Paris: Harmattan, 2014. 168p. €18.00.

Gauthier, Florence. *Triomphe et mort de la révolution des droits de l'homme et du citoyen, 1789–1795–1802.* Paris: Syllepse, 2014. 387p. €22.00.

Grenot, Michèle. *Le souci des plus pauvres Dufourny: La Révolution française et la démocratie.* Rennes: Presses Universitaires de Rennes, 2014. 426p. €23.00.

Horan, Joseph. "Fibers of Empire: Cotton Cultivation in France and Italy during the Age of Napoleon." PhD diss., Florida State University, 2013.

House, Jonathan M. *Controlling Paris: Armed Forces and Counter-Revolution, 1789–1848.* New York: New York University Press, 2014. 324p. $55.00.

Israel, Jonathan. *Revolutionary Ideas: An Intellectual History of the French Revolution from "The*

Rights of Man" to Robespierre. Princeton, NJ: Princeton University Press, 2014. 888p. $39.95.

Jégo, Yves. *La campagne de France, 1814.* Paris: Tallandier, 2013. 319p. €20.90.

Le Bozec, Christine. *La Première République, 1792–1799.* Paris: Perrin, 2014. 365p. €23.00.

Lentz, Thierry. *Les vingt jours de Fontainebleau: La première abdication de Napoléon, 31 mars–20 avril 1814.* Paris: Perrin, 2013. 294p. €23.00.

Linton, Marisa. *Choosing Terror: Virtue, Friendship, and Authenticity in the French Revolution.* Oxford: Oxford University Press, 2013. 323p. £65.00.

Marquis, Hugues. *Agents de l'ennemi: Les espions à la solde de l'Angleterre dans une France en révolution.* Paris: Vendémiaire, 2014. 349p. €22.00.

Parisot de Bayard, Jean-Christophe. *Louis XVII: Dernières nouvelles du roi-perdu.* Paris: Christian, 2014. 178p. €25.00.

Pichot-Bravard, Philippe. *La Révolution française.* Versailles: Via Romana, 2013. 294p. €24.00.

Pigeard, Alain. *L'oeuvre de paix de Napoléon, 1800–1815: 200 réalisations pour reconstruire la France.* Paris: Bisquine, 2014. 380p. €22.00.

Poirson, Martial. *La Révolution française et le monde d'aujourd'hui: Mythologies contemporaines.* Paris: Garnier, 2014. 553p. €49.00.

Renglet, Antoine, and Axel Tixhon. *Un commissaire de police à Namur sous Napoléon: Le registre de Mathieu de Nantes, 10 vendémiaire an XIII–28 août 1807.* Louvain: Presses Universitaires de Louvain, 2013. 329p. €25.00.

Rey, Marie-Pierre. *Un tsar à Paris: 1814, l'année où les Russes ont fait l'histoire de la France.* Paris: Flammarion, 2014. 329p. €22.00.

Rooney, Morgan. *The French Revolution Debate and the British Novel, 1790–1814: The Struggle for History's Authority.* Lewisburg, PA: Bucknell University Press, 2013. 223p. $85.00.

Sarrazin, Jean-Pierre. *Gabriel Julien Ouvrard: Grandeur et misère d'un financier de génie sous l'Empire.* Paris: Harmattan, 2014. 221p. €23.00.

Schnapper, Antoine, and Pascal Griener. *David, la politique et la Révolution.* Paris: Gallimard, 2013. 444p. €39.00.

Sciara, Giuseppe. *La solitudine della libertà: Benjamin Constant e i dibattiti politico-costituzionali della prima Restaurazione e dei cento giorni.* Soveria Mannelli: Rubbettino, 2013. 352p. €22.00.

Smith, Allyce. "Revolutionary Marriage: Family, State, and Natalism from the Ancien Régime to the Napoleonic Era." PhD diss., Florida State University, 2013.

Spary, Emma. *Feeding France: New Sciences of Food, 1760–1815.* Cambridge: Cambridge University Press, 2014. 428p. £65.00.

Tulard, Jean, and Marie-José Tulard. *Napoléon et quarante millions de sujets: La centralisation et le Premier Empire; suivi d'un Dictionnaire des 134 départements à l'apogée du Grand Empire.* Paris: Tallandier, 2014. 402p. €24.00.

Vincent, Bernard. *Lafayette.* Paris: Gallimard, 2014. 184p. €7.00.

Wang, Shan-Ching. "Kingship and Rituals in the French Revolution (1789–1793): The Guillotining of Louis XVI." PhD diss., St. John's University, 2013.

1830–1870

Chrastil, Rachel. *The Siege of Strasbourg.* Cambridge, MA: Harvard University Press, 2014. 320p. $39.95.

Dessaivre-Audelin, Louise. *L'impératrice au chevet des Amiénois victimes du choléra: Amiens, 4 juillet 1866.* Amiens: Encrage, 2014. 111p. €10.00.

Dirou, Armel. *La guérilla en 1870: Résistance et terreur.* Paris: Giovanangeli, 2014. 295p. €23.00.

Giuliani, Fabienne. *Les liaisons interdites histoire de l'inceste au XIXe siècle.* Paris: Publications de la Sorbonne, 2014. 477p. €29.00.

Horowitz, Sarah. *Friendship and Politics in Post-revolutionary France.* University Park: Pennsylvania State University Press, 2013. 227p. $79.95.

Massot, Jean. *Le Conseil d'Etat et le développement économique de la France au XIXe siècle: Actes de la journée d'études organisée au Conseil d'Etat le 20 mai 2011.* Paris: Documentation Française, 2014. 151p. €15.00.

Pilbeam, Pamela M. *Saint-Simonians in Nineteenth-Century France: From Free Love to Algeria.* Basingstoke: Palgrave Macmillan, 2014. 256p. £55.00.

Tega, Walter. *Tradizione e rivoluzione: Scienza e potere in Francia (1815–1840).* Florence: Olschki, 2013. 348p. €35.00.

Villette, Vincent. *Apprendre à voter sous la IIe République: Le suffrage de masse dans le département de la Seine, 1848–1851.* Paris: Indes Savantes, 2013. 301p. €29.00.

THIRD REPUBLIC

Aïache, Daniel. *La révolution défaite: Les groupements révolutionnaires parisiens face à la révolution espagnole.* Paris: Noir et Rouge, 2014. 131p. €17.00.

Allorant, Pierre, and Jacques Resal, eds. *Femmes sur le pied de guerre: Chronique d'une famille bourgeoise, 1914–1918.* Villeneuve-d'Ascq: Presses Universitaires du Septentrion, 2014. 467p. €29.00.

Amin, Samir, ed. *Sur les traces de Jaurès: Ouvrage collectif.* Paris: Temps des Cerises, 2014. 222p. €16.00.

Arbois, Julien. *La vie quotidienne des poilus: Témoignages intimes de la Grande Guerre.* Grainville: City Lights Books, 2014. 285p. €17.00.

Barrère, Joseph, and Dominique Delluc. *Adieu mes petits soldats de France: Album d'un maître d'école des Hautes-Pyrénées, Marsac et Villenave-près-Marsac, 1914–1919.* Saint-Sever-de-Rustan: Mémoire des Deux Guerres en Sud-Ouest, 2013. 147p. €24.00.

Bénézech, Alfred, and Michel Cécé. *Carnets de guerre (1914–1918): Témoignages croisés d'Alfred Bénézech à Genevoix, Giono, Cendrars.* Nîmes: Lucie, 2014. 163p. €16.00.

Béroujon, Marcel. *Lettres à ses parents d'un poilu de Thizy, décembre 1914–septembre 1919: Entre déluge d'obus et orgie de choux à la crème.* Paris: Harmattan, 2014. 319p. €33.00.

Bouchenot, Matthias. *Tenir la rue: L'autodéfense socialiste, 1929–1938.* Paris: Libertalia, 2014. 299p. €15.00.

Bowd, Gavin. *La vie culturelle dans la France occupée (1914–1918).* Paris: Harmattan, 2014. 304p. €31.00.

Brown, Frederick. *The Embrace of Unreason: France, 1914–1940.* New York: Knopf, 2014. 345p. $28.95.

Cadier-Reuss, Marguerite. *Lettres à mon mari disparu (1915–1917).* Paris: Harmattan, 2014. 280p. €29.00.

Candar, Gilles, and Vincent Duclert. *Jean Jaurès.* Paris: Fayard, 2014. 685p. €27.00.

Candar, Gilles, and Romain Ducoulombier. *Jaurès, une vie pour l'humanité.* Paris: Beaux Arts Magazine, 2014. 176p. €25.00.

Chuzeville, Julien. *Militants contre la guerre, 1914–1918.* Paris: Spartacus, 2014. 135p. €10.00.

Clemenceau, Georges. *Clemenceau: L'intégrale des articles de 1894 à 1906 publiés dans La Dépêche.* Ed. Georges Mailhos and Rémy Pech. Toulouse: Privat, 2014. 800p. €49.00.

Conner, Tom. *The Dreyfus Affair and the Rise of the French Public Intellectual.* Jefferson, NC: McFarland, 2014. 280p. $55.00.

Franc, Claude. *Les généraux français de la Grande Guerre.* Antony: ETAI, 2014. 191p. €39.00.

Gibson, Craig. *Behind the Front: British Soldiers and French Civilians, 1914–1918.* Cambridge: Cambridge University Press, 2014. 528p. $99.00.

Giraud, Henri-Christian. *1914–1918: La Grande Guerre du général Giraud.* Monaco: Rocher, 2014. 281p. €22.90.

Green, Nancy L. *The Other Americans in Paris: Businessmen, Countesses, Wayward Youth, 1880–1941.* Chicago: University of Chicago Press, 2014. 352p. $40.00.

Gros, Damien. *Naissance de la IIIe République.* Paris: Presses Universitaires de France, 2014. 527p. €32.00.

Gugliotta, Georges. *Le général de Galliffet: Un sabreur dans les coulisses du pouvoir, 1830–1909.* Paris: Giovanangeli, 2014. 346p. €23.00.

Hardier, Thierry, Jean-François Jagielski, and Rémy Cazals. *Oublier l'apocalypse? Loisirs et distractions des combattants pendant la Grande Guerre.* Paris: Imago, 2014. 438p. €24.00.

Heuclin, Jean, Jean-Paul Visse, and Jean-Charles Desquiens, eds. *La presse clandestine dans le Nord occupé, 1914–1918.* Valenciennes: Presses Universitaires de Valenciennes, 2014. 504p. €24.00.

Jankowski, Paul. *Verdun: The Longest Battle of the Great War.* Oxford: Oxford University Press, 2013. 336p. $34.95.

Jurquet, Albert. *Guerre à Mende: Journal de l'arrière-front, 1914–1918; Un témoignage inédit.* Toulouse: Privat, 2014. 328p. €20.00.

Kronenberger, Stéphane. "Des temps de paix aux temps de guerre: Les parcours des travailleurs étrangers de l'Est et du Sud-Est de la France (1871–1918)." PhD diss., Université de Nice, 2014.

Laborie-Rivière, Lisa. *Eté 1914: Nancy et la Lorraine dans la Grande Guerre.* Nancy: Musée Lorrain, 2014. 288p. €39.00.

Lafon, Alexandre. *La camaraderie au front, 1914–1918.* Paris: Colin, 2014. 541p. €24.50.

Lafon, Alexandre, and Colin Miège. *Une guerre d'hommes et de machines: Désiré Sic, un photographe du génie, 1914–1918.* Toulouse: Privat, 2014. 151p. €25.00.

Lalouette, Jacqueline. *Jean Jaurès: L'assassinat, la gloire, le souvenir.* Paris: Perrin, 2014. 384p. €24.00.

Lebecq, Pierre-Alban. *Paschal Grousset: Sport et éducation physique à la française, 1888–1909.* Paris: Riveneuve, 2013. 164p. €15.00.

Lefebvre, Gaston, and Jean-Corentin Carré. *Carnet de route d'un poilu: Un de l'avant, 9 octobre 1914–27 novembre 1917; suivi de Le plus jeune héros de la guerre.* Brignais: Traboules, 2014. 259p. €18.00.

Le Gall, Erwan. *Une entrée en guerre: Le 47e régiment d'infanterie de Saint-Malo au combat, août 1914–juillet 1915.* Talmont-Saint-Hilaire: Codex, 2014. 277p. €29.00.

Le Mouel, Guy, and Henri Ortholan. *Le général de Langle de Cary, 1849–1927: Un Breton dans la Grande Guerre.* Janzé: Hérissey, 2014. 299p. €20.00.

Marchal, Anselme, Marie-Catherine Villatoux, and Paul Villatoux. *L'extraordinaire épopée du lieutenant Marchal: Pilote de missions spéciales pendant la Grande Guerre, d'après le récit de l'aviateur publié en 1919.* Paris: Histoire et Collections, 2014. 310p. €22.00.

Marcus, Paul. *Jaurès et Clemenceau: Un duel de géants.* Toulouse: Privat, 2014. 236p. €16.00.

Martin-Laval, André, Fernand Martin-Laval, and Antoine Martin-Laval. *Trois frères en guerre: Martin-Laval, une famille de Marseille en 1914 1918.* Toulouse: Privat, 2014. 734p. €28.00.

Maurer, Dorothee-Elisabeth. "'This Astonishing Chaos of a Modern World': Gender, Nationality, and French-American Relations, 1871–1919." PhD diss., University of Nebraska–Lincoln, 2014.

McAuliffe, Mary Sperling. *Twilight of the Belle Epoque: The Paris of Picasso, Stravinsky, Proust, Renault, Marie Curie, Gertrude Stein, and Their Friends through the Great War.* Lanham, MD: Rowman and Littlefield, 2014. 417p. $29.95.

Meyer, Benoît. *Dictionnaire de la Der des Der: Les mots de la Grande Guerre (1914–1918).* Paris: Champion, 2014. 348p. €19.00.

Morillon, Marc, and Jean-François Falabrègues. *Le Service de santé, 1914–1918.* Paris: Giovanangeli, 2014. 160p. €35.00.

Moulinet, Daniel. *Prêtres soldats dans la Grande Guerre: Les clercs bourbonnais sous les drapeaux.* Rennes: Presses Universitaires de Rennes, 2014. 331p. €19.00.

Nicloux, Jean-François. *Les diables de fer: Leur sang et leur gloire; Le 29e bataillon de chasseurs à pied dans la Grande Guerre.* Parcay-sur-Vienne: Apart, 2014. 445p. €29.00.

Paganelli, Dominique. *Il a tué Jaurès: Complément du titre.* Paris: Table Ronde, 2014. 213p. €16.00.

Patard, Charles. *Si on avait écouté Jaurès: Lettres d'un pacifiste depuis les tranchées; Notes de guerre et correspondance, 1914–1917.* Ed. Isabelle Jeger. Toulouse: Privat, 2014. 130p. €14.00.

Pignot, Manon. *Paris dans la Grande Guerre, 1914–1918.* Paris: Parigramme, 2014. 189p. €19.00.

Porte, Rémy. *Joffre.* Paris: Perrin, 2014. 426p. €23.00.

Prost, Antoine. *Si nous vivions en 1913.* Paris: Grasset et Fasquelle, 2014. 137p. €11.00.

Read, Geoff. *The Republic of Men: Gender and the Political Parties in Interwar France.* Baton Rouge: Louisiana State University Press, 2014. 289p. $45.00.

Renard, Jean. *Jean Renard, 1914–1918: Carnet de route.* Neuville-sur-Oise: Banc d'Arguin, 2014. 236p. €20.00.

Renaud, Patrick-Charles. *La guerre à coups d'hommes: La bataille des frontières de l'Est; Lorraine, août–septembre 1914.* Paris: Grancher, 2014. 431p. €25.90.

Rioux, Jean-Pierre. *La mort du lieutenant Péguy, 5 septembre 1914.* Paris: Tallandier, 2014. 270p. €20.90.

Roche, Albert. *Quand retentit le tocsin! 1914–1918; En Ardèche dans les cantons du Cheylard, Lamastre, Saint-Martin-de-Valamas, Saint-Agrève.* Polignac: Roure, 2014. 232p. €23.00.

Secondy, Louis, Jean-Luc Secondy, and Guilhem Secondy. *Les Héraultais dans la Guerre de 14–18.* Villeveyrac: Papillon Rouge, 2014. 288p. €20.00.

Segrétain du Patis, Joseph le. *Ecrire la guerre: Les carnets d'un poilu, 1914–1919.* Paris: LBM, 2014. 200p. €20.00.

Séguéla, Matthieu. *Clemenceau ou la tentation du Japon.* Paris: Centre National de la Recherche Scientifique, 2014. 469p. €25.00.

Sirot, Stéphane. *1884, des syndicats pour la République.* Latresne: Bord de l'Eau, 2014. 112p. €8.00.

Stéphany, Pierre. *C'étaient les poilus! Des hommes ordinaires plongés dans l'enfer.* Brussels: Ixelles, 2014. 349p. €22.00.

Valentin, Jean-Marc. *René Viviani, 1863–1925: Un orateur, du silence à l'oubli.* Limoges: Presses Universitaires de Limoges, 2013. 297p. €25.00.

Vernaz, Etienne. *En campagne: Lettres d'Etienne Vernaz, 1893–1914.* Ed. Jacques Péré, Evelyne Péré-Christin, and Annette Becker. Grâne: Créaphis, 2014. 61p. €19.00.

Vincler, Jeanne. *Août 1914 en Meurthe-et-Moselle: Dictionnaire des communes sinistrées.* Strasbourg: Quotidien, 2014. 274p. €31.00.

Vinson, Eric, and Sophie Viguier-Vinson. *Jaurès: Le prophète mystique et politique d'un combattant républicain.* Paris: Michel, 2014. 305p. €20.00.

Winock, Michel. *Les derniers feux de la Belle Epoque: Chronique culturelle d'une avant-guerre, 1913–1914.* Paris: Seuil, 2014. 196p. €16.50.

POST-1940

Adler, Alexandre. *Quand les Français faisaient l'histoire.* Paris: Grasset, 2014. 256p. €18.00.

Alliot, David. *Le festin des loups: Collabos, profiteurs et opportunistes pendant l'Occupation.* Paris: Vuibert, 2014. 279p. €19.90.

Autran, Pierre. *Robert Jardillier (1890–1945): Un socialiste humaniste et chrétien dans la tourmente.* Dijon: Editions Universitaires Dijon, 2014. 366p. €25.00.

Barbier, Claude. *Le maquis de Glières: Mythe et réalité.* Paris: Perrin, 2014. 466p. €24.00.

Baury, Michel. *Pourquoi Oradour-sur-Glane: Mystères et falsification autour d'un crime de guerre.* Rennes: Ouest-France, 2014. 281p. €17.00.

Bernard, Mathias. *Valéry Giscard d'Estaing: Les ambitions déçues.* Paris: Colin, 2014. 487p. €23.90.

Biscarat, Pierre-Jérôme. *Izieu: Des enfants dans la Shoah.* Paris: Fayard, 2014. 332p. €18.00.

Blanc, Julien, Cécile Vast, and Laurent Douzou. *Chercheurs en Résistance: Pistes et outils à l'usage des historiens.* Rennes: Presses Universitaires de Rennes, 2014. 172p. €16.00.

Blondeau, Yves. *Rester debout: La Résistance vue par ses acteurs.* Paris: Tirésias, 2014. 574p. €27.00.

Broche, François. *A l'officier des îles: Récit.* Paris: Pierre-Guillaume de Roux, 2014. 237p. €21.90.

Bruneau, Jean-Baptiste. *La Marine de Vichy aux Antilles, juin 1940–juillet 1943*. Paris: Indes Savantes, 2014. 285p. €26.00.

Buton, Philippe, Olivier Buttner, and Michel Hastings. *La guerre froide vue d'en bas*. Paris: Centre National de la Recherche Scientifique, 2014. 381p. €30.00.

Campion, Jonas. *Les gendarmes belges, français et néerlandais à la sortie de la Seconde Guerre mondiale*. Brussels: Versaille, 2011. 346p. €40.50.

Cauvin, Jean-Paul. "A New Machine for Thinking: Historical Epistemology in Twentieth Century France." PhD diss., Emory University, 2014.

Chambeiron, Robert, and Marie-Françoise Bechtel. *Résistant: Entretiens avec Marie-Françoise Bechtel*. Paris: Fayard, 2014. 186p. €15.00.

Chauveau, Frédéric, and Arnaud-Dominique Houte, eds. *Au voleur! Images et représentations du vol dans la France contemporaine*. Paris: Publications de la Sorbonne, 2014. 323p. €27.00.

Cheveigné, Maurice de. *Radio libre, 1940–1945*. Paris: Félin, 2014. 224p. €20.00.

Cheysson, Claude. *Claude Cheysson: Une force de conviction*. Paris: IBAcom, 2014. 273p. €20.00.

Corbin, Alain. *Sois sage, c'est la guerre: Souvenirs d'enfance de l'exode à la bataille de Normandie*. Paris: Flammarion, 2014. 154p. €15.00.

Cordier, Adeline. *Post-war French Popular Music: Cultural Identity and the Brel-Brassens-Ferré Myth*. Farnham: Ashgate, 2014. 188p. £60.00.

Creton, Laurent, Sébastien Denis, Pauline Gallinari, and Dimitri Vezyroglou. *Le cinéma une affaire d'état, 1945–1970*. Paris: Documentation Française, 2014. 283p. €18.00.

Croquet, Jean-Claude. *Des passeurs qui ont défié les Nazis: Entre Haute-Savoie et Suisse, 1940–1944*. Paris: Non Lieu, 2013. 141p. €19.00.

Croubois, Claude. *Les Tourangeaux dans la guerre, 1939–1945*. Riom: De Borée, 2014. 459p. €28.00.

Cupers, Kenny. *The Social Project: Housing Postwar France*. Minneapolis: University of Minnesota Press, 2014. 424p. $115.00 cloth, $35.00 paper.

Cuttier, Martine. *Terre d'Afrique des officiers dans la tourmente: Les Saint-Cyriens de la promotion "Terre d'Afrique," 1957–1959, témoignent pour l'histoire*. Paris: Dacres, 2013. 624p. €32.00.

Desquesnes, Rémy. *Le mur de l'Atlantique: De Dunkerque au Tréport*. Rennes: Ouest-France, 2014. 143p. €16.00.

Dias Vaz, Manuel. *La communauté silencieuse: Mémoires de l'immigration portugaise en France*. Bordeaux: Elytis, 2014. 253p. €20.00.

Ducange, Jean-Numa, Julien Hage, Jean-Yves Mollier, and Jean Vigreux. *Le Parti communiste français et le livre: Ecrire et diffuser le politique en France au XXe siècle (1920–1992)*. Dijon: Universitaires de Dijon, 2014. 211p. €18.00.

Dufour, Pierre. *La campagne d'Alsace: Automne 1944, hiver 1945*. Paris: Grancher, 2014. 352p. €22.00.

Duhem, Jacqueline. *Ascq 1944: Un massacre dans le Nord, une affaire franco-allemande*. Lille: Lumières de Lille, 2014. 266p. €22.00.

Dussault, Eric. *L'invention de Saint-Germain-des-Prés*. Paris: Vendémiaire, 2014. 251p. €22.00.

Effosse, Sabine, and Patrick Fridenson. *Le crédit à la consommation en France, 1947–1965: De la stigmatisation à la réglementation*. Paris: Comité pour l'Histoire Economique et Financière de la France, 2014. 318p. €28.00.

Escafré-Dublet, Angéline. *Culture et immigration de la question sociale à l'enjeu politique, 1958–2007*. Rennes: Presses Universitaires de Rennes, 2014. 259p. €20.00.

Estrada, Jérôme. *Les combattants de l'aube: Les compagnons de la Libération d'origine lorraine*. Woippy: Serpenoise, 2014. 175p. €31.00.

Fejérdy, Gergely. *L'Europe francophone et la Hongrie au début de la guerre froide: Les relations diplomatiques et culturelles entre les pays francophones de l'Europe occidentale et la Hongrie de 1944 à 1956*. Paris: Champion, 2014. 607p. €100.00.

Fondation Charles de Gaulle. *De Gaulle et le Liban, les Libanais et de Gaulle: Regards croisés sur une relation*. Paris: Geuthner, 2014. 66p. €15.00.

Frank, Robert. *La hantise du déclin: La France de 1914 à 2014.* Paris: Belin, 2014. 283p. €24.00.

Fredette, Jennifer. *Constructing Muslims in France: Discourse, Public Identity, and the Politics of Citizenship.* Philadelphia: Temple University Press, 2014. 222p. $89.50.

Gidel, Henry. *Les Pompidou.* Paris: Flammarion, 2014. 442p. €22.00.

Gillet, Jean-Claude. *Le combat nationalitaire de la fédération corse du Parti socialiste unifié, 1960–1990.* Ajaccio: Piazzola, 2013. 197p. €20.00.

Godard, Patricia, Lydie Porée, and Colette Cosnier. *Les femmes s'en vont en lutte! Histoire et mémoire du féminisme à Rennes (1965–1985).* Rennes: Goater, 2014. 300p. €14.00.

Grataloupt, Roger. *Les procès de la collaboration dans la Loire: La justice de l'épuration, 1944–1945.* Polignac: Roure, 2014. 272p. €25.00.

Grenard, Fabrice. *Une légende du maquis: Georges Guingouin, du mythe à l'histoire.* Paris: Vendémiaire, 2014. 603p. €26.00.

———. *Tulle: Enquête sur un massacre, 9 juin 1944.* Paris: Tallandier, 2014. 344p. €20.90.

Grimaud, Paul Emile. *Carnets d'un préfet de Vichy, 1939–1944.* Paris: Cherche Midi, 2014. 552p. €22.50.

Guéhenno, Jean. *Diary of the Dark Years, 1940–1944: Collaboration, Resistance, and Daily Life in Occupied Paris.* Trans. David Ball. New York: Oxford University Press, 2014. 368p. $29.95.

Hastings-King, Stephen William. *Looking for the Proletariat: Socialisme ou Barbarie and the Problem of Worker Writing.* Leiden: Brill, 2014. 345p. $154.00.

Hazan, Katy. *Rire le jour, pleurer la nuit: Les enfants juifs cachés dans la Creuse pendant la guerre, 1939–1944.* Paris: Calmann-Lévy, 2014. 204p. €20.00.

Hopquin, Benoît. *Nous n'étions pas des héros: Les compagnons de la Libération racontent leur épopée.* Paris: Calmann-Lévy, 2014. 331p. €18.00.

Jennings, Eric Thomas. *La France libre fut africaine.* Paris: Perrin, 2014. 350p. €23.00.

La Rocque, François de. *Pourquoi je suis républicain: Carnets de captivité.* Ed. Serge Berstein, Hughes de La Rocque, and Cédric Francille. Paris: Seuil, 2014. 342p. €21.00.

Lecat-Bringer, Emilie. *L'axe Frei-De Gaulle: Une parenthèse enchantée dans les relations franco-chiliennes, 1964–1970.* Paris: Nouveau Monde, 2014. 199p. €22.00.

Lecouturier, Yves. *Célébrités, héros et anonymes du D Day.* Rennes: Ouest-France, 2014. 187p. €15.00.

Lee, Daniel. *Pétain's Jewish Children: French Jewish Youth and the Vichy Regime, 1940–1942.* Oxford: Oxford University Press, 2014. 288p. £65.00.

Lefebvre-Filleau, Jean-Paul. *Chronique d'une libération: Paris et sa banlieue, 19–31 août 1944.* Sayat: De Borée, 2014. 347p. €26.00.

Linol, Franck, and Hélène Delarbre. *Oradour: Le dernier tram.* La Crèche: Métive, 2014. 108p. €20.00.

Loinger, Georges, Katy Hazan, and Michèle Schlanger-Merowka. *L'odyssée d'un résistant: Témoignage d'un centenaire, enfant d'Alsace.* Nice: Ovadia, 2014. 256p. €26.00.

Marc, Sandra. *Les Juifs de Lacaune (Tarn) dans l'après-guerre: Difficultés quotidiennes, réinsertion et aide du Cojasor, 1944–1949.* Paris: Harmattan, 2014. 247p. €27.00.

Marlière, Eric. *Des "métallos" aux "jeunes des cités": Sociohistoire d'une banlieue ouvrière en mutation.* Paris: Cygne, 2014. 195p. €20.00.

Mathieu, Yves. *Le réseau Ajax: Des policiers dans la Résistance.* Portet-sur-Garonne: Loubatières, 2014. 269p. €25.00.

Mazzeo, Tilar J. *The Hotel on Place Vendôme: Life, Death, and Betrayal at the Hôtel Ritz in Paris.* New York: Harper, 2014. 292p. $26.99.

Mencherini, Robert, ed. *Etrangers antifascistes à Marseille, 1940–1944: Hommage au consul du Mexique Gilberto Bosques.* Marseille: Gaussen, 2014. 151p. €25.00.

Moriceau, Jean-Marc. *Secrets de campagnes: Figures et familles paysannes au XXe siècle.* Paris: Perrin, 2014. 235p. €19.50.

Morin, Dominique. *Résistances chrétiennes dans l'Allemagne nazie: Fernand Morin, compagnon de cellule de Marcel Callo.* Paris: Karthala, 2014. 246p. €22.00.

Nosek, Roland. *Un espion nazi à Paris: Interrogatoire du SS-Hauptsturmführer Roland Nosek.* Paris: Histoire et Collections, 2014. 300p. €22.00.

Oppenheimer-Faure, Rodolphe, and Luc Corlouër. *Edgar Faure: Secrets d'état, secrets de famille*. Paris: Ramsay, 2013. 222p. €19.00.

Perrier, Gérard. *Vitrolles: Un laboratoire de l'extrême droite et de la crise de la gauche, 1983–2002*. Tarbes: Arcane 17, 2014. 260p. €20.00.

Petitpré, Gérard. *Les Trente Glorieuses de la Cinquième République, 1958–1988*. Paris: Harmattan, 2014. 249p. €26.00.

Quillévéré, Alain. *Bals clandestins pendant la Seconde Guerre mondiale dans les Côtes-du-Nord*. Morlaix: Skol Vreizh, 2014. 350p. €22.00.

Robert, André. *Jura, 1940–1944: Territoires de résistance*. Pontarlier: Belvédère, 2014. 375p. €22.00.

Roberts, Mary Louise. *D-Day through French Eyes: Normandy, 1944*. Chicago: University of Chicago Press, 2014. 240p. $25.00.

Sancet, Charles. *Les femmes des PTT et la Seconde Guerre mondiale*. Paris: Tirésias, 2014. 302p. €25.00.

Short, Philip. *Mitterrand: A Study in Ambiguity*. London: Bodley Head, 2013. 692p. £30.00.

Sirinelli, Jean-François. *Le siècle des bouleversements de 1914 à nos jours*. Paris: Presses Universitaires de France, 2014. 321p. €21.00.

Sirinelli, Jean-François, and Suzanne Berger, eds. *La France qui vient: Regards américains sur les mutations hexagonales*. Paris: Centre National de la Recherche Scientifique, 2014. 202p. €20.00.

Théofilakis, Fabien. *Les prisonniers de guerre allemands, France, 1944–1949: Une captivité de guerre en temps de paix*. Paris: Fayard, 2014. 784p. €32.00.

Tricaud, Sabrina. *L'entourage de Georges Pompidou (1962–1974): Institutions, hommes et pratiques*. Brussels: Lang, 2013. 453p. €50.00.

Vaïsse, Maurice. *De Gaulle et l'Amérique latine*. Rennes: Presses Universitaires de Rennes, 2014. 278p. €19.00.

Zay, Jean. *Ecrits de prison, 1940–1944*. Ed. Antoine Prost, Julian Jackson, Anne Simonin, and Robert Owen Paxton. Paris: Belin, 2014. 1,051p. €34.00.

COLONIALISM

Artigalas, Florence. *Les jésuites au Nouveau-Monde: Les débuts de l'évangélisation de la Nouvelle-France et de la France équinoxiale, XVIIe–XVIIIe siècle*. Matoury: Ibis Rouge, 2013. 180p. €25.00.

Association des Anciens de l'Union Nationale des Etudiants de France. *L'UNEF et la guerre d'Algérie: Actes du colloque du 12 octobre 2012*. Paris: ML, 2013. 179p. €15.00.

Barrière, Nicole. *Cessez-le-feu, 19 mars 1962: Cinquante ans, un regard témoin et littéraire*. Paris: Alfabarre, 2014. 239p. €25.00.

Bertin-Maghit, Jean Pierre. *La guerre d'Algérie et les médias: Questions aux archives*. Paris: Presses Sorbonne Nouvelle, 2013. 184p. €34.00.

Besnaci-Lancou, Fatima. *Des harkis envoyés à la mort: Le sort des prisonniers de l'Algérie indépendante, 1962–1969*. Ivry-sur-Seine: Atelier, 2014. 221p. €22.00.

Binot, Jean-Marc. *Le repos des guerriers: Les bordels militaires de campagne pendant la guerre d'Indochine*. Paris: Fayard, 2014. 350p. €22.00.

Bismuth, Hervé, and Fritz Taubert. *La guerre d'Algérie et le monde communiste*. Dijon: Universitaires de Dijon, 2014. 251p. €20.00.

Blais, Hélène. *Mirages de la carte: L'invention de l'Algérie coloniale*. Paris: Fayard, 2014. 346p. €25.00.

Blanchard, Pascal, Sandrine Lemaire, Nicolas Bancel, and Dominic Thomas, eds. *Colonial Culture in France since the Revolution*. Trans. Alexis Pernsteiner. Bloomington: Indiana University Press, 2013. 633p. $60.00.

Chaput–Le Bars, Corinne. *Quand les appelés d'Algérie s'éveillent: Denis, Philippe, Paul et les autres*. Paris: Harmattan, 2014. 396p. €38.00.

Conklin, Alice L. *In the Museum of Man: Race, Anthropology, and Empire in France, 1850–1950.* Ithaca, NY: Cornell University Press, 2013. 374p. $79.95.

Correale, Francesco. *La Grande Guerre des trafiquants: Le front colonial de l'Occident maghrébin.* Paris: Harmattan, 2014. 482p. €47.50.

Darmon, Pierre. *L'Algérie de Pétain: Les populations algériennes ont la parole, septembre 1939–novembre 1942.* Paris: Perrin, 2014. 522p. €25.00.

Daugeron, Bertrand. *A la recherche de l'Esprance: Revisiter la rencontre des Aborigènes tasmaniens avec les Français, 1772–1802.* Paris: Ars Apodemica, 2014. 347p. €38.00.

Diarra, Abdoulaye. *La Gauche française et l'Afrique subsaharienne: Colonisation, décolonisation, coopération, XIXe–XXe siècles.* Paris: Karthala, 2014. 340p. €27.00.

Fournier, Fernand. *Paroles d'appelés: Leur version de la guerre d'Algérie.* Paris: Harmattan, 2014. 230p. €25.00.

Gallois, William. *A History of Violence in the Early Algerian Colony.* New York: Palgrave Macmillan, 2013. 216p. £50.00.

Garcia, Cyril. *Trois historiens face à la guerre d'Algérie: Marc Ferro, Raoul Girardet, Pierre Vidal-Naquet.* Paris: Harmattan, 2014. 160p. €16.00.

Granier, Solène. *Domestiques indochinois.* Paris: Vendémiaire, 2014. 221p. €20.00.

Ha, Marie-Paule. *French Women and the Empire: The Case of Indochina.* Oxford: Oxford University Press, 2014. 304p. $110.00.

Haudrère, Philippe. *Les Français dans l'océan Indien, XVIIe–XIXe siècle.* Rennes: Presses Universitaires de Rennes, 2014. 330p. €20.00.

Hiddleston, Jane. *Decolonising the Intellectual: Politics, Culture, and Humanism at the End of the French Empire.* Liverpool: Liverpool University Press, 2014. 288p. £70.00.

Jobin, Guillaume. *Lyautey, le résident: Le Maroc n'est qu'une province de mon rêve.* Vol. 1. Paris: Magellan, 2014. 386p. €19.50.

La Guérivière, Jean de. *Colonisation: Carnets romanesques.* Paris: Bibliomane, 2014. 282p. €25.00.

Lara, Oruno Denis. *L'histoire au fil des isles: Etudes caraïbes.* Vols. 1–2, *XVIIe–XVIIIe siècles*; vol. 3, *La Tortue et Saint-Domingue, 1630–1703.* Paris: Harmattan, 2014. 242p., 229p., 361p. €26.00, €25.00, €37.50.

Leonetti, Guy, and Marie-Elisabeth Albert. *Mémorial Indochine, 1945–1954.* Paris: Giovanangeli, 2014. 191p. €35.00.

Lewis, Mary Dewhurst. *Divided Rule: Sovereignty and Empire in French Tunisia, 1881–1938.* Berkeley: University of California Press, 2013. 302p. $49.95.

Malmassari, Paul. *1830–1914, de l'armée en Afrique à l'Armée d'Afrique: Actes de la journée d'études, 10 décembre 2012.* Marseille: Riveneuve, 2014. 143p. €24.00.

Marchandiau, Jean-Noël. *J'avais 20 ans en Indochine: De Belleville à Diên Biên Phu, itinéraire d'un enfant des faubourgs.* Gennevilliers: Prisma, 2014. 257p. €22.00.

Mathieu, Jean-Marie. *Souvenirs de guerre d'Algérie: Un intellectuel sur le terrain face à la répression.* Paris: Harmattan, 2014. 148p. €15.50.

Narayanan, Anndal G. "*Le Silence de la Guerre?* French Combatants' Memoirs of the Algerian War, 1954–1988." PhD diss., University of North Carolina at Chapel Hill, 2013.

Osborne, Michael A. *The Emergence of Tropical Medicine in France.* Chicago: University of Chicago Press, 2014. 328p. $50.00.

Pervillé, Guy. *Oran, 5 juillet 1962: Leçon d'histoire sur un massacre.* Paris: Vendémiaire, 2014. 315p. €20.00.

Piat, Denis. *Pirates et corsaires à l'île Maurice.* Paris: Pacifique, 2013. 142p. €25.00.

Pichevin, Bernard. *Généalogies et histoire de Tahiti et des îles de la Société: La descendance des ancêtres prestigieux, les arii.* Pirae: Au Vent des Iles, 2013. 288p. €38.00.

Rushforth, Brett. *Bonds of Alliance: Indigenous and Atlantic Slaveries in New France.* Chapel Hill: University of North Carolina Press, 2012. 406p. $39.95.

Toussaint Louverture. *The Memoir of General Toussaint Louverture.* Ed. Philippe R. Girard. Oxford: Oxford University Press, 2014. 172p. $55.00.

Vastey, Pompée-Valentin. *The Colonial System Unveiled.* Trans. Chris Bongie. Liverpool: Liverpool University Press, 2014. 320p. $120.00.

Vidal, Cécile, ed. *Français? La nation en débat entre colonies et métropole, XVIe–XIXe siècle,* Paris: Ecole des Hautes Etudes en Sciences Sociales, 2014. 272p. €20.00.

Weber, André-Paul. *Régence d'Alger et royaume de France, 1500–1800: Trois siècles de luttes et d'intérêts partagés.* Paris: Harmattan, 2014. 220p. €22.00.

Winterhalter, Roger. *Si c'était à refaire . . . : Une fraternité plus forte que la guerre d'Algérie.* Paris: Manuscrit, 2012. 105p. €13.99.

Zimmermann, Bernard. *Les résistances pieds-noires à l'OAS.* Paris: Harmattan, 2014. 231p. €24.00.

Translated Abstracts

JULIA LANDWEBER

« Cette merveilleuse fève » : L'introduction du café dans le régime alimentaire et la culture française aux dix-septième et dix-huitième siècles

Cet essai examine l'adoption du café dans la culture française entre 1644 et 1788. Dans ces années, une boisson dont se méfiaient les Français (pour son amertume, les risques sanitaires et les associations avec l'Empire ottoman) est devenue une boisson bien-aimée, qui a donné son nom au nouvel espace du café, et a attiré une culture en plein essor de consommateurs intéressés par les nouveautés exotiques. Cette histoire offre des idées nouvelles sur plusieurs sujets, y compris la relation culturelle en évolution entre la France et l'Empire ottoman ; les changements dans les structures de sociabilité des classes moyennes urbaines ; le passage de la socialisation autour de l'alcool à la promotion des stimulants qui donne à réfléchir ; le rôle croissant des commerçants, des médecins et des pharmaciens dans l'évaluation de l'innocuité des nouveaux produits alimentaires ; la montée de la cuisine moderne, et la naissance d'un commerce mondial autour du café français au dix-huitième siècle.

PHILIPPE MEYZIE

The Construction of Renown of *Terroir* Products: Actors and Issues of This Gourmand Market in France (Seventeenth to Early Nineteenth Century)

The valorization of the geographic origin of food products emerged in France during the eighteenth century. For merchants, consumers, and enlightened amateurs (travelers, gourmets), identification with a town or province became a sign of quality. This well-structured, specialist market is similar to a luxury market in terms of demand and its sociocultural aspect. At once rooted in the practices of the ancien régime and responsive to economic innovation, the circulation and consumption of these foods produce a unique food market reflecting the importance of *terroir* in early nineteenth-century gourmand culture. By studying the reputation of these local products, this article investigates the actors and stakes of this French gourmet market.

MARTIN BRUEGEL

Le déjeuner ouvrier à l'extérieur dans le Paris de la Belle Epoque : Le modèle français des repas entre norme et pratique

En élaborant la notion anthropologique du « vrai repas » pour estimer le contenu calorique des déjeuners des ouvriers à l'extérieur autour de 1900, cette recherche montre que les hommes ont un accès plus facile que les femmes à ce qu'ils considèrent comme un repas roboratif. Mais tout le monde ne mange pas selon le modèle français du repas structuré en trois : hors d'œuvre, plat de résistance, dessert. Un secteur d'aliments à emporter propose des alternatives au modèle français et permet aux consommateurs

de tenir les normes à distance. L'histoire ou le retour du refoulé : l'ethnocentrisme contemporain qui accepte le modèle canonique comme une évidence a fait négliger aux chercheurs français cet espace informel où les règles de la bienséance n'exercent qu'une influence limitée sur les pratiques alimentaires. L'oubli dans lequel est tombée l'histoire de cette nourriture de rue a permis d'interpréter l'émergence de la restauration rapide comme une manœuvre étrangère et de qualifier de « malbouffe » les mets qu'elle propose.

PATRICIA TILBURG

« Sa coquetterie tue la faim » : Les ouvrières de la mode, le déjeuner, et la midinette, 1896–1933

Cet article propose la midinette comme un personnage clef de l'imaginaire parisien du vingtième siècle. Notamment, la représentation populaire de la pause déjeuner des midinettes glorifiait les séductions amoureuses et le charme pittoresque des travailleuses parisiennes. Ce charme était fondé, en partie, sur une alimentation légère, voire une sous-alimentation. L'ouvrière de la mode était saisie comme une adepte d'une sous-alimentation frivole et agréable, heureuse de sacrifier de la nourriture pour les plaisirs de la mode et du divertissement. Une nouvelle représentation de la sous-alimentation se trouve dans les descriptions de la midinette à travers la littérature populaire, la chanson, le vaudeville, et même les efforts réformateurs. La midinette sous-alimentée de l'imaginaire parisien du début de siècle ne mangeait pas pour s'engager plus profondément dans le marché capitaliste—en faisant de son corps une publicité séduisante pour la consommation urbaine.

KENNETH MOURÉ

La capitale de la faim : Les restaurants du marché noir à Paris, 1940–1944

Les restaurants parisiens du marché noir ont prospéré pendant l'Occupation. Les Allemands ont fustigé les autorités françaises pour leur incapacité d'arrêter ce commerce, soutenant que les repas luxueux consommés par les trafiquants du marché noir privaient les Parisiens des denrées essentielles. Une étude des restaurants parisiens du marché noir pourrait nous aider à éclaircir la nature des conflits franco-allemands sur le ravitaillement et le pouvoir relatif déterminant la « collaboration », à expliquer l'exacerbation progressive de l'opinion publique contre le régime de Vichy, et à mettre en lumière la créativité des restaurateurs qui trouvaient des méthodes alternatives pour alimenter leur commerce. On y voit aussi l'importance des exigences allemandes qui provoquaient l'étendue des activités du marché noir.